The Politics of Change in a Zambian Community

The Politics of Change in a Zambian Community

George C. Bond

The University of Chicago Press
Chicago and London

George C. Bond is associate professor in the
division of philosophy, the social sciences,
and education at Teachers College, Columbia
University.

The University of Chicago Press, Chicago 60637
The University of Chicago Press, Ltd., London

Library of Congress Cataloging in Publication Data

Bond, George C
    The politics of change in a Zambian community.

    Bibliography: p.
    Includes index.
    1. Yombe (African people)—Politics and government.
I. Title.
DT963.42.B66   320.9′689′404   75-12228
ISBN 0-226-06408-5

To Lucy Mair

Contents

Preface

When I undertook my fieldwork in Uyombe, Zambia, from 1963 to 1965, I had two main aims. My first aim was to provide general ethnographic coverage of a people, the Yombe, who had not been studied before, and thus to fill a gap in the ethnography of Central Africa. My second aim was to carry out a study of politics at the local level during the final phases of colonial rule.

Local politics forms the context in which national institutions and organizations penetrate the integument of rural societies and confront indigenous political traditions and the interests of rural elites. There is a growing body of anthropological literature on this theme, but there are as yet very few studies of local politics that are concerned with the transitional period between colonial rule and independence and few that have traced the rise to power and prominence of a new party-based elite within an African chiefdom. During the struggle for Zambian independence, the colonial system of local government lost much of its legitimacy among Africans, many of whom questioned the right of government officers to exercise authority. Authority ceased to be contained solely within colonial structures, and thus provided the politically astute with the opportunity to manipulate the shifting social environment to their advantage. They were able to create new political structures to challenge the authority of local government.

Put differently, the drive for independence released new forces in rural societies, provided new opportunities for political action, produced new coalitions and alignments, and created a fluid situation of ambiguity and uncertainty. Under these conditions it was often difficult for me as a fieldworker to discover regularities in the political behavior of the Yombe. It became apparent that a single anthropological approach could not encompass the multiple facets of rapid political change. My training had been within the tradition of structural functionalism, and although I used elements of this approach to develop the structural context in which to examine political behavior and process, I soon recognized that it could not adequately handle the irregularities, inconsistencies and contradictions of a situation of political upheaval, one in which a new political system was being constructed through the dialectical interaction of internal and external forces.

Most studies of Central African peoples have been undertaken by anthropologists associated with Manchester University. I made use of some of the methods and techniques of a "Manchester approach," such as situational analysis and social dramas, in order to discover the way in which individuals behaved in a number of situations and to establish the constraints which regulated their choices and decisions. Such an approach reaps a rich ethnographic harvest, but it can also lead to the pursuit of the particular and to the selection of only those cases which represent principles derived from the local system. Although it may be possible to account for social behavior in terms of these principles, there are also those principles which are produced by the interaction of local and national political and economic forces. Rural societies in Central Africa have often been treated as if they were closed social systems in a state of equilibrium, with only temporary disruptions of the equilibrium. Ever since colonial rule was first imposed, however, the possibility that these rural societies may establish new equilibriums has been minimal indeed. There has been a constant intrusion of external forces and the construction of new political forms and structures. This was perhaps most apparent during the last phases of colonial rule.

In this book I have attempted to combine structural analysis with an actor-oriented approach. My final concern was to look for the dialectical components of political life in the interaction of contrasting social forces, patterns, and interests and to explore the growing relationships of subordination and dependency of the common folk of the villages to the new political elites of a small town. By making implicit use of elements of a dialectical approach, I believe that I was able to represent the fluid nature of the situation which obtained during the period of fieldwork and also to suggest trends which were discernible not only in Uyombe, but also in other small-scale communities in rural Africa.

I entered the field, with some trepidation, at a time of considerable political tension. European colonial officers had told me that the Yombe were highly suspicious of strangers, and uncooperative. Fortunately, I had also spoken with Africans who assured me that I would be well received and cared for. Needless to say, the Africans were correct. The Yombe were more than generous with their hospitality, friendship, and time. They allowed me to participate fully in their personal lives and the life of the community. During the first six months of my stay, the old men devoted much of their time to instructing me in their customs, recounting the history of the chiefdom, their clans and lineages, and teaching me Tumbuka. I cannot, of course, mention individually all these senior men, but I do wish to express my gratitude to them and especially to Chief John Punyira Wowo and to the late Mr. Isaac Chitundozya Kumwenda and Mr. Matthew Chilembo.

Among the younger men who helped to make my stay in Uyombe a most valuable experience there are those to whom I am particularly indebted. Mr.

Ewell Wowo, Mr. Evans Kumwenda, Mr. Adon Chilembo, Mr. Henry Wowo, and Mr. Adamson Musukwa guided me around hazardous political pitfalls, served as my tutors, and provided me with hospitality and warm enduring friendship. I also wish to express my thanks to Mr. Tepson Mbambara, Mr. Beanwell Munyenyembe, and Mr. Kanyenyere Gondwe, who at different times acted as my assistants in the tasks of taking censuses, surveys, administering questionnaires, transcribing taped speeches, collecting genealogies, measuring fields and yields, and performing other duties of anthropological research. Many Yombe women provided me with food, information, and kindness, allowed me to attend their church, their political meetings, and their informal evening gatherings around their fires. I am especially indebted to Edina Nyamuwowo, who saw that I was properly fed, Lucy Nyamuwowo, who saw to it that I was in church on time, to Agnes Nyamunthali, who bolstered my spirits, and to my neighbors, who shared their morning and evening gossip.

I owe a special debt of thanks to President Kaunda of Zambia, who took of his precious time to see that a young graduate student received proper treatment and encouragement, and to the late Yatuta Chisiza, who helped me in many important ways.

Parts of this book appeared in a dissertation presented at the London School of Economics and Political Science in 1968. The dissertation was supervised by Professor Lucy Mair, whose encouragement, gentle patience, and pointed criticism I acknowledge with gratitude and respect. I wish also to thank David Boswell, Robert Groves, Robert Jay, Philip Staniford, and Christopher Turner for their stimulating and fruitful comments on the dissertation. Elizabeth Colson, Lucy Mair, William Shack, Elliot Skinner, and Joan Vincent were kind enough to read and comment on the book in manuscript. The deficiencies in style, argument, and reasoning are exclusively mine.

I wish to express my deepest thanks to my parents, J. Max Bond and Ruth Clement Bond, for their constant encouragement. I am grateful to my wife, Alison Murray, for her help in preparing this book. I acknowledge my debt to my uncle, the late Horace Mann Bond, to my brother J. Max Bond, to Martin Kilson, and to Kenneth Simmons, all of whom encouraged young blacks in their academic careers. I owe a special debt of gratitude to William Shack, who has provided constant encouragement and support. I wish to express my lasting gratitude to the Yombe; I hope that I have in no way broken the faith. I am grateful to Columbia University and the Institute for African Studies, Columbia, for summer grants which allowed me to work on this book.

I have used pseudonyms to obscure the identities of all but one of the important principal characters, and many place names have been altered. The ethnographic present has been used to refer to the twenty-two months of fieldwork from 1963 to 1965, although the reader will appreciate that Yombe society is constantly changing.

1
Introduction

In the 1950s and 1960s independent African countries were in the making, and political change was observable in the field. During the struggle for independence in Northern Rhodesia (Zambia), and shortly afterward, new forces were being released. Indigenous elites were vying with European rulers and with one another for authority and power.

The last phases of European colonial rule were marked by an intensification of political activity (and religious strife) in both urban and rural areas. Authority and power were gradually being transferred from European rulers to the leaders of African national political movements. During this transitional period the ambiguities and inconsistencies of political life increased so that individuals and groups could manipulate social and political arrangements in pursuit of competing interests. This is not to say that the existing order of Northern Rhodesia was completely swept away. There was pronounced continuity; the basic order of the society persisted.

This study of politics at the local level deals with political continuity and change in Uyombe chiefdom, a small community in the Northern Province of Zambia, where the ruling clique came into conflict with a new, party-based elite. It traces the rapid rise to power and prominence of a new rural elite, and explores the manner in which these new men contested the authority of the chief and his men, the "old guard." It looks at the type of local politics produced in the struggle for power between the new elite and the old guard which had successfully entrenched itself during the period of British colonial rule. The new elite, consisting of educated royals and commoners, party officers, and entrepreneurs, established progressive coalitions which served both national and local interests and sought to rationalize the local political system, thus enabling it to deal more efficiently with contemporary problems such as rural development and Zambian independence.

A rigorous structural approach which assumes homogeneity, consistency, and stability (van Velsen 1964, p. xxiii) proved inappropriate for the study of Uyombe chiefdom politics. Firth's concept of social organization (Firth 1964, pp. 30–88) was far more useful since it draws attention to the processes by which individuals choose between alternative courses of action, manipulate norms and values, and adopt or reject roles in the pursuit of their interests and social goals. In order to demonstrate these processes I make use of extended case studies, "not as 'apt illustrations' of structural principles, but as a constituent part of the analysis" (van Velsen, 1964, p. xxv). Such studies not only illustrate principles but show how principles are contravened, so that opportunities are created for action which may undermine the principles themselves.

For the purposes of this monograph a useful definition of politics is the one offered by Mair. She suggests that in the "wider fields of social relationships there are always and everywhere persons with conflicting and competing interests, seeking to have disputes settled in their favour and to influence community decisions (policy) in accordance with their interests. This is politics" (Mair 1962, p. 10), and it is exactly this which I make the principal focus of my study. Mair's view allows for a unified consideration of political behavior, processes, events, and those forces which during 1963 to 1965 were shaping and transforming the political life of Uyombe.

Two principal themes run through this book; one is social forces and the persistence of social principles, and the other is the actions of individuals and the process of political change. The social forces operating within Uyombe chiefdom suggest the more general patterns and trends that are molding rural communities in Central Africa. They are in part embodied in the political activities of the principal political figures treated here. These social forces (or processes) form the basis for choices and shifting political alignments. The social forces operating within Uyombe may be viewed in terms of oppositions. They are related to differences in orientation (local or national) and conflicts of interest, and stem from the interaction of territorial communities, or groups and associations.

Muyombe, the capital of the Uyombe chiefdom is the social, political and commercial center of Uyombe and illustrates the importance of the small town for local development and change in the rural areas of Zambia. It links the lesser village communities of the chiefdom into the more inclusive frameworks of administration and politics. The policies of the central government, the province, and the district are considered by the local elite living in Muyombe before they are presented to villagers. The relation of Muyombe to the lesser village communities of the chiefdom has created a dynamic field of political competition. Concerned essentially with the allocation of scarce resources between the capital and local units, this competition is characteristic of most newly independent countries.

A second sphere of political activity in Uyombe is generated by relationships between the six branches of the royal Wowo clan, whose members form the "traditional" ruling stratum of Yombe society. At present two royal branches, Chapyoka and Njera, are the main competitors; the chief, John (Punyira) Wowo, who represents the "old guard," is from Chapyoka, and the deputy chief, who represents the "new men," is from Njera. The struggle between these two men and the interests they represent is a central theme of this study.

The relationship of the royal Wowo clan and the Native Administration to the local constituency (a unit of political party organization, here referred to as the subregion branch) of the United National Independence Party (UNIP) forms yet another sphere of chiefdom political activity. The UNIP subregion branch has provided the "new men" of the chiefdom with a basis of political support which they have used to gain authority and power within the chiefdom, the chiefdom government, and the Native Administration. Local UNIP officers hold important positions on such bodies as the chief's council (now known as the area committee) and its executive body, the development committee. The local, party-based elite often competes with the royal clan and the Native Administration for control of the chiefdom. During the period of this study (1963–65) the spheres of competence of many institutions and statuses were ambiguous, allowing much room for maneuver and manipulation. The party-based elite was attempting to extend its control at the expense of the royal clan and the Native Administration. It may be said that the contending parties no longer shared the basic values upon which the "legitimacy" of the political system rested (Rex 1968, p. 116).

Yet another division within Yombe society cuts across group affiliations and has its influence on political relationships. This is the division between more and less educated persons. The more educated are those who have completed standard VI (at least eight years of schooling), are proficient in English, and are or have been employed, for example, as clerks or teachers. The less educated are persons who have completed no more than standard IV (six years of schooling or less), speak poor English or none at all, and who have been previously employed abroad (outside Uyombe) in unskilled jobs. The prominent political leaders of the chiefdom—at least between 1963 and 1965—were mostly drawn from the ranks of the more educated, and these men often cooperated in originating policies and imposing them on the chiefdom. The less educated leaders are now, however, increasing their control, since with Zambian independence many of the more educated have left Uyombe to take up appointments in the civil service or the political party.

The interaction in the Uyombe chiefdom between a small rural town and lesser communities, between "traditional" and new elites, and between the more and the less educated generates fields of political activity which demonstrate social forces not peculiar to Uyombe. These forces are part of developing trends in rural communities throughout Central Africa. The use of the concept "political field" makes it possible to explain some of the processual dimensions of social life which are giving rise to such trends. A political field involves those activities which affect the distribution of power within a society. It encompasses more than the structural or institutional arrangements of a society, since it includes the practical working arrangements (Long 1968, p. 9). The practical arrangements of a society involve individuals and their choices, as well as the contingencies of social life. They include those situations in which individuals pursue their interests and social goals, seek to control resources and people and to deny the control and interests of others. They are most apparent in events which flow across the boundaries of groups and bring individuals from different groups together for political purposes (Swartz 1968, pp. 1–2). Events also allow one to observe the maneuvers of individuals; the way in which they manipulate statuses, roles, relationships; and the rules, norms, and values of a society. Through them one may observe the process of political change.

2
The Yombe and
Their Country

The Yombe, a Bantu-speaking people, inhabit a small corner of Isoka District in the Northern Province of Zambia. In 1963 they numbered 11,593 or 14% of the total population of the district,[1] which covers some 5,340 square miles and is part of that mountainous country between lakes Tanganyika and Malawi through which there has been much migration of populations (M. Wilson 1958, p. 1). No fewer than eight ethnic or tribal groupings are represented in the area, and Isoka District is often referred to as the "Mixed Tribes Area." Many of the smaller ethnic (or tribal) groups are offshoots or fragments of larger populations which are concentrated in southern Tanzania and northern Malawi. The ethnic composition of some of the six chiefdoms which make up the district reflects this diversity, but the chiefdom of Uyombe is not one of them; its population is overwhelmingly Yombe, speaking Tumbuka, a Bantu language.

Uyombe chiefdom lies between ten and eleven degrees south latitude and is part of the northern lobe of the eastern plateau system which rises above more than five thousand feet into the Nyika plateau. It is that most eastern tip of Isoka District which intrudes into Malawi and is bordered to the south by the chiefdom of Kambambo in Lundazi District (Zambia), to the northwest by Chifungwe, and to the east by the chiefdoms of Ntaliri and Nkamanga in Malawi. A narrow uninhabited strip of Lundazi District separates Uyombe from the chiefdom of Hewe and forms part of the border between Zambia and Malawi. The neighboring peoples are the matrilineal Senga to the south and the patrilineal Fungwe, Nyika, and Tumbuka to the northwest and southeast.

The Yombe are more intimately allied to their more numerous fellow Tumbuka speakers in the Northern Province of Malawi than they are to their neighbors in Isoka District, sharing many features of social and political organization. With few exceptions the pattern of kinship among the Tumbuka-speaking peoples is based on agnatic descent. Cattle are used in bridewealth, and residence is virilocal. Most Tumbuka are peasant cultivators who

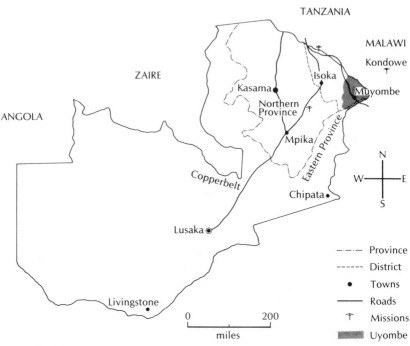

Map 1. Zambia

practice subsistence agriculture. Their political organization is based on the recognition of chieftainship. The mythical charters of the royal clans of the different chiefdoms all relate that their founders crossed Lake Malawi from the east as a party of hunters and traders, possibly before the end of the eighteenth century. Members of the party went their separate ways, settled in different areas, and established themselves as rulers over the indigenous peoples. (For information on Tumbuka and related peoples see Tew 1950, p. 51; Brelsford 1956, pp. 76–81; M. Wilson 1958, pp. 38–40. For history see Young 1932, p. 34; Tew 1950, pp. 52–55.)

The different branches of the Tumbuka-speaking cluster have never been ruled by one paramount chief. The Yombe and Wenya used to send tribute to Kyungu, the ruler of the Ngonde (G. Wilson 1939, p. 15), while other Tumbuka sent tribute to the Chikuramayembe of Nkamanga. Today each branch is an autonomous chiefdom. These chiefdoms are often divided by district, provincial, and even international boundaries, yet among them all there is a consciousness of kind which is reinforced by language, custom, and practice, and by common historical and religious experience. This consciousness has been in part a reaction to their subordination by the conquering Ngoni, who displaced, scattered, or assimilated some Tumbuka populations and raided others, among them the Yombe (Murray 1922, pp. 28–39; see also Young 1932, pp. 131–36). The Tumbuka expressed their reaction to Ngoni domination by rejecting Ngoni practices and by resuscitating or creating rituals which demonstrated their distinctive identity (Abraham 1932, p. 22).[2]

Uyombe covers some 625 square miles. There are numerous thickly forested hills and mountains, in which troops of baboons live. Between the hills and mountains there are stretches of well-watered, undulating countryside. Some parts of the eastern area of the chiefdom rise abruptly into the Nyika plateau, and other parts rise into high clusters of hills along the border with Ntaliri in Malawi. In the south, toward the Shiri river, there is a gradual descent into flat, forested land. In the southwest an area of scrub bush gradually descends into the Makutu Protected Forest area. The northwestern part of the chiefdom ascends into the dense forests of the Makutu mountains.

The numerous hills, mountains, and stretches of forest are criss-crossed by perennial rivers and streams. The four main rivers are the Luhoka, the Bemba, the Vumbo, and the Shiri, the latter forming the southern border of the chiefdom. It is along these rivers and their streams that most of the villages are situated. The rivers provide the most regular supply of water. During the rains they become torrents, flooding their banks, but toward the end of the dry season they are mere trickles with deep pools of water scattered in their beds. From these rivers, women and children fetch water in clay and metal pots or debes (empty four-gallon kerosene tins) for domestic uses such as drinking, cooking, and bathing. It is along the flood plains of rivers and streams that maize and beans are most often cultivated, and during the rains they appear as green ribbons crossing the chiefdom. Millet is planted on the rising foothills and slopes of high hills and mountains. Exceptionally, there are no settlements and few gardens near the lower reaches of the Luhoka river in the southwest. This can be seen from Map 2, which also shows that the most densely settled areas are in the north and to the east of the Vumbo and Bemba rivers. The southwestern part of the chiefdom is rich in game; here larger animals such as elephants and buffalo are killed by local hunters.

In the more densely populated areas, cultivation, seasonal grass fires, and the cutting of trees for building purposes, firewood, and millet gardens have left little of the original forest growth. As yet, with a population density of some seventeen persons per square mile, there is no great scarcity of arable land. It is only near villages that any scarcity arises, so that villagers may have to walk great distances to their fields. Some may even take up residence on their gardens and return home only after harvesting their crops. Otherwise, fertile land is plentiful and it is not subject to rent, sale, or inheritance; rights to cultivate it are easily acquired.

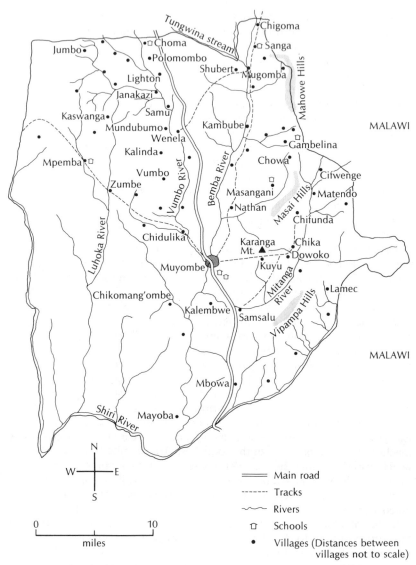

Map 2. Uyombe Chiefdom

MALAWI

MALAWI

Tungwina stream

Chigoma

Choma

Sanga

Jumbo

Polomombo

Shubert

Mugomba

Lighton

Janakazi

Mahowe Hills

Samu

Kaswanga

Kambube

Mundubumo

Wenela

Gambelina

Kalinda

Chowa

Cifwenge

Mpemba

Vumbo

Zumbe

Masangani

Matendo

Nathan

Masai Hills

Chifunda

Chidulika

Karanga
Mt.

Chika

Dowoko

Muyombe

Kuyu

Chikomang'ombe

Lamec

Kalembwe

Samsalu

Mitanga
River

Vipampa Hills

Mbowa

Shiri River

Mayoba

N
W — E
S

0   10
miles

Main road

Tracks

Rivers

Schools

Villages (Distances between
villages not to scale)

Population

The Yombe form a very small proportion (0.2%) of the total population of Zambia (Kay 1967a, p. 45), and they constitute only 14% of the total population of Isoka District. The official Zambian census of 1963 put the population at 11,593. The main feature of the Yombe population is its youth; 63.2% are below the age of twenty-two. Only 18.4% of the total population is both male and aged over twenty-two; it is from this small percentage that incumbents of political posts and the main leaders of Yombe society are recruited.

Uyombe's population is slightly denser than that of Isoka District as a whole, which has an overall density of fifteen persons per square mile. It is difficult to ascertain its exact distribution, since the 1963 census and other government reports give more detailed information about other areas of the district than they do about Uyombe. For all other areas, the 1963 census gives population by village, but for Uyombe most enumeration areas are vague—for example, "Muyombe Jumbo" and "Lubuzi Luhoka." It can be seen from map 2 that villages between Muyombe and Jumbo would also include many of those along the Luhoka river. The absence of a definition of enumeration areas renders an accurate assessment of population distribution impossible.

Economy

For the Yombe the year is divided into two seasons, the rains and the "drys," which clearly demarcate the activities of village life. The rains, averaging thirty to forty inches a year, begin in late November or early December. The onset of the first rains marks the beginning of a period of intense agricultural activity; the cultivation of such crops as maize, millet, and beans becomes the primary preoccupation of villagers. Since the Yombe do not irrigate, and cultivate only during the rainy season, it is the period of hardest work. Villagers may leave their homes to take up residence on their maize gardens. But even though they are dispersed for as long as five or six months, they remain responsible to the headman and he for them. The rains begin to taper off in April and May and come to an end in late June or early July. During the dry season the only major agricultural activity is the preparation of millet gardens for planting after the first rains. It is not, however, a period of idleness. Villagers use this time to mend and replace agricultural and domestic implements and to repair or build houses, woodsheds, and granaries. They clean the villages, clear paths, mend bridges, and participate in chiefdom "self-help" schemes such as building dispensary and school buildings. These activities continue until the rains return.

The Yombe are peasant cultivators. Throughout the chiefdom there are few variations in agricultural techniques, in agricultural implements, and in the crops cultivated. Maize, finger millet, and beans are the main crops grown and form the staple diet. Maize is planted in December and early January and harvested in May and June. Beans are planted twice a year between the rows of maize. Millet gardens are prepared by cutting branches from trees and burning them during the dry season. In January the burned area is sown, and the millet is harvested in late June and early July. Many ritual observances are associated with the sowing and harvesting of millet, which is used for making the beer, *finga,* which is offered to the ancestors, *viwanda* (sing. *ciwanda*). In addition to the staple crops, the Yombe grow groundnuts, cassava, bananas, and a variety of other minor crops such as sweet potatoes and pumpkins.

Maize and millet are made into a thick porridge, *sima,* which is served at every meal together with a side dish of relish, *dendi.* The relish is usually beans, though vegetables, *mpangwe,* are also frequently served. Meat is not a regular part of the Yombe diet, but it is one of the preferred relishes. It is served mainly when there are visitors. The combination of maize and millet porridge with red beans provides the Yombe with a nutritious diet. Although numerous cases of smallpox, chicken pox, and pneumonia were brought to the dispensary in Muyombe, while I was in the area, there were few cases of malnutrition.

The principal agricultural implements are hoes and axes, and although district agricultural officers and the Kasama Marketing Co-operative have encouraged the Yombe to use ox-drawn plows, their efforts have met with little success. However, in 1965 two men within the chiefdom began training oxen in anticipation of purchasing plows. They hoped to get Native Administration permission not only to disregard village boundaries but to enclose large areas of land. The Native Administration was favorably disposed to their long-term plans, but no definite decision was reached because they had not yet acquired their plows. The use of ox-drawn plows may bring about changes not only in agricultural techniques but also in the relationship of the Yombe to the land, which is their basic productive resource.

There are no local industries or home crafts in Uyombe. The main local source of money is the sale of crops, maize, beans, and some millet. Once a year the Kasama Marketing Co-operative sends trucks to Uyombe to purchase maize and beans. It opens seven markets for two weeks in July or August, and if all the roads are in good repair, its trucks go there. Maize is the main crop exported by the Yombe. Money is also derived from the sale of eggs and fruit to teachers and the other representatives of district government living in Muyombe.

In 1964 the Kasama Co-operative was paying three shillings and six pence for a debe of maize kernels, and eight shillings for a debe of beans. The annual sale from the whole chiefdom usually amounts to more than £1,200. The Yombe cultivator is aware that the produce he sells to the Co-operative brings a much higher price in Isoka, the district headquarters, and other larger centers than that which he receives from the Co-operative. In Isoka, a day and a half's ride by truck from Muyombe, a tin of maize sold for ten to fifteen shillings in 1964 and a tin of beans for eighteen to twenty shillings. Most Yombe argue that because the prices offered for their crops are so low, they have little reason to increase their productivity. Maize, millet, and beans are also bought by local and Malawi traders, who may exchange a yard of cloth valued at two shillings and six pence for a debe of maize or millet, and two yards for a debe of beans. The crops are then sold in Malawi markets at a considerable profit.

In 1965 there were eighteen shops, one bottle store, and six (working) maize grinding machines in the chiefdom. Most of the shops were situated along the main motor road. Ten were in the capital, Muyombe, four were in Wenela and Polomombo, and only four were in villages off the main road. Shops were usually owned by individuals, though a few were joint enterprises. Many owners had begun their small enterprises by trading used clothes, cloth, and even candy for maize, millet, and beans and then transporting and selling the crops for cash in Malawi.

Shops tend to be small and only sell essential domestic items such as salt, sugar, and needles and thread. The few larger shops in the capital are stocked with a greater variety of goods, ranging from small domestic items to hoes, cloth, bicycle parts, and sometimes cot beds. The owners of these larger shops do not usually live on the premises but employ assistants who occupy rooms in the rear of the shop. They also employ one or two tailors who sew dresses for women, trousers for men, and school uniforms for children.

The shop owners and those employed by them are all Africans. None of the eighteen shops is owned or controlled by a non-African, nor are the small tea rooms, the six maize-grinding machines, and the one petrol pump and bottle store. In 1960 the chief gave permission for an Asian trader to establish a shop in Muyombe. Local shop owners and traders protested so vehemently against Asian commercial intrusion that he withdrew his consent. Though local shop owners buy their goods from Asians in Lundazi District, Asians have been unable to establish commercial enterprises in Uyombe itself.

Many shop owners are highly educated by Zambian standards and form part of the local rural elite. Because they are concerned with improving commercial opportunities, the more educated shop owners have played an active part in politics. They are members of chiefdom councils and committees which have explored ways of getting better prices for produce, improving the network of roads and tracks, and acquiring loans from the Zambian government. In May and June of 1965, shop owners held a series of meetings to organize themselves into a Traders' Co-operative Association. Their purpose was to explore ways of getting government loans for local African businessmen and to acquire goods at wholesale prices instead of having to purchase them at retail prices from Asian traders. Though these goals had not been achieved when I left Uyombe in September 1965, their very existence shows how a small but highly educated section of the community is establishing a framework for the pursuit of commercial interests. Some of those involved are not only shop owners and traders but also hold posts in the Native Administration, sit on chiefdom committees, and are important figures in the local branches of UNIP. They are at the core of an emergent commercial African elite in the rural areas, which is interested in getting the government not only to assist small African business but also to provide loans for peasant cultivators.

Because there is little opportunity for earning money within Uyombe, most men (but very few women) at some point in their lives seek employment "abroad" (that is, outside Uyombe) in the main industrial and urban centers of Central, Southern and East Africa. From the tax register kept by the local Native Administration, I estimated that at any one time 25% to 35% of the adult male taxpayers were abroad. There is some variation in the rate of labor migration from different parts of the chiefdom. For example, the 1963 tax register indicates that from Luhoka parish, which included seven villages in the west-central area of the chiefdom, 91 or 44.5% of the 204 de jure male taxpayers (including men exempted or living abroad but still registered) were abroad. From Zabathali parish, which included ten villages in the northeastern part of the chiefdom, 23% of the de jure male taxpayers were abroad. These figures should be taken as only very rough estimates; men return and others leave without their presence or absence being entered in the tax register. Moreover, boys may leave before their names have been inscribed. The late 1950s and early 1960s was also a period marked by political protest and by social and religious strife. As part of this insurgent protest, which culminated in Zambian independence, many men refused to report their movements or pay tax. In 1964 the Yombe refused to pay any tax at all.

Most men tend to spend from two to seven years working abroad in other parts of Zambia or in Rhodesia, South Africa, Tanzania, and Malawi. In 1963, of 216 men abroad from 27 villages, 72% were in Zambia, 10% in Rhodesia, 9% in South Africa, 5% in Tanzania, and 4% in Malawi. Like the Mambwe of Zambia and the Tonga of Malawi (Watson 1958, p. 6; van Velsen 1960, p. 268), Yombe labor migrants maintain a stake in the home society by sending money and goods to kinfolk living in Uyombe, by returning every so often for extended visits, and by receiving home folk when they visit. The money which they send home helps to support not only their relatives but also local shop owners. The labor migrants also send money to the Native Administration to assist in such schemes as building dispensaries and school blocks. In other words, labor migrants are in no way lost, nor do they entirely remove themselves from Yombe society. They are concerned with what happens at home, and those left at home are concerned about them.

Communications

The chiefdoms of Uyombe and Chifungwe form a "pocket" of Zambia that intrudes into Malawi. In 1965 no road suitable for motor vehicles connected them with other parts of Zambia. The main graded dirt road that passed through Uyombe from south to north was owned and maintained by Malawi and it linked Uyombe to the commercial and administrative centers of Katumbi, Rumpi, and Muzuzu to the south and to Fort Hill (Citipa) to the north, all of which are in Malawi. In order to reach Isoka, the District headquarters, and other parts of Zambia by motor vehicles, it was necessary to travel through Malawi territory and to pass through the checkpoints of the international boundary between Zambia and Malawi.

From the main Malawi road which runs from south to north, four tracks branch off to other parts of the chiefdom. The first leaves the main road at Samsalu (the central village of Njera branch of the royal clan) in the south and follows the course of the Mitanga river eastward as far as Chifunda, the central village of Chapyoka branch of the royal clan. In 1963–64 this track was unsuitable for motor vehicles, but under the leadership of the headman of Chifunda repairs have since been made by villagers to accommodate the trucks of the Kasama Marketing Co-operative. Two tracks branch off from Muyombe. The first follows the northeastern course of the Bemba river and enters the neighboring chiefdom of Ntaliri. The second runs to the northwest and ends at the village of Mpemba along the Luhoka river. The final track is in the north and links the main Malawi road with the one that enters Ntaliri. It was constructed by the citizens of Ntaliri to facilitate the transportation of their crops to the main road. For the most part it is the Yombe who are responsible for maintaining these four tracks. During the rains the numerous essential bridges are swept away, and the tracks often remain impassable even in the dry season. For villagers, especially those who live far from the main road, the condition of these tracks is extremely important. If the trucks of local and Malawi traders and of the Kasama Marketing Co-operative cannot reach the majority of villagers, the villagers cannot sell their surplus produce unless they themselves take it to one of the Kasama Co-operative markets, which open for only two weeks, or to the shops of local traders.

Though the road system is poorly developed and inadequately maintained, it would be a mistake to consider Uyombe an entirely remote and isolated corner of Zambia. There is much more communication within the chiefdom and with the outside world than there has been at any time in the past. Communication between villages and neighboring chiefdoms has been facilitated by the bicycle. The Yombe use bicycles with great skill to negotiate the network of narrow paths which link the numerous settlements of the chiefdom. Bicycles are rapidly displacing women as the primary mode of transporting heavy loads over long distances, and the Malawi Public

Works Department trucks, which pass through Uyombe, provide another means of transport. They are not supposed to carry produce and passengers but they often do so for a fee.

The daily Malawi bus service links Uyombe to the outside world. One bus travels south in the morning and one north in the afternoon. They make three stops in Uyombe, of which the longest and most important is at Muyombe, where the buses can refuel and passengers buy refreshments. It is there also that the Zambian government mailbags are collected and deposited. This service links Uyombe with Rumpi in the south and Nakonde in the north. Connections can be made at Rumpi with buses traveling to different parts of Malawi, and at Nakonde with buses going north into Tanzania and south to Isoka and the main urban and industrial centers of Zambia.

Another means of communication with the world outside Uyombe is the transistor radio, which enables the Yombe to follow events in Zambia, Malawi, Tanzania, and, if they are interested, other parts of the world. Radio Zambia and Radio Malawi broadcast daily programs in Tumbuka, Nyanja, Bemba, and English—languages which are spoken by many Yombe. Most local civil servants, traders, and local UNIP officers living in Muyombe have radios. Newspapers are not a very important means of communication. Although a Bemba schoolteacher at the upper primary school in Muyombe was an agent for the *Central African Mail*, an African newspaper, copies were usually two to three months late in arriving, very few in number, and they circulated only within Muyombe. Because there were so few subscriptions the service was discontinued after six months. A final means of communication with other parts of Central and Southern Africa is provided by the constant movement of individual Yombe to and from the centers of urban employment.

Historical Background

There is insufficient historical evidence to determine how long the Yombe have lived in Uyombe or where they came from. The myths of the six branches of the royal clan of Uyombe chiefdom all suggest that their founding ancestors came with a party of hunters and traders who crossed Lake Malawi from the east and founded the royal clans of the present Tumbuka chiefdoms. If Cullen Young is correct, this party of traders began to establish its control over the indigenous populations between 1780 and 1800 (Young 1932, p. 27). The ancestors of the Wowo found the area which is today Uyombe inhabited by the Bisa. Accounts differ as to whether the Bisa were absorbed, killed, or driven out of the country. In any event, the Wowos became the uncontested rulers, and their chief, whose praise name is Mlowoka ("he who crossed over") gained control of the external trade in ivory. It would seem however that Uyombe chiefdom was a tributary of

Ngonde and that Yombe chiefs were nobles of the Ngonde ruler, Kyungu, and sent him tribute (G. Wilson 1939, p. 15). Though these factors suggest that Uyombe was nominally under Kyungu, members of the royal Wowo clan deny any political subordination to Ngonde. They claim that Uyombe has always been an independent chiefdom and that in the dispute over chieftainship, Kyungu was consulted as an equal among equals.

The present inhabitants of Uyombe do not seem to be the descendants of the original population but an amalgam of different peoples who fled from the ravages of Ngonde, Bemba, and Ngoni wars and Arab slave raiders. Many Yombe are the descendants of refugees who settled in the area, accepted the Wowos as rulers, and assimilated local customs and practices. Their clan names and myths indicate the diversity of their ethnic origins. There are, however, few Ngoni clan names and few Yombe claim Ngoni descent. This is not surprising since the Ngoni never settled in Uyombe, as they did in other Tumbuka areas.

In these other Tumbuka-speaking areas the northward movement of the Ngoni disrupted social and political life. In the 1840s the Ngoni marched through Nkamanga, but it was not until 1855 that there was the "smash-up of Nkamanga," as Cullen Young describes it (Young 1932, p. 116). The Ngoni settled in the area, and those Tumbuka-speaking peoples who were not conquered or assimilated were raided or forced to give tribute. Even though the Yombe were not conquered, they lived in constant apprehension of Ngoni raids and old men tell stories of hiding from Mombera's warriors. While the Nkamanga and Henga underwent Ngoni rule and were assimilated, the Yombe remained on the periphery of Ngoni domination.

During the nineteenth century the Yombe, like other Tumbuka, lived either in villages or in small scattered hamlets hidden in the bush (Murray 1922, p. 148). Both types of settlement were related to defense, and either one form or the other was readily adopted depending on the nature of the danger at hand. Elderly Yombe agree that there were no more than fifteen major settlements in Uyombe—some were able to name only eight or nine—and that some of these had palisades built around them. The chief (or king, *themba*) ruled from his capital, Muyombe, which was not a permanent settlement, since it moved with the chief. The other villages were under village chiefs. Scattered hamlets were attached to the major settlements. The six branches of the royal Wowo clan had their own villages: Kalinda, Kaswanga, and Vumbo were in the north and Samsalu, Cika, and Chifunda, were in the south. Mbamba, Mpemba, and Zumbe were the villages of the three official councillors of the chief, and their heads formed the interregnal council when he died; together with members of the royal Wowo clan, they selected the new chief. Four of the remaining five villages were under commoners. The last village, Mbowa, which was situated near the border between Uyombe and Hewe, was under a noted warrior hunter of the royal Wowo clan. The village was mainly an outpost, and when Ngoni warriors were seen or disputes arose with Chief Katumbe of Hewe, the head of

Mbowa would summon the "sisters' sons," *bapwa* (sing. *mupwa*), of the royal clan to form a first line of defense. This suggests the important role of "sisters' sons," who were expected to help and, if necessary, defend the royal clan against its enemies. Even today the sisters' sons of the royal clan often refer to themselves as the spears and guns of the royal clan and remind its members that it was mainly sisters' sons who fought against the Ngoni at Mbowa in the South and at Chigoma in the north.

Stockaded villages were probably the most striking feature of the settlement pattern of Zambia in the nineteenth century, but they were not the typical form (Kay 1967*b*, p. 9). During this period of warfare and raiding, unless a people was numerous and militarily strong, large villages were a liability rather than an asset. Most Yombe and other Tumbuka peoples were neither numerous nor militarily strong, and lived in small scattered hamlets hidden in the bush. The palisaded villages provided those living in scattered hamlets with a place of refuge from small parties of Ngoni warriors or Arab slave raiders as well as from lions which often passed through the chiefdom. But the villages could not withstand large numbers of Ngoni warriors. Chigoma, a large village in the northern part of Uyombe, was destroyed more than once. However, Uyombe was never the main focus of Arab and Ngoni raids even though the raiders did pass through it on their way to other parts, and battles were fought on its borders, at Mbowa and Chigoma. The activities of Arab slave raiders ended in 1896, when Mlozi, an Arab slave trader based on Karonga, was defeated by the British. Two years later, in 1898, the British also subdued the Ngoni.

Even before the suppression by the British of the Arab slave trade and the Ngoni raids, the Yombe and other Tumbuka peoples were being gradually exposed to Western influences. The principal form of Western contact was with the Presbyterian missionaries of the Free Church of Scotland. In 1875 a party of Presbyterian missionaries under Captain Young arrived in Malawi and founded a station at Cape Maclear (Laws 1934, p. 7). The mission consisted of a number of skilled persons, the most important of whom was to be Dr. Robert Laws, an ordained Scots medical missionary who became the founder of Livingstonia (or Overtoun) mission at Kondowe. Cape Maclear was a convenient base for exploring other parts of the lakeshore, but the climate was poor and Africans were few in that area (ibid., p. 16). In 1881 the mission moved to Bandawe in Tonga Country (van Velsen 1959; see also Long 1962). In 1894 Dr. Laws left Bandawe and established a new mission in the salubrious heights of Kondowe above the Henga Valley. The Kondowe Livingstonia mission was to have a profound influence on the inhabitants of Uyombe as well as on the Tumbuka peoples of the Henga Valley, Nkamanga, and Hewe. Under Dr. Laws the purpose of the Livingstonia mission was not only to make Africans good Christians but also to educate them and to provide them with training in practical skills such as bricklaying, carpentry, masonry, and the rudiments of Western medicine. He intended that Livingstonia-trained Africans would return to their villages and develop African industrial life (*Livingstonia Letter Book* 1906, pp. 22–29). Most Livingstonia graduates, however, did not return to their villages but were employed by government, European planters and merchants, and large mining concerns in Southern and Central Africa (Livingstone 1932, p. 311).

The Livingstonia mission became the center of Christian activity, education, and Western influences throughout what has now become northern Malawi and northern Zambia. From it, other mission stations were founded. Although Uyombe remained at the periphery of the Livingstonia Synod, never having its own mission, African evangelists from Livingstonia led by David Kaunda, the father of President Kenneth Kaunda, went through the chiefdom in 1899, encouraging the Yombe to undertake training to become members of the Central African branch of the Free Church of Scotland, which in 1924 became the Church of Central Africa, Presbyterian (C.C.A., P.). But most Yombe did not begin to accept Christianity until John Punyira Wowo, a member of Chapyoka branch of the royal clan and now chief, was converted and attended Livingstonia. After completing his studies, he returned to Uyombe as an evangelist, and he and his brother Jere toured the chiefdom, persuading the Yombe to join the Free Church and to send their children to Livingstonia to be educated. John Wowo's home village, Chifunda, the central village of Chapyoka branch of the royal clan, became a Christian village and the center of local innovation and experiments. With new skills learned at Livingstonia, some villagers built two-story houses made of brick. John Wowo was instrumental in getting Livingstonia to found local mission schools, and by 1926 there were eleven schools in the chiefdom staffed primarily by Yombe. The Yombe teachers at these local primary schools formed the core of a new Christian- and Livingstonia-educated elite whose most prominent figures were John Punyira Wowo and his close cognatic relatives. Because they were Christians and taught at mission schools, they became the leading members of the local Free Church congregation when it was founded in the late 1920s. The local Free Church has been not only the center of Christian activity but also, since 1927, John Punyira Wowo's principal source of political support. Its leading elders and deacons have been his agnates and sisters' sons.

The eleven mission schools in Uyombe enrolled both boys and girls. Of a total enrollment of 469 in 1926 there were 253 (or 53%) boys and 216 (or 47%) girls (*Livingstonia Letter Book* 1927, pp. 787–88). Because these were vernacular schools, Yombe had to attend Livingstonia mission at Kondowe for training in English and to acquire special skills. The presence of eleven schools in Uyombe staffed primarily by Yombe, and the size of the enrollment, demonstrate the influence of Livingstonia mission and the West. A new elite, which was Christian and highly educated by Zambia standards, was in the process of formation, and at the same time it was undertaking the initial training of its successors who were to come into their own some twenty to thirty years later. Many of those who attended local mission schools in the late 1920s and the 1930s are now prominent in the commercial and political life of Yombe society. For the most part they were not educated at Livingstonia mission in Malawi. In the 1930s those pupils who had completed Yombe schooling were directed to Lubwa, a Presbyterian mission in Chinsali District which had been founded in 1904 by David Kaunda. It was at Lubwa mission that Yombe youths came into contact with persons of .diverse ethnic backgrounds, and it was there that they were influenced by men who were to become founders and organizers of Zambian independence movements.

By the turn of the century the influence of Free Church of Scotland missions had become widespread in Northern Nyasaland and in the adjacent territory of Northern Rhodesia. Livingstonia, Mwenzo (founded in 1894), and Lubwa became the principal centers of education of an African elite. They also provided Africans with opportunities for employment at the missions themselves or at one of their village schools. Those Africans who were employed by the missions received a wage, though not a large one, and were able to remain in the rural areas without seeking employment in the growing industrial and urban centers of the south. These "new men" stood apart from the uneducated elements of the indigenous ruling stratum of chiefs and headmen and often formed themselves into nonethnic (or nontribal) associations (van Velsen 1966, p. 379). The growth of these associations and the new educated element of the population which they represented provided the rural areas with a literate and vocal nucleus of leaders who were willing to protest against the policies of the mission (*Livingstonia Mission Council Book* 1921), of the British South Africa Company (Mbeelo 1971, pp. 241–42), and subsequently of British colonialism. Though Yombe educated at these missions were not themselves involved in such protests, it was within this atmosphere that they received their religious and educational training. They were themselves "new men."

During the period that Presbyterian missionaries were establishing missions in what is now Northern Malawi and Zambia and were providing Africans with a Western education and training in practical skills, the British South Africa Company under Cecil Rhodes was acquiring possession of the mineral rights of Northwestern Rhodesia and was extending its administrative control over Northeastern Rhodesia. With the suppression of the Arab slave trade and the defeat of Mpezeni's Ngoni, Northeastern Rhodesia, which included Isoka Division (or District), was effectively brought under the administration of the British South Africa Company. In 1899 the company's deputy administrator for Northeastern Rhodesia transferred his headquarters from Blantyre in Nyasaland to Fort Jameson in Northeastern Rhodesia. The village of Fife became the administrative center for Isoka District.

The British South Africa Company concentrated its efforts on developing the resources of the northwest. The northern territories of both Northeastern

Rhodesia and Nyasaland were regarded merely as areas which would supply African labor for the industrial and urban centers of the south. To keep the expenses of administration in Northeastern Rhodesia to a minimum, the company imposed a system of administration which was in many ways similar to protectorate policies of indirect rule. Native commissioners made use of indigenous rulers, and chiefs and their headmen were responsible for preserving law and order among their people. There were no formally constituted "native" courts or treasuries, the adjudication of cases being handled for the most part by indigenous tribunals. The more serious of these cases were referred to the native commissioner. For more effective administration, the company attempted to regulate patterns of population distribution. In both Northern Nyasaland and Northeastern Rhodesia many Africans were dispersed in small hamlets and villages, a type of settlement pattern which made administration and the collection of a hut tax difficult. In 1906, native commissioners were instructed to amalgamate small dispersed settlements into large villages (Kay 1967b, p. 11). This policy of amalgamation facilitated administration but did not take into account indigenous patterns of land usage and methods of cultivation. These two factors and the conflict between displaced headmen and villagers doomed the scheme to failure, and in 1911 the company rescinded its instructions (ibid.). But the general problem of population movement and distribution was one with which each new administration has had to deal.

The British South Africa Company imposed taxes on the African population (Gann 1969, p. 101), delegating to the native commissioners the task of collection. The native commissioners, in their turn, elicited the cooperation of chiefs and headmen. The hut tax was an important factor in stimulating the African to leave his home community in order to seek wage employment abroad, and it was primarily during this period of Zambian history that labor migration became an established pattern. The native commissioner and labor recruiters often relied upon the cooperation of local rulers to recruit African laborers. Thus, company administration did not seriously disrupt traditional patterns of authority but preserved law and order, collected taxes, and otherwise ruled through chief and headman.

When, in 1924, the administration of Northwestern Rhodesia and Northeastern Rhodesia by the British South Africa Company came to an end, the two territories became the British protectorate of Northern Rhodesia. Five years later the embryonic elements of indirect rule apparent in the administrative policies of the British South Africa Company were strengthened and expanded. The ordinances of 1929 restricted the powers and authority of the chiefs and provided uniformity in the system of local government throughout the protectorate. They provided for the recognition of chiefs and the establishment by the governor of Native Authorities and Native Courts. The chiefs became Native Authorities with their own staffs, each consisting of a clerk, court assessors and Kapasus (or messengers). Chief's councils were set up, consisting of chief's traditional advisors. In 1936, new ordinances were enacted. They did not alter the essential features of the ordinances of 1929 but they elaborated the form of Native Courts and provided for the establishment of Native Treasuries. This series of ordinances formed the basis of indirect rule and provided the framework of African local government in the rural areas. Local chiefs were no longer autonomous rulers. Instead they were at the base of a uniform and inclusive system of British colonial administration. Their immediate European superiors, the district commissioners, were themselves subordinate administrative officers, who were in their turn responsible to provincial commissioners and the governor and to the Northern Rhodesian Legislative Council in Lusaka and the Colonial Office in Britain. Thus, decisions taken in London or Lusaka could affect the daily life of Northern Rhodesian villagers.

At the same time that ordinances were being enacted to create a system of local government, steps were taken to regulate patterns of settlement. This took the form of what has become known as the "taxpayer rule." Native Authorities were instructed that new villages could be formed only if there were a minimum of ten taxpayers, whose dwellings had to be within hailing distance of that of the headman. It became apparent to district commissioners that neither they nor the Native Authorities could enforce this rule, and in 1945 it was revoked and replaced by the parish system. Under this system, individuals would not be restricted to villages but would be allowed to build and cultivate anywhere within an area designated a parish. By establishing units of administration larger than the village of ten taxpayers, it was hoped that social and economic development would be enhanced (Kay 1967b, p. 15).[3] According to Kay, the parish system failed for two reasons. The first reason was that in the postwar years there was not sufficient investment of capital and skills to bring about the intended development, and the second reason was that many provincial and district commissioners were basically opposed to the scheme (Kay 1967b, pp. 16–17). A third factor was that local headmen, at least in Uyombe, saw in the parish system a threat to their authority and prestige; they would no longer control villagers and might even become subordinate to a parish authority. This combination of factors brought an end to the parish system, which for all practical purposes was either forgotten or, more often, overlooked. Though Uyombe has nominally retained its parishes, they are rarely used as units of administration.

The postwar period was also one in which the Native Administration system was revised. The chief's councils were to include, in addition to village headmen and traditional advisers, elected and nominated councillors, some of whom were to have executive departmental functions and were to be educated commoners (Hailey 1956, p. 84). Thus, a new element was brought into local government, one which did not necessarily derive its status from the traditional order but rather from its possession of western education and skills. This revision of the Native Administration system did not have a great deal of significance for the Yombe until about 1961.

During the late 1950s and the early 1960s, nationalistic activity intensified not only in the urban centers but also in the rural areas. In the Northern Province this unrest was expressed in the widespread disturbances of 1961, which involved the burning of schools and the destruction of roads and bridges. Partly in response to the general unrest in the rural areas, a new Native Administration ordinance was enacted in 1960 which provided for the appointment of deputy chiefs to assume the administrative duties of aged, infirm, or otherwise incompetent chiefs (*Northern Rhodesia Government Gazette* 1960, p. 218). In Uyombe, where support for the nationalist movement was deeply rooted, the introduction of this ordinance opened the way for the election of a deputy chief who was a strong and active supporter of the Zambian national independence movement. In 1961, local branches of the United National Independence Party were founded in Uyombe. The branches provided commoners with an effective channel of political expression and allowed them to gain power. In the same year, the local branches of UNIP were formed into a "constituency," the unit of UNIP organization between the regional party and the local branches — hereafter referred to as a subregion branch. The subregional branch had its own central committee, which managed the affairs of its constituent branches and linked them to the regional party organization.

Because the chief of Uyombe had failed to perform many of the duties expected of a Native Authority, in 1962 the district commissioner of Isoka District introduced the post of deputy chief for Uyombe, ensuring that it was filled by election. The candidates were all members of the royal clan, and the electorate consisted of the adult male members of the six branches of the royal clan. With the support of the local UNIP subregion branch, Edwall Wowo of Njera royal branch was elected.[4]

The district commissioner of Isoka permitted Edwall Wowo to assume most of the chief's duties and to undertake reforms which increased popular participation in chiefdom government and allowed for more rapid development. In 1962 the government made the following administrative changes: the chief's council was renamed the "area committee," and the deputy chief was allowed to nominate UNIP subregion officers and other educated men as members of it. A number of other committees were created. Under the deputy chief's administration the most important has been the development committee, which has become the policy-making body of the area committee. From the development committee, ad hoc committees have been appointed to handle different problems of chiefdom government. In his attempt to centralize chiefdom government and at the same time to provide greater popular participation, the deputy chief has been opposed by the chief and his supporters as well as many village headmen who have seen in his reforms a threat to their own authority.

Chiefdom Government

The present structure of Uyombe chiefdom government is the outcome of historical and political processes which continue to play a part in structuring political relationships. Two interrelated and overlapping frameworks of local government may be distinguished: one is "traditional," and the other was created to secure effective control of an African majority by a small number of British administrative officers. This composite structure is briefly summarized in figure 1. The chart provides only a minimal and preliminary identification of important posts, councils and commitees.

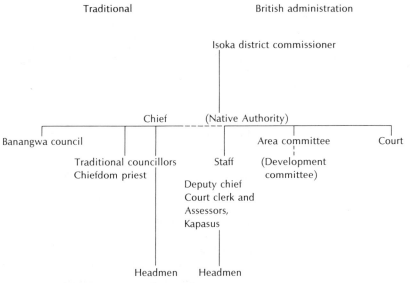

Figure 1. Chiefdom Government (1962-65)

Traditional posts are those of the chief, his three traditional councillors, the chiefdom priest (*musofi*), and village headmen. The chief is the head of the chiefdom, holds his post for life, and is a member of the royal clan. The royal clan consists of six branches but only the adult male members of Chapyoka, Njera, and Chipanga branches are eligible for the chieftainship. The chieftainship is supposed to rotate among these three chiefly branches; a chief's sons or another member of his branch are not supposed to succeed him. Two other branches, Kaswanga and Vumbo, participate in the selection of a new chief, but their members may not themselves hold the post. The last branch, Polomombo, does not even have the right to take part in the selection. Though the chief is chosen from the royal clan and selected primarily by its adult members, the three traditional councillors, the headmen of

Mbamba, Mpemba, and Zumbe, play an important part. They are the ones who take charge of the chiefdom when a chief dies, arrange for the selection of a new one, and represent the interests of commoners. The chief is supposed to seek their advice on all important chiefdom matters. Subordinate to the chief are the village headmen. Although they are appointed by the chief, he may not dismiss them without the approval and consent of the royal clan council, the Banangwa council. They are in charge of their own villages but they are also responsible to the chief. The chiefdom priest is appointed by the chief, his principal duties being to maintain the graves of chiefs and to perform rites at these graves in times of crisis such as droughts and plagues.

The Banangwa council consists of members of the six branches of the royal clan. Because members consider themselves the owners of the chiefdom, their council deals with matters such as rights of chiefdom residence, village boundaries, and the dismissal of headmen. The Banangwa Council has the right to review the way in which members occupying chiefdom posts conduct public affairs and to hear important disputes between royals. Any person who habitually breaks traditional customs and practices may be summoned before it. Because commoners do not belong to it and may not attend its meetings unless invited, they must seek royal spokesmen to represent their interests. This indicates the exclusive nature of the council as well as the power it held in the past. Though its control over commoners has declined, it is still an important political arena in which royal branches, segments, and individuals seek support and compete for power.

The chiefdom government also includes those posts and councils established during British rule. This administration system consists of the chief (Native Authority), his staff, the area committee, and the chiefdom court. The chief's staff includes the deputy chief, a court clerk, two court assessors, and Kapasus (messengers). They are minor civil servants appointed and paid by government to deal with the business of administration. The chief, who is subordinate to the district commissioner (now the district secretary) is in charge of the chiefdom. He is expected to maintain law and order, carry out government policies, and to initiate minor legislation relating to matters such as village sanitation and rural development. He is supposed to be in charge of chiefdom councils and committees and the head of the chiefdom court. In 1962 most of these duties were taken over by the deputy chief.

The area committee (formerly the chief's council) includes the chief, his staff, headmen, and other prominent persons of the chiefdom. Its approval is necessary for the use of chiefdom funds and labor and the passing of minor regulations. It is from this body that other committees derive their authority. The development committee is the executive body of the area committee; its members are either nominated by the chief or elected by the area committee. Its main purpose is to originate development schemes and to persuade members of the larger body to vote for them. Other committees

have been created, for example, the night school committee, the Vinkakanimba Day committee, and the Lenshina (or Lumpa) rehabilitation committee, to deal with special matters. Village headmen are also part of this
structure of administration.

Political and Religious Groups

The two main political groups in Yombe society are the royal clan and the
UNIP subregion branch. Both the royal clan and the subregion branch are
concerned with regulating chiefdom affairs. The councils and committees of
chiefdom government form a series of arenas in which the two groups
compete for support and power. The prevalence of one or the other may also
affect the way in which the staff of chiefdom government carries out its
duties.

The royal clan, an exogamous, agnatic descent group, bases its claim to
rule on descent from the conquerors of the chiefdom. Its adult male
members (numbering about 5% of the total adult male population) refer to
themselves as "free people," *Banangwa*. They form the traditional ruling
stratum, and from their numbers the chief is selected. Though their council,
the Banangwa council, is part of local government, the council is basically a
meeting of kinsmen to discuss matters affecting their joint estate, the chieftainship and the chiefdom. The relations between members are supposed to
be governed by norms of agnatic kinship, which stress cooperation, unity
and equality. These norms are not always followed, particularly when
disputes over rights and status arise between branches. A man's primary
loyalty should be to his own branch and he is supposed to protect its
interests against the claims of other branches.

The six branches of the royal clan are themselves political groups, and
they compete for control of chiefdom affairs. They have their own interests
for which they seek support from other royal branches, the UNIP subregion
branch, the churches, and the headmen. The two principal competitors are
Chapyoka and Njera, mainly because the chief is Chapyoka and the deputy
chief Njera. The competition of these two men pervades the political life of
the chiefdom and their branches attempt to marshal support for them in the
royal clan, in the subregion branch, in the churches, and among commoners.

The UNIP is a national mass party; its membership is open to everyone and
easily acquired by purchasing a card. Hence at the local level it includes
commoners and royals alike. A branch was formed in Muyombe during the
period 1960–61 by men returning from abroad. Its officers organized a
number of local branches throughout Uyombe and in parts of the neighboring chiefdom of Ufungwe. These branches were combined to form a "constituency" (subregion branch). The Muyombe branch officers became the
"constituency cabinet" (or subregion committee) responsible for the activi-

ties of local branches and their executive committees, and they have maneuvered themselves and their supporters into important posts in chiefdom government. They are members of its councils and committees and hold some offices. They are also the main advisers of the deputy chief, who was elected through their influence when the post was created in 1962.

While Christianity has not replaced the traditional ancestor worship, it has been an important catalyst of social change. It has provided the Yombe with a new set of beliefs and practices and a new basis for social alignment that transcends the narrow boundaries of their agnatically based ancestor cults.

The present composition of Christian churches in part reflects political cleavages in the royal clan and developing patterns of social differentiation. In 1965, the Free Church of Scotland had a membership of only 250; but the small membership conceals its historical significance as the church of the new educated elites and of those who aspire to elite status. Most members describe themselves as civilized and consider many practices of the independent African churches and other religious movements as "uncivilized." This attitude stems from their basic Western orientation, the educational and occupational qualifications of church leaders, and the historical contact with the Livingstonia mission.

The Free Church of Scotland was the first European mission church to form a congregation in Uyombe. Within this congregation there rapidly developed a core of Livingstonia-trained men and women who were elders and deacons and who thus controlled church affairs. Many church officers were Chief Punyira's cognates and loyal supporters. Chief Punyira selected his personal adviser from them and appointed church members to headmanships when these posts fell vacant. By the 1930s the new Livingstonia-trained elite controlled both the Free Church and the chiefdom, and the Free Church became identified not only with the new elite but also with the chief and his royal branch. In 1965, while there were elders and deacons who still supported the chief and his branch, there were many who belonged to other royal branches or who were members of and loyal to UNIP. The Free Church remains the church of the new elite, and though many of the young political leaders are suspended members, they still attend services regularly.

In the mid-1930s the Watchtower movement and two independent African churches, Jordan and National, founded congregations in Uyombe. None of the local figures who played a prominent part in organizing these churches belonged to the chief's royal branch; few of them were highly educated men. Since the mid-1930s the head of Watchtower has been Chongo Wowo of Chipanga royal branch, who joined the movement while working abroad. Though he has tried to build up a large membership in Uyombe, he has had little success; in 1965, the movement had only about fifteen adult members. Since the movement specifically forbids its members to take part in politics, politically interested royals and commoners have not joined it.

The Jordan and National churches have not suffered from such restrictions on political activity. They were both founded by Malawians who, objecting to European-dominated mission churches, sought to make Christianity compatible with African beliefs, practices, and customs. In Uyombe the most active Jordan and National evangelists were not men who were part of the Livingstonia elite. Some of these evangelists belonged to the royal clan, although not to the chief's branch. Bwana Samsalu and his eldest son Esaw, prominent members of Njera branch, organized Jordan churches throughout the chiefdom; and in 1965, their village was a Jordan stronghold. Some National leaders were also royals, but mostly belonging to Chipanga, Kaswanga, and Vumbo.

Jordan and National, which share many beliefs and practices, have recruited most of their members (about six hundred between the two churches) from villagers and not primarily from the Muyombe elite. Their leaders consider the Free Church their main rival for religious authority.

The Lumpa church provides a more recent example of royals attempting to make use of a religious movement to advance their position in the chiefdom. It was a prophetic movement founded by a Bemba woman, Alice "Lenshina" Mulenga, in Chinsali District. In 1953, Alice Mulenga received her prophetic calling, subsequently founding the Lumpa church at Kasomo near to Chinsali. In Uyombe the first branch was formed in Kalinda, the central village of Polomombo (the deprived branch of the royal clan), and the movement was almost entirely an experience of the northwest. By 1955 there were eight local churches, with many of their preachers and judges Polomombo or from the local villages. However, 1960–61 saw the rapid rise of Uyombe UNIP branches and the realization by most Yombe that UNIP and not Lumpa was the important political force. Many Polomombo and headmen withdrew from Lumpa and joined UNIP. The Lumpa church and UNIP grew progressively antagonistic in Chinsali, Uyombe, and other parts of Zambia. In 1964 this antagonism erupted into violence; Lumpa churches were banned and members detained. In Uyombe the detainees numbered 255.

In Uyombe, Christian churches may provide the basis for political coalitions and a source for recruiting political support. A church elder may attempt to represent the interests of his church within the royal clan, UNIP, and on the councils and committees of chiefdom government. Conversely, he may represent the interests of these bodies within the church and attempt to gain its backing. This produces situations in which the choices of participants as to which interests they will support and whom they will back are not always predictable. An individual may attempt to select a role or status from his role and status sets in order to redefine the situation and produce a realignment of support in his favor. This type of maneuvering often leads to ambiguity and indecisive political encounters between the main political and religious groups.

The period of my fieldwork, 1963–65, coincided with the period of rapid movement toward independence in Zambia, and of working out how to manage that independence once it was achieved. New policies stemmed on the one hand from government and on the other from UNIP, the dominant African nationalist political party, which was gradually taking over the reins of government. The spheres of authority and competence of both the British colonial government and UNIP had not been clearly defined. In this context of rapid political change the institutions of local government assumed a certain flexibility, allowing for the representation of new interests. Local civil servants, UNIP subregion branch officers, and villagers alike were uncertain as to the nature of the relationship between the local government and the UNIP subregion branch. On the very morning of Zambian independence, 24 October 1964, the chief went to the home of the UNIP committee secretary to inquire whether he was still the chief or whether the secretary would assume his post.

3

The Territorial Framework: The Village and the Capital

In developing African countries the relation of the national capital to lesser, nonindustrial communities generates a dynamic political field based upon competition for the use of limited national resources. The economic and social development of the national capital draws upon the resources, (for example, revenue, labor, and skills) of lesser communities, and thus may hinder their development. Although the chiefdom of Uyombe is not in every respect a microcosm of Zambia as a whole, Yombe political life reflects the relationship of Muyombe, the capital, to lesser territorial units. Muyombe is the center for a new rural elite of former clerks, schoolteachers, and other government employees. This elite, which is highly educated by Zambian standards, has entered into chiefdom politics, and its most active members belong to chiefdom councils and committees which make decisions about local development; the distribution and location of basic services such as education, health, and commerce. In general, this elite has preferred to concentrate basic services in Muyombe, and its members have argued that advance in the chiefdom as a whole depends on the rapid development of Muyombe. It aspires to have Muyombe recognized as a rural township and thus become eligible to receive financial support from the Zambian government. Villagers, on the other hand, argue that services should be distributed throughout the chiefdom. This disagreement is the major issue between Muyombe and the villages.

Under British rule, the territorial arrangements of Uyombe were transformed, and Muyombe was made distinct from other villages. This change in the position of Muyombe relative to the subordinate peripheral communities increased their dependence upon the center and, at the same time, broadened the areas for competition and conflict with it. In former days, Uyombe had many of those features which Southall describes as characteristic of "segmentary states" (Southall 1953, pp. 241–49). It was distinctly a territorial unit, and all settlements within the area nominally recognized the superiority of the *musumba*—the chief and his village. The boundaries of the chiefdom, like those of the larger villages, were marked by rivers, hills, and other natural features. Large stockaded villages such as Jumbo in the northwest, Chigoma in the northeast, and Mbowa in the south were situated near the borders to guard against the encroachment of neighboring chiefdoms on Uyombe land. Old men still remember the boundary skirmishes with the Ngoni and with the neighboring chiefdoms at Chigoma and Mbowa.

In precolonial days, Muyombe was the administrative center of the chiefdom and had a specialized administrative staff recruited primarily from its senior residents, the chief's close cognatic kinsmen and trusted commoners. The lesser communities in many respects were reproductions of Muyombe. Although the chiefdom had a centralized government, there were other foci of administrative authority, notably the central villages of the areas belonging to the six branches of the royal clan. The heads of these villages had the same order of authority over their subordinate villages as the chief had over his. They are even said to have put villagers to death for disobedience, a right supposed to be held only by the chief. The six branches of the royal clan together considered the chiefdom, its land, its people, and the chieftainship itself to be part of their joint estate. The branches of the royal clan might fight among themselves but they would stand together against their nonroyal subjects.

Each large settlement was a replica of the capital and thus had the potential of changing its allegiance from one power pyramid to another— placing itself under the hegemony of a neighboring chief or even Kyungu, the ruler of the Ngonde, another segmentary state (Southall 1953, p. 253)—or attempting to establish itself as an autonomous political community. To prevent secessionist movements, the chief had to rely upon forces which were similar to those available to the secessionists. In the early 1900s such a situation arose in a dispute between two rival claimants for the chieftainship; one claimant was from Polomombo branch of the royal clan and the other one was from Njera branch. Polomombo's attempt at secession was prevented by the timely intervention of the European native commissioner. The dispute was settled in Njera's favor and the Polomombo Wowo were not allowed to secede. Muyombe was recognized as the only administrative center. The Native Authorities Ordinance of 1929 not only defined the territorial boundaries over which Native Authorities had jurisdiction but also recognized the residence of Native Authorities as centers of authority. From then on it was no longer possible for a community to secede without the consent of the Protectorate Administration. As far as Isoka District was concerned, the administration pursued an active policy of amalgamation (Hudson 1965). Thus, under British rule Uyombe ceased to be a loosely knit political community of more or less homologous territorial units, interconnected through the chief and his capital and by the framework provided by the royal clan (the principal land-owning group of Uyombe chiefdom). The Protectorate Administration penetrated the integument of Yombe society through Muyombe, not only locking local settlements into a single political framework but also linking them to the wider administration system of Isoka District, the Northern Province, and the protectorate government of Northern Rhodesia.

In the process of becoming the center of Uyombe chiefdom's local government, Muyombe became more than just another village. It assumed a multiplicity of functions as the main locus of education, commerce, and political and religious activity for the chiefdom as a whole. It now constitutes that critical juncture through which district, provincial, and even national institutions and organizations penetrate into rural life. In Muyombe, decisions are made concerning not only the life of villagers but also the allocation of limited public resources. The direction of chiefdom development is therefore determined in Muyombe and other settlements are now more dependent upon it than they were in the past. Because it provides a number of basic services, villagers show a marked concern over whether the limited resources will be used to build schools, dams, and dispensaries in Muyombe or near to their own village. Villagers expect their headmen to represent village interests on the councils and committees of chiefdom government and to challenge the development of Muyombe at the expense of other settlements.

The conflict of chiefdom and village interests is a recurrent theme in Yombe politics. The important figures who are actively engaged in shaping the political affairs of the chiefdom are the core of the new rural elite, which seeks to have local decisions made in its favor and aspires to enter into the more inclusive arenas of district and provincial politics. These men have chosen to live in Muyombe, at the synapse of Yombe political life.

Villages

The village is a territorial unit under a headman, *fumu* (pl. *mafumu*). It consists of a discrete cluster of dwellings with a surrounding area of land usually bounded by such natural features as streams, hills, or large trees. The size of a village may vary from four or five huts to sixty or more. The Yombe speak of the settlements as *mizi* (s. *muzi*), though they may refer to the smaller ones by the diminutive *kamuzi*. The word *muzi* may be applied to any permanent settlement, regardless of size. The Yombe distinguish settlements that have been recorded in the Tax Register kept by the local government from those that have not received this official recognition. I shall refer to settlements inscribed in the Tax Register as administrative villages.

An administrative village is an officially recognized subdivision of the chiefdom.[1] Its headman has been nominated by the chief and approved by the district commissioner. His name is listed in the Tax Register kept by the local government, and he is responsible for his area and the people who live in it. Although sixty-five villages are inscribed in the Tax Register, in 1964 there were in fact fifty-eight. There are also other villages whose headmen derive their authority from the administrative headmen on whose land their settlements are situated. These settlements and their inhabitants are considered by the Native Administration to belong to the administrative villages.

There is yet another type of settlement. In the cultivation season, villagers may move to huts, *vilindo* (sing. *cilindo*), situated on their gardens. This saves them from having to walk every day to the gardens and permits them to protect their crops from the ravages of such wild animals as small deer, baboons, and wild pigs. Residence "on the farm," as it is sometimes called, is supposed to be seasonal but in fact may become permanent. If it does, a new village will appear. Many Yombe prefer to live in small, dispersed, residential units, as they commonly did at the turn of the century. The Native Administration attempted to prevent this by requiring all villagers to return to their villages at the end of the maize harvest in July and to stay there until the rains begin in late November.

The physical layout of Yombe villages has changed considerably since the last century. Elderly Yombe say that villages were then built around a central area in which a circular shelter, the village *Mphara*, was situated. The Mphara was an important center of village activity. Married men usually ate their main meal of the day there and spent the rest of the evening discussing local affairs. Cases were heard and meetings were held there. Today, few villages have a Mphara, but its significance may be seen in the fact that Yombe refer to the Native Administration building in Muyombe as a Mphara because men assemble there to discuss important problems.

The huts of the village chief were normally sited on the periphery and were easily distinguishable because of the high reed fence which surrounded them. The grass huts of other villagers tended to be grouped in discrete clusters around the Mphara. Close agnatic ties are said to have been the main basis of clustering. Other general features of the villages were boys' houses, which the Yombe also call *mphara*, girls' houses (*ntanganini*), and cattle kraals. The latter were usually situated on the outskirts of a village.

Since few villages today have a Mphara, the focus of daily life has shifted to the household, though a man takes an active interest in the affairs of those neighbors and friends with whom he may share the evening meal. Few villages now have boys' houses, though they existed as recently as fifteen years ago. Common residence in a boys' house formed the basis of lasting friendships which are still extremely important, since political cliques may be based on them.

In the garden settlements a man usually builds a small pole and mud hut where he and his family live from late November until July. The adjacent gardens may be those of married sons, fellow villagers, or people from other villages. Another pattern is for several men to build houses together. This type of settlement may develop into a village.

Though a woman must live with her husband, there are few restrictions on where a man may settle. Land is abundant; it is not subject to rent, sale, or individual inheritance, and a man is in no way tied to it. He can easily acquire access to land by applying to the headman who controls it. Few headmen refuse to let people from other villages cultivate gardens in their area, though they may keep the best land nearest the village for themselves and their villagers.

Because headmen want as many villagers as they can attract, it is not difficult for a man to move from one village to another. The procedure for joining a village is simple. The usual practice is for the stranger, *mulendo* (pl. *balendo*), to approach a relative or friend already living in the village and ask him to play the part of an intermediary or messenger (*nkaramba*). The intermediary speaks to the headman about the stranger and vouches for his character. Then the stranger must himself approach the headman, who usually gives him permission to settle, tells him where to build his house, points out land already in use, and should report the move to the Native Administration. Once this permission has been given the newcomer is no longer looked upon as a *mulendo* but as a permanent resident, *muzengezgiani* (pl. *Bazengezgiani*).

The Headman

The headman and his close agnatic kin are also *bazengezgiani;* but in addition they consider themselves and are considered by other villagers to be the owners of the village, *beneco ba muzi*. As the head of the village the headman decides whether the village should move, on account either of the exhaustion of the soil or of sickness or many deaths, or of attacks by lions. In recent years headmen have found it more attractive to site their villages near the roads and main paths.

Though a village may move and individuals may leave it, it may nevertheless be regarded as an enduring social unit. The headman is known by its name, and his successor assumes the same name. Both the post and the title are vested in the agnatic group whose members trace descent from the founder. The chief usually selects a headman's successor from the founding agnatic group, though he has the authority to appoint someone else, who then becomes the village owner, *mwene muzi*. The chief may also give a man permission to found his own village and assign him land on which to do so. But a man with initiative may collect a group of relatives and friends and found his own settlement. If he can gather a sufficient following, he may apply to the Native Administration for official recognition, but when he dies his successor will be appointed by the chief.

The headmen of the central villages of the six branches of the royal clan are the only ones who are not chosen or invested with authority by the chief. When one dies, the senior members of the royal clan select a successor from among the eligible members of the branch.

The Headman's Duties

The Yombe attach considerable value to the position of headman of an administrative village. The post gives an ambitious man control over land and people, and if his village is large, he gains power, influence and prestige within the chiefdom. Branches of the royal clan and the UNIP subregion may seek the support of a headman of a large village, and, if he can reconcile the potentially conflicting demands of the royal clan and the party, he may become a decisive figure on the councils and committees of the Native Administration and the subregion branch.

Because the administrative headman is deemed to be the owner of the village, he is entitled to one thigh from each animal killed on village land and to one day's labor from each villager at planting time. The economic value of the thigh and the one day of village labor does not secure for him a standard of living superior to that of fellow villagers, since demands are constantly being made on his resources. Nonetheless, headmen attach great importance to receiving the labor and especially the thigh, which symbolizes their rights over land and people. If they do not demand it, other headmen may encroach upon their territory. The heads of settlements built on the land of an administrative headman are not entitled to the thigh; the headman has delegated authority to them and they are subordinate to him.

Failure to present a headman with the thigh can lead to a fight and even a court case. Villagers, however, are increasingly reluctant to give it. Many argue that because they have purchased a gun and license from the government they should not be expected to give a portion of their kill to the headman, especially if they do not reside in his village.

The headman is a nonsalaried agent of chiefdom government whose reward stems from his control of land and people. An essential requirement of his position, therefore, is a following. It is from him that a person gains the right to settle in the village and to use village land. Fallers found, among the Soga of Uganda, that control of land and people without tribute or a salary was not a sufficient reward for the headman. Without some form of income the Soga headman was unable to fulfill his "traditional" obligations of hospitality, which constituted a serious drain on his own personal resources. His failure to provide hospitality lost him the respect of villagers and undermined both his role as the hereditary leader of his village and his effectiveness as an agent of the African local government (Fallers 1956, p. 175). The delicate position of the Soga headman is in part resolved in the case of the Yombe headman. In Uyombe the headman is expected to dispense hospitality from his own granaries, but villagers are expected to help him with contributions of food and beer. Thus, the full burden of providing hospitality and even assisting destitute villagers falls not only upon the headman but also upon the whole village. The headman is the one who receives and distributes the contributions of his fellow villagers, and he is expected to be more generous than others.

The headman is responsible to and for his villagers. He is expected to provide for the needy and, on those occasions when he makes offerings to his ancestors for village welfare, to provide villagers with food and beer. Both villagers and the chief expect the headman to maintain order, arbitrate minor disputes, and attend villagers when they have an important case in the Native Administration court in Muyombe. There are, however, major cases which do not reach the Native Administration court. They may involve either witchcraft accusations or offences which are common but demand severe penalties. The headman may attempt to arbitrate such cases with the assistance of senior villagers and headmen of other villages or arrange for them to be heard by the chief in the privacy of his compound.

The headman is responsible for organizing and coordinating village activities such as cleaning the village and keeping paths and bridges in good repair; he also leads village hunts. He represents the village to other headmen, the Banangwa council, the chief, and, on occasions, the representatives of UNIP. He holds a seat on the area committee, where he represents the interests of his villagers. He may argue for schools, roads, and bridges in his area. Many local development schemes such as the building of new blocks for schools and the dispensary and the construction of a dam in Muyombe are based on "self-help," the use of unpaid village labor and the skills of local men. Most villagers are reluctant to contribute money, labor, and skills for local schemes that do not benefit them directly. Hence, they expect their headman to try to get development schemes in their area and, at the same time, to protect them from having to contribute to schemes undertaken in other parts of the chiefdom—especially in Muyombe, which, many villagers argue, has received more than its share. Because the headman sits on the area committee, which must approve the schemes proposed by the development committee, villagers expect him to put their names forward when paying jobs become available. Headmen make frequent visits to Muyombe to gather as much information as they can on new schemes, the prospect of jobs, and the general economic and political situation of the chiefdom.

While representing the interests of his villagers, the headman is also the agent of chiefdom government and, in addition, must be responsive to the demands of the UNIP subregion branch. He is the one who must see that villagers obey the laws of the chiefdom and the orders of the chief. This need not create problems for him unless the policies of the chief are contrary to the interests of villagers. When such a situation arises, he must attempt to reconcile conflicting demands. He may, as Kuper argues for the Kalahari village headman, use the support of villagers to avoid carrying out the demands of chiefdom government, or he may use his position as the agent of chiefdom government to coerce his people (Kuper 1970, p. 357). The backing of villagers depends on the issues involved. An ineffective or habitually insubordinate headman, however, runs the risk of being dismissed from his post by the Banangwa council. This last factor is important for two reasons.

First, leaders of village factions who aspire to the headman's post may support the chief against the headman and the village interests he represents. Second, because headmen are appointed by the chief but can be dismissed only by the Banangwa council, aspiring faction leaders must not only get support within the village but also establish links with powerful royals who may advance their claims on the Banangwa Council.

A headman's agnates, though they may live in other villages, consider the headman's post theirs and themselves the owners of his village. The claim is not a legal one, but the chief usually appoints a headman's successor from the same descent group. While a headman is still in office, his ambitious agnates may begin to recruit other agnates and villagers both as followers and to gain the favor of the chief and other senior members of branches of the royal clan.

Gluckman's discussion of the Central African headman stresses the delicacy of the headman's position arising from the conflict of demands and principles (Gluckman 1963, p. 151). Nonetheless, the Yombe headman has much room for maneuver. True, he is subject to conflicting demands which stem from his position in the village and from his position in chiefdom government, but there are options open to him for mobilizing support against recalcitrant villagers on the one hand, and unpopular government policies on the other. The subregion branches of UNIP have introduced new sources of power and provided alternatives to established patterns of political alliances.

From the early 1960s, neither the chief nor the headmen were sure of their positions under the colonial government and their standing with UNIP. Most Yombe headmen performed duties that were not part of their official roles. For example, a stranger who stayed in a village would be asked for his UNIP card and, if he did not have one, would be advised by the headman to purchase one and report his presence to the local branch. If for any reason the headman was suspicious of the stranger, he would send for a branch officer. It was not unusual for headmen and villagers to refuse to cooperate with local representatives of government departments unless they had been told to do so by local UNIP officers. They would also seek the advice and even consent of local UNIP officers prior to accepting many Native Administration policies.

The Headman: Village and Chiefdom Links

Gluckman has observed of Central African villages that "the kinship links between the headman and his followers may vary from tribe to tribe, or within a tribe, and within a single village there may be different kinds of kinsmen, but the headman is always regarded as the senior kinsman (Gluckman 1963, p. 148). Within Uyombe, villages are the basic residential units and headmen are the principal figures who are expected to represent the

interests of the common folk in public life. The composition of a village and
its politics may affect the grass roots support of chiefdomwide leaders. A
headman may or may not be able to mobilize support for himself and for his
royal patron on the basis of his kin ties with fellow villagers. His own agnates
may be his strongest adversaries, for they too consider the village theirs and
thus want to control it. One can analyze village composition by describing
the various kinship, affinal, and other links between the adult heads of
houses and the headman. In the description that follows I take the headman
as the focal figure, not because he is necessarily the senior kinsman within the
field of domestic and kinship relationships within the village, but because he
holds a political post. Many headmen are the heads of agnatic groups and
may be senior cognates for some villagers, but other villagers may be their
affines or not related to them at all. The headman derives his importance
from the fact that he is the official representative of the villagers to other
headmen and to the chief and that he sits on the councils and committees of
chiefdom government.

An examination of the relationship of 64 adult house heads to the
headmen in five villages suggests the type of variation found in the social
composition of Yombe villages. The five villages are situated in different
parts of the chiefdom, and each has its own history. B and E were some five
to seven miles to the south of Muyombe; A was about ten miles and C some
fifteen miles to the northeast; and D was about twenty miles to the north.
Each of the five headmen was at least sixty years old, had at least two wives,
and was the head of an extended family and the senior member of his
agnatic descent group. Most of the 64 house heads were men; the five
women heads were all living with their male agnates.

Table 1 shows the relationship of the 64 adult house heads to their headmen. The villages are arranged according to the approximate dates of their
founding. I have not given a date for the founding of village A because its
headman claimed that it was one of the original settlements in the chiefdom,
if not the oldest. An individual with more than one kinship link with the
headman is classified by the relationship which the people regard as the
more significant one for residence.

The first feature shown by the table is that only 22 (34%) of the 64 house
heads are primary or classificatory agnatic kin of the headman. This is
significant because older Yombe emphasize agnatic kinship as an important
principle of residential affiliation. There is evidence that close agnates do in
fact live in the same village. Of the 22 house heads who were agnatically
related to the five headmen, 19 were one step removed (16 were the headman's sons and 3 were his brothers) and 2 were two steps removed (brothers'
sons) from the headman. The remaining house head was a classificatory son.
This points to the preponderance of real over classificatory agnatic kin, again
emphasizing the importance of close agnatic kin relationships in contrast to
more distant ones. This should not, however, obscure the possible range of
variation between villages; 8 of the 11 house heads of village D were the

headman's close agnates, but in village C none were the headman's agnates, a point discussed below. A third feature is that 26 (41%) of all the house-heads are the headmen's affines, and all but one of these affinal links are primary ones. Eleven of the house heads are only two steps removed from the headman; in 7 cases the headman is the father of the house head's wife, in 3 cases the brother, and in 1 case the daughter's husband. Of the 14 remaining house heads who are linked affinally to the headman, 2 are three steps removed from the headman, 3 four steps, and 9 more than four steps. The one remaining house head is a classificatory affine. A fourth feature of these five villages is the small number of house heads who are the head-man's cognates. Nine (14%) house heads were the headman's cognates—an arrangement which was a marked feature only of village C and is related to its early history. But though cognatic relationships do not appear an important factor in choice of residence, it is from them that a political figure selects his trusted allies and it is through them that he may gain the backing of persons not related to him. Seven (11%) of the adult house heads were not related to the headman at all.

In a society which stresses the principle of agnatic affiliation as a basis for

Table 1. Relationship of 64 House Heads to Headman in Five Villages

	Village A	Village B	Village C	Village D	Village E	All Villages
Year founded	?	1929	1932	1940	1943	
Age of headman	75	75	65	70	60	
No. of house heads	10	11	17	11	15	64
Sex of house heads						
Men	9	11	14	11	14	59
Women	1	—	3	—	1	5
Agnates						
Primary	4	3	—	8	6	21
Classificatory	—	1	—	—	—	1
Total	4	4	0	8	6	22
% of total	40	36	0	73	40	34
Cognates						
Primary	—	—	8	—	—	8
Classificatory	—	1	—	—	—	1
Total	0	1	8	0	0	9
% of total	0	9	47	0	0	14
Affines						
Primary	5	5	6	2	7	25
Classificatory	—	1	—	—	—	1
Total	5	6	6	2	7	26
% of total	50	55	35	18	47	41
Unrelated						
Total	1	0	3	1	2	7
% of total	10	0	18	9	13	11

residence, it is surprising that about two-thirds of the 64 house heads did not belong to the headman's descent group and so could not claim to be owners of the village. These villages are not agnatic units, and the headman, though part of the fabric of village life, is not enmeshed in a localized kin group consisting solely of his agnates. Many house heads are the headman's affines but are also the affines of other members of his descent group. They may owe no special loyalty to him. If, for example, the headman is the son-in-law of a house head, he is considered subordinate to him and not a senior kinsman. Yet those men who have married his daughters and paid only a small portion of the bridewealth are considered subordinate to him, though not to his lineage. The headman's agnates expect him to represent their claims as owners of the village, and to oppose competing claims from persons, including his affines, whom they regard as "strangers." Yet, at the same time, the headman's agnates may seek the support of these "strangers" against him.

The way in which the five villages were founded accounts for some of the variations in their social composition and also makes clearer the relationship of each headman to the royal clan. Three of them may be termed "commoner" villages, one is a "sister's son's" village, and one a "royal" village. The relationship of headmen to branches of the royal clan is important for understanding chiefdom politics. The rivalry between the six branches of the royal clan (and also between the segments of branches) is manipulated by ambitious commoners, while at the same time senior members of the royal clan make use of commoners to promote their own interests. A headman who is a commoner needs a friend on the Banangwa council to represent and protect his interests and those of his villagers; in turn, members of the royal clan need the support of headmen on the area committee. If one party fails to support the other, either one may look for and find backing elsewhere.

Village A

The headman of village A is Tim. Although he and his agnates are commoners, they claim that Mwene Labeta—the founder of their descent group, Vidi—entered Uyombe before the founding ancestors of the royal clan and built a village at the foot of Kalanga mountain, the ritual center of the chiefdom. If this version of Yombe "history" is accepted (members of the royal clan do not accept it), not only is theirs the oldest settlement but the Vidi are the owners of the chiefdom. Because the Vidi have on occasions made this claim in public, their relationship with many senior members of the royal clan is strained, and Tim's tenure as headman at times precarious. Most villagers are Tim's agnates or affines, but the village is torn by factional disputes, which arise from his attempt to retain the allegiance of villagers and to secure the headmanship for a member of his own segment of Vidi after his death. His main rival is Didi, his classificatory son and the head of another segment of the lineage, who aspires to the headship of both lineage and village.

In the course of their disputes over rights and status, both Tim and Didi not only attempt to marshal the support of fellow villagers but also seek the backing of senior members of the royal clan. Tim has sought the support of Bwana Samsalu the head of Njera branch and Didi that of the chief. Bwana Samsalu and the deputy chief are the chief's main adversaries. These disputes between Tim and Didi and their attempt to gain support of royals for their conflicting claims has introduced chiefdom rivalries into village politics and undermined Vidi claims. They have also made other Yombe wary of settling in the village. (For a detailed discussion of this case see Bond, 1972)

Village B
Village B, a "royal" village, was founded in 1929 by Kaleb, the son of chief Vwalamawoko, who ruled from 1915 until 1927. After Vwalamawoko's death, Kaleb settled in the new capital founded by the new chief, Punyira (John Wowo), even though sons of previous chiefs should not, traditionally, live in the village of the reigning one. Both Kaleb and Punyira belong to the Chapyoka branch of the royal clan. Punyira suspected Kaleb of practicing witchcraft against him and told him to leave the capital. Kaleb left and founded his own settlement. Even though Chief Punyira had the right to remove potential rivals from the capital, his action permanently alienated Kaleb and his segment of Chapyoka. The fact that Kaleb belonged to the royal clan may account for the slightly higher percentage of affines among the heads of houses in his village. Most of these are his daughters' husbands. Kaleb is protected from the intrusion of royal rivalries into his village, since as a royal he himself has access to the Banangwa council as well as having a seat on the area committee.

Village C
The social composition of village C, a "sister's son's" village, sets it apart from the other four. Most of the house heads are either cognates or affines of the headman. The village is an offshoot, though not a satellite, of Chifunda, the central village of Chapyoka branch of the royal clan. Its founder, Motta, left Chifunda in 1932 and founded his own settlement two miles away. Motta's mother was a member of Njera branch of the royal clan, and when Motta founded his new village, two of her sisters and their husbands went with him. They were subsequently joined by one of her sister's sons. Thus the core of the settlement consists of the descendants of four royal women of Njera, and it is this feature which has shaped the social composition of the village.

Motta is a loyal and trusted sister's son of Njera. Because he considers the interests of Njera as a whole to be more important than those of segments, he has often been called upon to arbitrate disputes within Njera. He has the ear of royals and is a party to their private councils, and, as a result, his favor is sought by other commoners.

Another prominent commoner, Yotta Chila, is attached to his village. The location of his brick houses reflects his social and kinship relationships. Yotta built his houses about half a mile from the village site near to the boundary that separates village C from Chifunda. He is Motta's wife's mother's half brother, but he is also Chief Punyira's sister's son. As a young man he attended Livingstonia mission and was among that small number of Livingstonia graduates who, under the leadership of chief Punyira, became teachers in local mission schools and evangelists of the Free Church. He is a Free Church elder of long standing. Though he does not participate in village politics, he is a trusted sister's son of Chapyoka and is a party to its most initimate affairs. He is a member of chiefdom councils and committees as well as those of the Free Church, where he actively represents and defends Chapyoka interests. Both he and Motta have privileged positions with respect to royal branches, and at another level they form an important bridge between them. They are the loyal sister's sons not only of royal branches but also of Wowo as a whole. When members of the royal clan attempt to exclude the sisters' sons of one branch or otherwise restrict their privileges, the sisters' sons of the different branches join together to protest their exclusion and remind their royal relatives that they have fought their battles and have been their main protectors. In these situations Yotta and Motta are often the main spokesmen for the sisters' sons.

Village D

Mugo, the headman of village D, is a commoner, but he is connected to Njera, since his paternal grandmother was a gift from a Njera chief, and his father was given a village by a Njera chief. This village disintegrated owing to internal disputes, but in 1940 Mugo founded a new village on the same land. Its core consists of Mugo's sons, who are eight of the eleven house heads. Two of the others are husbands of his daughters who have not completed their payments of bridewealth. Mugo is an outspoken opponent of the chief, whose hostility he incurred by giving game to the head (a senior kinship position) of Njera instead of to the chief. Although he is an open supporter of Njera, senior members of Njera do not seek his council, and he is considered by some to be too independent. Bwana Samsalu has, however, assigned him the task of keeping a watchful eye on an ambitious headman in the area, who is a sister's son of Njera but has on occasions backed the chief against them.

Village E

Village E was founded as the result of a conflict between two segments of a commoner lineage over the distribution of bridewealth. Dan, the head of one segment, who was a village headman, wanted to share the payment with the chief, his mother's brother. Jake, a member of another segment and not related to the chief, protested the proposal and, in his anger, killed the bridewealth cattle. He and his brother then left the village and settled temporarily in village B, where the headman, although a member of the chief's branch of the royal clan, was an adversary of the chief. A year later, in 1943, Jake and his brother founded their own village. Although many of Jake's sons and brother's sons are working abroad, six of the fifteen adult house heads are his close agnates. The seven who are his affines belong to the same descent group. Their affinal links with Jake are of recent origin and were not the reason for their settling in the village. The head of this group came to the village because he and Jake were friends and hunted together, and he considered him to be a good headman, concerned with the welfare of his villagers and willing to support their demands. Jake's frequent failure to enforce Native Administration policies has brought him into conflict with his superiors, who often summon him to the capital for failing to perform his duties. He usually receives a severe reprimand and a warning that if he cannot carry out his duties, he will be dismissed from his post.

There is, for example, a Native Administration ruling that all villagers must return home after the maize harvest, about the first week in July. The residents of village E leave in December and take up residence on their gardens about two to three miles from the village. In July 1965, neither Jake nor his villagers returned. When the Native Administration heard of this, Jake was summoned to the capital. He offered two explanations for his failure to enforce the regulations. First, there had been outbreaks of smallpox in the chiefdom during the past year. Jake admitted that he had not assembled his villagers for vaccination, arguing that the traditional Yombe practice was for people to live apart until the epidemic was over and appropriate chiefdom rituals had been performed. Second, as the chairman of the local branch of UNIP he was following UNIP policies, which directed villagers to live on their gardens in order to increase agricultural productivity. The deputy chief told him that if he could not carry out his duties and lead his villagers, he would be brought before the Banangwa council and dismissed from his post.

There were other reasons for the disobedience. With other men of the village, Jake was engaged in potentially dangerous but profitable illegal activities. He was leading his villagers, but not in a way approved by the government. Jake appealed to Yombe traditional practices at the same time as he attempted to use his post as a UNIP branch chairman to account for his failure to enforce Native Administration rules. In other words, the founding of UNIP branches has provided headmen with new sources of political support. Jake is not allied to a branch of the royal clan, but he may use his post in the UNIP subregion branch to protect his villagers against them. Because on this occasion he overstepped the bounds of his position, he was warned not only by the deputy chief but also by his superiors within UNIP for attempting to use his post for his personal interests.

The rivalry between segments of the royal clan leads royals to seek the support of headmen and other commoners. They open to ambitious headmen and commoners alternatives in seeking support for their own interests against those of other persons—fellow commoners and even royals. An important cluster of political relationships stems from women. The members of segments and branches of the royal clan look to their intimate cognatic relatives to represent and defend their interests and to render other special services. From these intimate relatives, royals select their most trusted advisers and derive their most loyal allies. The founding of branches of UNIP has provided headmen, commoners, and royals alike with new opportunities for gaining power within the political context of the chiefdom and even access to the more inclusive arena of the district. Headmen may assist the subregion branch of UNIP in carrying out its policies and, in return, they look to it for support against the royal clan and the Native Administration. If the headman is an astute politician, he may use the different political forces within the chiefdom to his advantage.

I would suggest that the political ambiguity in Uyombe is characteristic of African countries not only during the transition from colonial rule to independence but also in the years following independence. The situation in Uyombe reflected the attempt of national Zambian leaders to work out suitable policies for governing Zambia. While national leaders were devising new policies, Native Administration and UNIP subregion officers were attempting to understand and impose them on villagers. The headman of village E, for example, was correct in arguing that local UNIP officers had discussed a proposal that villagers should live on their gardens in order to increase agricultural productivity. But a few months later, these same officers told the villagers that they must return home after the harvest. They even considered amalgamating villages to produce larger communities with the intention of centralizing basic services. Because the headman of village E was a UNIP branch chairman, he was a party to many of these discussions, which took place in the subregion branch headquarters in Muyombe. Policies devised in Lusaka had eventually filtered down to Muyombe, where local administrative and UNIP officers interpreted and shaped them to suit local conditions. It fell to the same officers to clarify the relationship between the Native Administration, the royal clan, and the UNIP subregion branch.

The Muyombe Cluster: A Small Town

Muyombe might be called a small town (Southall 1961, p. 1).[2] It is more than a village, yet it lacks most of the characteristics of an urban center. This type of small town differs from the average Central African village in function rather than size. Although such a town may be situated in a single ethnic (or "tribal") context, it does not strictly conform to the social and residential patterns of other local settlements. It may be termed Janus-faced, since it services the surrounding countryside and at the same time forms the principal gateway into larger social and political arenas. As the seat of local administration, such a town links a number of settlements in a wider administrative framework. It is an important local trading center and may also have an upper-primary or secondary school.

It is through such small towns that higher-level economic and political transactions are mediated before reaching the rank-and-file villagers. Middleton has observed that they are "the main loci for the dissemination of external influences to the rural areas, and it is in them that the new elites and middle classes are largely recruited" (Middleton 1966, p.33). They may include a local foreign population of civil servants and traders, but such ethnic diversity is not always present. Muyombe is characterized by the homogeneity of its population.[3]

Although a small town such as Muyombe remains essentially part of the rural social system, and may be comparatively unaffected by dramatic political upheavals outside, it is nonetheless oriented toward a wider community and so can provide the rural population with avenues for social and political mobility. It is the social middle ground in which the skills and behavior learned in urban communities gain significance for rural life.

The Cluster

The administrative village of Muyombe, consisting of the chief's village—Muyombe proper—and seven other settlements, is the capital and the administrative, political, and commercial center of Uyombe chiefdom. According to the 1963 Zambian census it has a population of 490. Thus it is larger than other Yombe villages and most Zambian rural settlements. Settlements with populations in excess of 200 persons are uncommon in rural Zambia (Kay 1967a, p. 29). There are only forty-six rural townships with populations between 100 and 2,500 (Kay 1967b, p. 46). Muyombe thus falls within the population range typical of rural townships (Kay 1967a, p. 18).

The cluster of settlements that make up the administrative village of Muyombe are Muyombe and Bula Ula (its permanently attached hamlet), Chimilira, Musantha, Kasalawuka, Muzira, Bula, and Kakhoma. The area encompassed by the cluster is roughly circular, covering about four square miles. Muyombe village is at the center. Musantha, Bula, and Chimilira lie to the north, and Muzira, Kakhoma, Bula Ula, and Kasalawuka to the south. The distance from Muyombe to any one settlement varies from only a hundred yards to more than two miles. The settlements are divided by such natural boundaries as streams. They derive their names from the founders or from local natural features.

Muyombe's headman is Chief Punyira. The headmen of the seven other settlements, who belong to the Muyombe advisory committee (established in 1962), derive their authority from Chief Punyira. Although the inhabitants refer to the settlements as villages, their headmen are not officially recognized and thus lack the rights associated with the post.

Muyombe village is peculiar in three respects. It is the chief's village and the capital; the inhabitants are dispersed at the end of each chief's reign; and each chief founds his own village, called Muyombe, on a new site. In the past, the process of founding a new capital began with a chief's death. No public announcement was made, and during the funeral ceremonies no one was supposed to demonstrate grief. Messengers summoned the chiefdom priest, *Musofi,* the chief's councillors, who were the headmen of Mbamba, Zumbe, and Mpemba villages, and the senior men, *banangwa,* and women, *bakamba,* of the royal clan. These were the people who would select the next chief. Once they were assembled, the chief was buried in his compound, along with much of his personal property and two or three of his subjects, usually his slaves.

Together with his followers, the new chief would go through the capital driving out the late chief's main supporters, his close agnatic kin, and his sisters' sons. Older Yombe explain that other inhabitants would leave voluntarily because they feared that the spirit of the late chief would cause them harm if they stayed. A simpler explanation is that there was no longer a reason for villagers to remain in the old capital, once it had ceased to be the political center of the chiefdom. The locus of power and wealth had shifted elsewhere. The new chief would leave with his followers to found his own village, in which the sons of any former chief were foridden to live. A former chief's close agnates (and loyal followers) were also forbidden to reside in the new capital; so they would return to the central village of their branch of the royal clan, settle in other villages, or attempt to found their own village. The practice of forbidding the late chief's agnates and followers to settle in the capital reduced the likelihood of internal intrigue and rivalries, lessened the possibilities of subversion from within, and provided the chief with a base of political support from which he could secure control of the chiefdom. Such a situation does not obtain in the present capital. The very processes which have transformed Muyombe into the dominant center of chiefdom government and differentiated it from other villages have restricted the authority and power of the chief to determine residence. Today, many of the chief's most active adversaries live in the capital, take an active part in the political life of Muyombe, and have systematically attempted to divest him of control of the town. Though the chief may appeal to traditional practices, he lacks the power to expel his opponents.

It may be argued that the inability of rulers to expel their rivals from the centers of authority has produced conflict in many of the capitals of independent African states. In developing African countries it is the elites in the towns who have instigated political crises, and not the peasants in the countryside. Similarly, in Muyombe it is from the local elite living in the capital that the chief has met his strongest opposition.

It was through the dispersion of the agnates of dead chiefs that the central villages of the six royal branches came to be founded. Sons of a dead chief often founded a village near to the site of their father's capital. Village B, whose headman is Kaleb, is the central village of the sons and grandsons of Chief Vwalamawoko. One reason for Kaleb's antagonism towards the chief and other heads of segments of Chapyoka royal branch is that he attempted to separate from Chapyoka and to have his segment recognized as a royal branch in its own right.

While royal and commoner villages had fixed territories, a chief could move his village to any part of the chiefdom. In thrity-eight years, Punyira has moved Muyombe four times, twice because the village was dirty and he considered it unhealthy, and twice in order to bring it nearer to the main motor road. These moves have gradually brought Muyombe from the south toward the center of the chiefdom. Because Muyombe now has buildings constructed of permanent materials, it seems unlikely that it will be moved again, even after the death of the present chief.

One of the seven settlements attached to Muyombe is the permanently attached hamlet of the chiefdom priest, *musofi*. The priest must dwell outside the chief's village but not at too great a distance. The present priest, Gideon Mukonda, resides about a mile from Muyombe in a hamlet known as Bula Ula which consists of five houses.

The six other settlements may be divided into two categories, according to origin. Their relation to Muyombe proper suggests the political arrangements of the chiefdom. The settlements in the first category are those founded by men from Muyombe: Chimilira, Musantha, and Kakhoma. The heads are Jean Wowo, the daughter of Chief Punyira's elder brother Jere; Ruti Wowo, Chief Punyira's son; and Pauta Chila, his sister's son. They were all appointed by the chief and are his trusted agents. The villages in the second category were founded by men from villages other than Muyombe, namely, Kasala-wuka, Muzira, and Bula. The heads of the first two are members of the royal clan; the head of the third is a commoner.

The heads of settlements founded by persons from Muyombe were or are the chief's advisers and loyal supporters. In the early 1930s Dandi Konda, a Livingstonia graduate and active member of the Muyombe Free Church congregation, married Jean Wowo, Punyira's elder brother's daughter. The chief told him to found a settlement beyond Chimilira stream, about a mile and a half from Muyombe. Dandi opened a store and had a profitable business for many years. Because he was a trusted and generous "son-in-law," Punyira gave him another wife from Chapyoka royal branch. In 1958, when Dandi died, Punyira appointed Jean as nominal head of Chimilira, thus securing the post for Chapyoka branch. In 1964, Chimilira consisted of thirteen houses.

The founding of Musantha illustrates the political rivalries which have tended to divide not only Muyombe but also Chapyoka royal branch. In the 1930s, Bena Wowo, Jere's only son, was selected by Punyira to assist him in his duties. With his forceful personality he became a highly respected and popular figure. Whenever Punyira went away, Jere and Bena took charge. In 1938 Punyira was absent for a month or so. On his return he stopped at Jumbo, a village on the northern border whose headman was loyal to him, and there learned that Bena had usurped the chieftainship. Punyira summoned the senior men of the royal clan. Finding that they supported him, he sent word to Bena to leave Muyombe and cross the Bemba river. With Jere, a sister and her husband, a friend and his family, and Mwatu, the son of one of his grandfather's slaves, Bena left Muyombe, crossed the Bemba and founded Musantha village two miles to the north. His settlement grew rapidly.

In 1957, Bena impregnated Mwatu's daughter, whereupon Mwatu threatened to kill him. Punyira and other senior members of the royal clan did not intervene, and so Bena fled to the Congo (Zaire), where he died. Punyira sent his sisters' sons to fetch the corpse for burial in Uyombe, appointing his own son Ruti, who had been away for seventeen years, as head of Musantha. Punyira and Ruti have sought to have Musantha recognized as an administrative village, which would secure Ruti against the right of a successor to drive him out. Their attempt has, however, been opposed by the deputy chief and his allies on the Muyombe advisory committee, by the UNIP subregion branch, and by the house heads in Musantha. In 1964, Musantha had thirty-three houses, a lower-primary school, small shops, and two maize-grinding machines.

Kakhoma is the last settlement to have originated from Muyombe. In 1956, Pauta Chila, the younger brother of Yotta Chila of village C, left Muyombe with his family, crossed Kakhoma stream, and built two sun-dried brick houses. The present settlement, about a hundred yards from Muyombe, has seven houses and a maize-grinding machine.

The three settlements founded by men from elsewhere are Kasalawuka, Muzira, and Bula. In the 1930s, Chongo Wowo founded Kasalawuka; and in 1945, Unka Wowo founded Muzira. Both Chongo and Unka are the sons of former chiefs and so could not live in Muyombe. The chief gave Chongo permission to settle about two miles away, near his birthplace and the grave of his father, Chief Chisusu, who ruled from 1870 to 1901. Unka was permitted to settle about a mile away, near the site of the capital of his father, Chief Kolelawaka, who ruled from 1901 to 1902. Chongo and Unka are the heads of important segments of Chipanga and Njera, the two royal branches which are the main rivals of the chief and his branch, Chapyoka. Their settlements are small, removed from the road, and together consist of only nine houses. Bula was founded in 1945, when Esaw Gondwe left Nathan's village and asked Chief Punyira for a place to settle. He was assigned a site about two miles to the north of Muyombe. Bula consists of eight houses.

The residents of these seven settlements are linked to Muyombe proper through their heads. The type of relationship of the adult house heads to the heads of six of the seven settlements may be contrasted with the social composition of the five villages already considered.

Table 2 shows the relationship of the adult house heads to the heads of the six settlements. Because an overall census was not taken of Musantha, it is not included in the table. The social composition of Muyombe proper is discussed in some detail below.

The total number of adult house heads of the six settlements was 34; 29 were men and 5 were women. Of the 34 house heads only 8 (24%) were the settlement head's agnates, 3 (9%) were cognates, 8 (24%) were affines, and 15 (43%) were not related to the settlement head. The most striking contrast between these six settlements and the five villages is in the number of adult house heads who are not related to the heads of settlements. In the five villages previously considered, only 7 (11%) of the 64 house heads were not related to the headman, while in these six settlements 15 (43%) of the 34 house heads are not related to the settlement head. Kinship and affinal relationships to the settlement head would therefore seem to be of less significance in the social composition of the six settlements. The advantages of living near the center seem to have been more important than kinship ties in attracting people to these settlements.

Table 2. Relationship of 34 Adult House Heads (29 Men, 5 Women) to the Heads of 6 Settlements

Agnates		Affines	
Primary	8	Primary	6
Classificatory	0	Classificatory	2
Total	8	Total	8
% of total	24%	% of total	24%
Cognates		Unrelated	
Primary	1	Total	15
Classificatory	2	% of total	43%
Total	3		
% of total	9%		

Muyombe Village Proper

Muyombe village is situated at the confluence of the Bemba and Vumbo rivers and many of its houses front the road. Map 3 shows its physical plan. The Native Administration building consists of a court and a small room which serves as the chief's office and a post office. The UNIP subregion branch has built its headquarters next to Punyira's compound (house 1). The "Isoka Superior Native Authority" has built a lower and upper primary school and contributed financial support to the construction of a dispensary with two wards. There is an agricultural office and the zinc shed of the Uyombe office of the Kasama Marketing Co-operative. Government-owned houses of the local staff of the health, agriculture, and education departments are situated to the south of the main village near the stream which separates Muyombe from Kakhoma. Most of the officials are from other parts of Zambia, and, because they do not regard Uyombe as an agreeable posting, they remain peripheral to the life of the community. They are drawn into the arena of chiefdom politics only in their capacity as representatives of local departments of the government.

Muyombe village is the main shopping center of the chiefdom. The seven stores are owned by local Africans, who have effectively prevented Asians

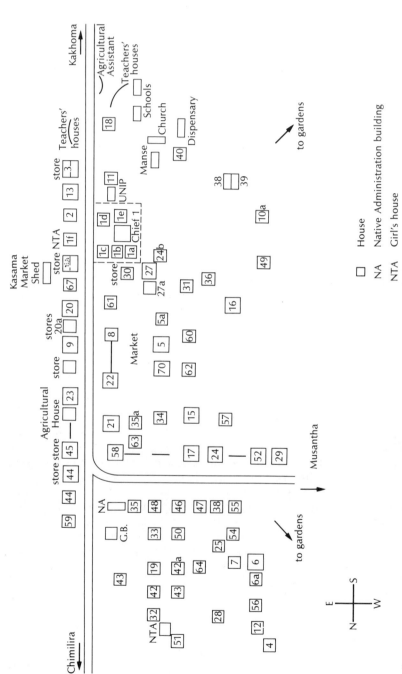

Map 3. Muyombe Village Plan

and other foreigners from establishing businesses. Labe Enda owns the largest and most prosperous store (houses 20 and 20a). In 1965 he paid £250 for a petrol pump, and he has built a bottle store. The two daily buses, one going south to Rumpi and the other north to Fort Hill, both in Malawi, stop in front of his stores. Labe and another store owner, Ado Chila, employ tailors who make dresses for women, trousers and shirts for men, and school uniforms for children. There are also two maize-grinding machines in Muyombe, but only one of them works.

Muyombe village, with its large brick church and manse, is the headquarters of the Uyombe congregation of the Free Church. Such sects as the National and Jordan churches have requested Punyira's permission to build churches in Muyombe but have always been refused, since Punyira supports the Free Church.

The concentration of important administrative, commercial, educational, and religious services in Muyombe proper makes it the focus for major chiefdom activities. Villagers look for new trends to Muyombe and its residents. They recognize that it is the central community which links them into more inclusive administrative and political frameworks, and that its residents attempt to control and shape the direction of chiefdom development.

In addition to public buildings there are the houses of local residents. Map 3 shows the physical distribution of houses but not other buildings. In 1964 I administered a questionnaire to the heads of sixty-three households in Muyombe; the head of the sixty-fourth had recently died. An examination of map 3 shows that there are more than sixty-four actual houses, for the houses of women whose husbands are living in the village are counted as part of the husbands' households. Where the household heads are women, the husbands are either dead or living away from the chiefdom or in nearby villages.

Of the 63 household heads included in the survey, 46 (73%) were men and 17 (27%) were women. The total number of inhabitants was 385, roughly averaging 6 persons per household. There were 50 men and 101 women over eighteen. Of the women, 65 were the wives of the 46 male household heads. Children accounted for 59% of the population.

The Yombe emphasize that a person intending to settle in a village should know someone already living there. The link may be one of kinship or friendship. Different types of kinship play their part in determining residence. This may be seen with respect to the 63 household heads in Muyombe village: 30 (47%) are settled with agnatic kin, 9 (14%) with cognatic kin, 14 (23%) with affinal kin, 9 (14%) were not linked to others when they settled, and one (2%) lives with a patri-clansman. There appears to be a preference for settling with agnatic kin—a tendency even more marked when only the 46 male heads of households are considered. Of these, 26 (57%) have settled with agnatic kin, 8 (17%) with cognatic kin, and 5 (11%) with affinal kin; 6 (13%) were linked to others when they settled.

As one might expect, 9 (53%) of the 17 female heads of households have settled with the agnatic kin of their husbands, of whom 8 are dead and one is away. Four (24%) of the other female heads have settled with their own agnatic kin, one (6%) with cognatic kin and the last three (18%) are under men living in nearby villages.

The bias toward agnatic relationships in determining residence does not apply to the relationship of the 63 house heads to the headman. The relationships of the adult house heads to Punyira suggests a difference between Muyombe and the five other villages in which kinship and affinal relationships with the headmen were more significant.

Table 3 shows the kinship relationships to Punyira of the 63 adult house heads in Muyombe. Of the 63 house heads, only 6 (10%) are his agnates, 4 (6%) are cognates, 4 (6%) are affines, while 49 (78%) are not related to him. In this respect Muyombe differs considerably from the other settlements considered. Within the five villages, only 7 (11%) of the 64 house heads were not related to the headman, and within the six settlements, 15 (43%) of the 34 house heads were not related to the settlement heads. But within Muyombe itself, 49 (78%) of the 63 house heads are not related to Punyira. Most residents of Muyombe live there not because they are the chief's relatives but because residence in the capital gives them opportunities not available elsewhere.

Table 3. Relationship of 63 House Heads (46 Men, 17 Women) to the Headman of Muyombe

Agnates		Affines	
Primary	1	Primary	2
Classificatory	5	Classificatory	2
Total	6	Total	4
% of total	10%	% of total	6%
Cognates		Unrelated	
Primary	3	Total	49
Classificatory	1	% of total	78%
Total	4		
% of total	6%		

Clusters of house heads can be identified in Muyombe. Based primarily upon kinship, these clusters are the nuclei of political support for prominent political figures, not only in Muyombe but in the chiefdom as a whole. Members of a cluster may be scattered throughout the village. The central figures of clusters may not themselves be prominent in the present political context, though they were in the past. They were (and are) loyal to the chief, but they have been gradually displaced by younger men. It is mainly within the cluster that house heads look for assistance in domestic and political matters, and they are often linked by reciprocal services. But any one of them may have ties with the members of other clusters and may in fact be included in them. Such men form important links between clusters, and their access to different ones gives them political influence and, at times, power.

Chief Punyira's Muyombe, founded in 1928, has thus been an on-going social unit for more than 38 years. Most of the original inhabitants were part of Punyira's following. They were drawn from three sources: Punyira's kin group—his close agnates and sisters' sons—Chifunda, the main village of Chapyoka branch, and the Free Church. Because Punyira was a prominent elder of the Free Church, his village attracted active church members from other parts of the chiefdom. Even though he was suspended in 1933 for taking a second wife, he has sought to maintain Muyombe as a Free Church center.

Punyira's compound is the focal point of the village (see house 1 in map 3); it consists of the houses of his five wives. Across the road is a building (1f) that was once a store but now serves as a girl's house, for his daughters. Next to it is the house (2) of his son Davy, who recently returned from the Zambian copper belt to get married. Ruti is his only other adult son in Uyombe; seven are away. Thus, in 1964, the adult members of the agnatic core of the village were Punyira and Davy. Other house heads in Muyombe are members of the royal clan, but they do not belong to Punyira's branch, Chapyoka, and are not considered to be the owners of the village.

The seven house heads who are related to Punyira settled in Muyombe because of him. One is his son Davy and the other six are related to him through women. House heads 3, 33, and 11 are his cognatic kin, and 4, 5, and 58 are his affines. Of the seven house heads which make up this cluster, Sam Kara (3) is the only one who takes an active part in the political life of the capital as well as the chiefdom. He is an important trader, an elder of the Free Church congregation, and a member of chiefdom committees. He settled in Muyombe because he is Punyira's sister's son. This relationship is important. It links two descent groups and establishes rights and obligations between them. A man may turn to his sisters' sons for aid and assistance, and may also look for support against his more distant agnatic kin. A man in high office draws his personal advisers from his sisters' sons. In their turn they gain access to power and may be appointed to political posts. Sam is one of Punyira's advisers and confidantes and supports him against the members of other royal branches in Muyombe.

Two other members of Punyira's cluster, Jake and Peter Wali (4 and 5), lived in Hewe in Malawi. In 1932 Jake set a trap for a wild animal but instead killed a man whose kinsmen demanded compensation. Jake appealed to Punyira, who sent ivory. In return, Jake gave Punyira his sister Anni for a wife, and Jake and his brother Peter moved to Muyombe. Both Jake and Peter are loyal subjects, but their support is of limited value to the chief. As clients they are entirely dependent upon the chief; they have no relationships which they could mobilize in his behalf. Moreover, because they lack the skills which come with extended schooling, they are not suitable for chiefdom councils and committees. The other members of Punyira's cluster do not take an active part in politics.

The second important focal point in the village is Edwall Wowo (6 and 6a), the deputy chief, who is Punyira's classificatory grandson. Eight house heads are linked to him and make up his cluster. Three of these (7, 8, and 9) are women and do not participate in politics. Though house heads 10 and 12 are Edwall's agnates, they too do not take part in politics. His main support comes from Kenon Mbamba (13) and his younger brother Samson (14) and James Gonde (21).

These three men are all related to Edwall through women. Kenon and Samson are his mother's brother's sons and James is his mother's sister's son. They are Edwall's personal advisers and are active members of chiefdom councils and committees, where they support him against his rivals. James is married to the older sister of Eric Enda, the Uyombe UNIP committee's secretary and thus is an important link between Edwall and Eric. Both men consult him on village and chiefdom affairs.

Both Punyira and Edwall, then, are the centers of clusters most of whose male house heads are linked to them through women. In Punyira's case this is partly because all but two of his adult sons and grandsons are away. The two house heads who are Edwall's male agnatic kin neither help him with domestic tasks nor take an active part in village affairs. Instead, Edwall helps to support them and derives most of his political backing from his cognatic kin.

Two men over seventy are the focal points of house head clusters. Isaac Enda (15), who was one of the original settlers, and Mat Chila (27) came to Muyombe to join Punyira. Most of the house heads of their clusters are in fact members of their extended families, *mbumba*.

Isaac spent his childhood in Chifunda and was one of the first teachers and Free Church elders in Uyombe. He is Punyira's classificatory sister's son, a relationship which he emphasizes but one which his sons Labe (16) and Eric (17) repudiate. Eight house heads are linked to Isaac; four (16, 17, 18, 19) are his close agnatic kin, his sons or brothers's sons, two (20 and 22) are his daughters' sons, one (23) is his sister's daughter, and one (21) is his daughter's husband.

With the exception of James Gonde (21), Isaac considers the heads of these households to belong to his extended family. Labe, as Isaac's eldest son, is the de facto head of the cluster. Many of its members live in Muyombe because of him and have received financial assistance from him. House head 20, Isaac's daughter's son, came to Muyombe because of him; Labe paid his school fees, made his marriage payments, and gave him a job as clerk in his store, which is the largest in Uyombe. Labe told house heads 18 and 19—Isaac's brother's sons, who lived in Hewe in Malawi—to come to Muyombe. He also helps to support the households of Isaac's sister's daughter (23) and his younger brother Eric (16), who is the UNIP committee secretary during his service as an unpaid political party organizer.

Most of the male house heads of Isaac's and Labe's cluster are active in politics and hold posts on village or chiefdom committees. They are also active in the UNIP subregion branch.

Other house heads are linked to individuals within this cluster by affinal and friendship ties. An example is Simon Nyeka (26), who is Eric's wife's (Gale) mother's brother. He and his sisters (25 and 26) settled in Muyombe because they preferred Muyombe to Mpemba, a distant village, and because they wanted to be near Gale. Simon, a Livingstonia graduate, a veteran of the Second World War, and a former teacher, is the Uyombe UNIP committee vice-chairman. Though he is married to Punyira's sister's daughter, he supports Eric in his political undertakings.

Mat Chila (27) is the center of another cluster. In 1934, Punyira summoned him to Muyombe and appointed him court assessor. Though he, like Isaac, was an active member of the Free Church, he is not related to Punyira. Four house heads are linked to him; three (28, 29 and 30) are his sons, and one (31) is a classificatory cognatic kinsman. Because Mat is an old man, the de facto head of this cluster is Eddi (28), his eldest son and apparent heir. Eddi was formerly the Muyombe UNIP branch chairman, but in 1962, when Mat retired, Edwall appointed him court assessor. Eddi's younger brother Ado, a shop owner, is vice-secretary of the Uyombe UNIP committee. He and Eric Enda lived in the same boys' house and herded cattle together; thus they are intimate friends, and they support each other in most political matters. Both Grandy (30) and Gipso (31) have been members of the Muyombe advisory committee but seldom take an initiative there and do not usually engage in village and chiefdom politics. They merely carry out Ado's decisions.

It should also be noted that there is a generational cleavage. Isaac and Mat, who are old men, support Punyira. Because they no longer play a part in the political life of the village, the importance of their support is peripheral. Their sons are Punyira's opponents and have attempted to gain control over the village as well as the chiefdom. This study is largely concerned with their activities.

The Muyombe Advisory Committee

The Muyombe advisory committee has jurisdiction over the eight settlements that make up the small town of Muyombe. It was created in 1962 by Deputy Chief Edwall with two aims. The first, shared with others of the new elite, was to develop Muyombe in order to claim recognition as a "rural township." In a dispute with Ruti, the head of Musantha, Edwall explained why he set up the committee and why he would not recognize Musantha as an administrative village. He said: "My aim is not to have many villages. I am trying to make one village. If we have a township we will receive more services and even financial assistance from the government." Edwall's aspirations included such improvements as providing electricity for Muyombe, a reservoir to supply buildings and dwellings with running water, and a hospital. The second aim was to reduce considerably the chief's control over Muyombe. The heads of settlements are members of the committee and must abide by its decisions. If the committee had had no other members, the chief's supporters would have been in the majority. But it also includes eighteen persons appointed by the Native Administration, i. e., Deputy Chief Edwall. Most of its officers do not support the chief. Edwall is the president, and Eddi Chila, whom he appointed court assessor, is the chairman. The vice-chairman, Tisi Koko, the secretary, Tanga Wowo, and the vice-secretary, Ado Chila, are all UNIP committee officers. Ado's younger brother is the treasurer, and Mwatu, a noted diviner, is the vice-treasurer. Most of the other appointed members are UNIP officers or Edwall's relatives.

Although Punyira is the headman of Muyombe, most of his duties are gradually being assumed by Edwall and the Advisory Committee. Punyira does not have the resources to carry out his traditional obligations—for example, to provide hospitality for strangers. The responsibility of providing strangers and important guests with hospitality has fallen to Edwall and to such organizations as the Muyombe UNIP branch and the Free Church. Most of Punyira's adult sons are away, and only his eldest son, Pack, and his grandson, Baldwin, send him money and clothes. Villagers are supposed to make his millet gardens, but only the members of his household and his extended family cluster do so. Though hunters are supposed to give him a thigh from all game killed in his area, most of them either keep it for themselves or send it to Edwall, who has it taken to Punyira. The harvest of Punyira's own gardens and his meager salary are used to support his many dependents.

As a Christian, Chief Punyira does not make public offerings for the welfare of the village. Though he sometimes performs them in his own compound, no one is supposed to know that he does. He is concerned with the moral conduct of villagers. He may assemble the adult men of Muyombe village cluster and tell them that they must not commit adultery or use magic to steal each other's crops. Villagers who are guilty of such practices are believed to be revealed to him in dreams. Because many Yombe believe that important events are revealed to the chief through dreams, he may attempt to use this belief to regulate village and even chiefdom activities. For example, village hunts or the banning of a prophet from his calling may be postponed because the chief has foreseen misfortunes. Villagers may bring disputes to him, or he may summon someone for failing to meet an obligation to a relative. Increasingly, however, such secular duties are being assumed by Edwall, who cannot claim the ritual duties, since he is neither the headman of Muyombe nor the chief of Uyombe.

The advisory committee has taken over many other duties of the chief. It maintains law and order and lays down rules for village sanitation and development schemes. It organizes villagers for village and chiefdom activities. For example, when the people of the chiefdom objected to building a dam in Muyombe, the advisory committee assumed responsibility for the scheme. When the residents of Muyombe must assist in development schemes in other villages, members of the advisory committee organize villagers into work parties and supervise them. The committee also organizes local hunts to protect the surrounding gardens from pests. It sees that villagers maintain the paths leading into Muyombe. Should villagers fail to take part in these activities, the committee may take them to court and have them fined. Thus, the advisory committee has assumed most of Punyira's duties and those of the other heads of settlements. It has become one of the means by which Edwall and other "new men" are attempting to transform the capital and, at the same time, divest Chief Punyira of his authority.

In summary, the imposition of colonial rule brought about changes in the relationship of Muyombe, the capital, to other settlements within and outside Uyombe. Uyombe ceased to be an autonomous political community and became one small unit of administration in the fabric of colonial rule. As it became part of a new bureaucratic order, its capital became the locus of new institutions of administration. Other settlements in Muyombe were subordinated and made dependent upon it.

The "new men" have contributed to the commercial and social development of Muyombe as the center of Uyombe; most shops and all but one of the chiefdom's maize-grinding machines are in Muyombe. These new leaders have attempted to have services located there and not distributed in other settlements. As a result, two of the five lower-primary schools and the chiefdom's only upper-primary school and dispensary are in Muyombe. This means that for Western medical treatment and for the schooling necessary to enter Isoka Secondary School, one must go to Muyombe or leave the chiefdom.

Muyombe is the center of the political life of the chiefdom, and many of its residents are important political leaders. Chief Punyira might reasonably be expected to be content with figurehead status, letting Edwall assume power and do the work. Instead, Punyira takes every opportunity to assert his power. Edwall has therefore attempted to gain control of the capital through the advisory committee, which has assumed most of Punyira's duties and those of the heads of the other settlements. The political rivalries and cleavage within the capital are also found at the level of the chiefdom. At this level other groups such as the royal clan and the UNIP subregion branch enter the political struggle.

4

The Structure of Political Groups: The Royal Clan

In the rural areas of many independent African countries a second political field, based upon a struggle for local political control, is often generated by the relation of the "traditional" ruling stratum, which owes its position to "tradition" and the British colonial system, to the "new men," who derive their position from neither traditional nor colonial sources. During the period of struggle to gain independence, many leaders of African nationalist movements declared their intention not only to Africanize the civil service but also to dismantle and replace the institutions of colonial administration, which, in the rural areas, were based upon chieftainship and the explicit recognition of the royal groups—dynasties, clans, lineages, or families— from which chiefs were recruited.

All independent African countries have attempted to Africanize the upper echelons of their civil service, but few have created new institutions of local government to replace the chief (or the Native Authority system) as the local agent of the government in the rural areas. The framework of local administration imposed under British colonial rule has thus remained sub-stantially intact. In countries such as Zambia and Malawi, chieftainship has not been abolished. The acceptance of the institution of chieftainship by national rulers secured the position in the political system not only of the chief but also of the royal groups within which these posts were vested. Mair suggests that one reason why most rulers of independent African countries did not abolish the institution of chieftainship was that it held symbolic significance for the rulers themselves. They could not repudiate chiefs on the one hand and then, on the other, assert the value of historic tradition (Mair 1969, pp. 83–84). Another reason for retaining chiefs is that many African countries do not have the financial resources to create new institutions in the rural areas and to staff them with qualified personnel (Skinner 1968, p. 199). Whatever the reason, in Zambia the chief remains the local agent of the government, and the royal group from which he is selected continues to occupy a prominent position in local political affairs. In a situation where the chief and the royal group cannot be displaced by local adversaries, they may nevertheless become involved in an ongoing struggle for power with local representatives of national political parties. The politics of Uyombe chiefdom provides an example of this type of struggle, one in which neither the chief nor the representatives of UNIP has the authority and the power successfully to eliminate the other from the arena of chiefdom politics.

Within Uyombe chiefdom, the royal clan and the Uyombe UNIP committee (the central committee of the subregion branch), are both concerned with the regulation of chiefdom affairs. Decisions affecting these may be made either within the chiefdom government or outside it by the Uyombe UNIP committee. The founding of the UNIP subregion branch not only opened the political system to greater participation by all segments of the community — including women — but also produced changes in the position of the royal clan and its relation to commoners.

The royal clan's preeminence in authority, power, and privilege is based upon a mythical charter, which asserts that its members are the agnatic descendants of the conquerors of the chiefdom. Though the different branches appeal to different versions of the charter, the charter itself is considered by royals and commoners alike to validate their claims to rule.

The members of the royal clan refer to themselves and are referred to by commoners as *Banangwa*, the free people.[1] The Mambwe of Zambia (Watson 1958, p. 147) and the Nyamwezi of Tanzania (Abrahams 1967, p. 35) use similar terms (*anang'wa* and *banangwa,* respectively) to indicate the sons of royal titleholders. Among the Yombe, however, Banangwa refers to all the men of the royal clan; royal women are known as *Bakamba*. The Banangwa are the rulers, and it is from them that the chief and headmen receive their authority, power, and privileges. They reserve the right to review the conduct of the chief, and only they may depose headmen or expel commoners from the chiefdom. Within the framework of chiefdom government, they use the Banangwa council to preserve their rights and privileges against those of commoners. The council is the principal arena in which branches struggle for power. When the royal clan is concerned with exercising or protecting its joint rights, it operates as an undifferentiated group. At other times it segments into six political units, which compete for power.

The royal clan has provided the chiefdom with a coherent political frame-work, while its council has served as a check on the chief's powers and the potential rivalry of royal headmen. A marked characteristic of Yombe chiefs in the precolonial and colonial periods was the desire to reduce the authority and power of the royal council and royal headmen and to undermine the rights of other branches to royal status.

Royal Clan Structure

The royal clan is a corporate descent group whose members have joint rights in chieftainship and the chiefdom. The Uyombe royal clan is the largest single corporate group of this type in the chiefdom, comprising about 5% of the adult male population. The percentage of royals to commoners may seem small when compared to other African societies, but the pattern of rotational succession to the chieftainship, the intense competition for it, and the struggle to maintain royal clan status have effectively restricted the size of the royal clan and the number of its branches. Unless a branch can maintain its rights in chieftainship, it gradually loses its status, and its members fall into the ranks of commoners. Though commoners also belong to clans, their clans are not corporate political units; the effective corporate group for them is the lineage. Commoner clans do not have councils; members do not meet as a body nor do they have joint rights in an estate. The royal clan also possesses a more elaborate organizational framework, which may be employed to impose its will on similar kinship-based units.

Although the royal clan is the dominant political group in Yombe society, royal status does not carry with it any distinctive or special economic privileges, rights, or opportunities. Within Uyombe, few opportunities are available for accumulating wealth in land, cattle, or money. There is no private or commercial ownership of land. Agricultural produce is sold either to the cooperative or on the open market. These marketing opportunities are open to everyone, and money derived from selling crops is not sufficient to produce major differences in wealth. There is no difference in the number of cattle owned by royals and commoners because the necessity of paying bridewealth, which is the same for royals as for commoners, prevents the accumulation of cattle. The main source of cash and goods is labor migration. The demands of kinsmen for marriage payments, schooling, debts, and the numerous court cases and fees prevent individuals and groups from amassing sizable sums of money and goods. Ambitious men may attempt to conserve and invest their earnings in small commercial enterprises, but most such enterprises are unsuccessful. The struggle between branches, then, concerns not so much economic resources as their rights and status within the royal clan and their attempt to control the chiefdom and its affairs.

The royal clan is divided into two named, primary lineages, Vinkakanimba and Polomombo. Vinkakanimba is the name of one of the founders of these lineages, whose descendants are divided into two segments stemming from his sons, Mughanga and (Winga) Musenga. The descendants of Mughanga are divided into two named branches, or *nyumba* (Houses): Kaswanga and Vumbo; and those of Musenga into three *nyumba*: Njera, Chipanga, and Chapyoka.

Branches are composites of smaller segments. Relationships within the branch are primarily those of kinship, while those between branches are primarily political. It is through the branches that the interests of commoners are articulated.

The political arrangements of Yombe society bear a striking resemblance to those of Mambwe society, where "the lineages of the royal clan form the framework of the political system." Although Watson (1958, p. 37) observes that "the cohesion of Mambwe society appears to depend on the dominance of the royal clan," a similar observation would not be entirely appropriate for the Yombe, even though royal clans are significant in the political arrangements of both the Mambwe and the Yombe. The Yombe royal clan does provide a cohesive element, though the conflict between its branches has also been a constant source of disruption.

Polomombo, the second primary lineage, is not recognized by Vinkakanimba as belonging to the royal clan. Its members, however, claim that their founder was the elder brother of Vinkakanimba, and the *Isoka District Note Book* of 1906 records Polomombo as a royal group. Today, chiefs are not chosen from this lineage, its members do not participate in the selection of the chief, and until recently it was excluded from the Banangwa council. Their re-inclusion was the result of one of Edwall's maneuvers. Though Polomombo segments into two branches, these branches may be considered a single political group.

Each royal branch has its own central village; those of the chiefly branches are in the south of Uyombe and the nonchiefly ones in the north. Samsalu is the village of Njera branch, Cika that of Chipanga, Chifunda that of Chapyoka, Kaswanga that of Kaswanga, Vumbo that of Vumbo, and Kalinda that of Polomombo. Most of the members of a branch do not reside in its central village but are scattered throughout the chiefdom. Even so, they consider the village as theirs and look to its headman to represent them in their dealings with other branches.

The headmen of these villages are usually the heads of the royal branches; the one exception is Chifunda. But village headmanship and branch headship are separate posts, not always occupied by the same person. The headmen of these villages are not appointed by the chief but by members of the royal clan. Selection is by no means random. As a royal headman grows old, he delegates most of his duties to his genealogical successor, retaining only his right to perform rituals. When he dies, it is this acting headman who is chosen by the royal clan.

The head of a branch is the senior man within it. For example, though Bwana Samsalu belongs to the junior segment of Njera branch, he is the head of the whole branch, since he is the only living male of the senior generation. Among the Musenga branches, Punyira is the only other man of the same generation. He is the head of Chapyoka; and, although he is older in years than Bwana Samsalu, he is junior and subordinate to him, since Njera is accepted as the senior branch. The head of Kaswanga also claims to be of the same generation as Bwana Samsalu and Punyira, but his claims are not accepted by them; they consider him to be their classificatory son.

The head of a branch has ritual authority over its members. He performs rites to the founder on behalf of all branch members. The head of a segment, on the other hand, can only perform rites to the founder of his segment and to the spirits of its dead members. These rites are believed to secure the well-being of the segment but not the branch.

The head of a branch may arbitrate disputes between its members and segments. He is also supposed to represent the branch in its dealings with other branches and on the Banangwa council. In fact, the heads of branches rarely come to council meetings; most are old men who have withdrawn from active participation in chiefdom politics and have assigned this task to their heirs apparent.

Variations in a Charter

The members of the traditional ruling strata of many African societies base their claims to special status, rights, and privileges on their own particular versions of "historical" events. These accounts of past events distinguish royal groups from commoners and establish the precedent that only royals are entitled to rule and to enjoy political authority. They are presented as accurate statements of past events. Following and extending Malinowski, social anthropologists have used the concept of the mythical charter. Though based upon and shaped by past events, such charters may be regarded as political statements and part of the inventory of ideological forms entitling one section of a society to rule another.

Among the Yombe, the mythical charter of a descent group cannot be considered apart from social action. It is neither autonomous nor insulated from social and political events. Although it contains ideals and rules, it does not dominate Yombe political life. It is not that man is in full control of myth, any more than myths control man, but the two, as part of the same ideological and political order, stand in a dialectical relationship. The significance of Yombe mythical charters is ultimately associated with the political interests of royal branches. Yet myths are bound by those past events which have produced their structural form and shaped their content; that is, "they use a structure to produce what is itself an object consisting of a set of events" (Lévi-Strauss 1966, p. 26). Though political events affect the content of the myth and may be incorporated into it, the events are ordered with respect to the structural form of the myth. Those who manipulate the content of the mythical charter are in part constrained by the structure of the mythical form, but they must also take into account the practical considerations of political life, one feature of which is to discredit the claims of others to authority based upon the "historical" charter of the royal clan. In other words, myths may be used instrumentally by contending royal branches to uphold, validate, and justify different vested interests and to denigrate the claims of rival branches. This is reflected in the fact that there is no single accurate or authentic myth but a number of different versions of the same one.

There are two parts to the mythical charter of the royal clan—the "historical" and the genealogical. Each branch has its own version of these two aspects. The "historical" part is presented as an accurate account of past

events. It concentrates on the upper reaches of the genealogy, the founders
—Vinkakanimba and Polomombo—of the two primary lineages of the royal
clan. Relating how they came to Uyombe chiefdom, it validates the claims of
the descendants to status within the royal clan. Many of the elements of the
different versions of the charter are the same, but they are combined in
slightly different ways. If these elements are considered as the "facts" in the
arguments over status and chieftainship, it is not surprising that the members
of the six royal branches rearrange them in order to further their respective
political interests.

There is variation in the extent or range of the genealogical knowledge
possessed by different branches of the royal clan. The knowledge of members
of chiefly branches is wide and detailed, while that of members of
nonchiefly branches is narrow and fragmentary. Because the primary
contest between chiefly branches centers on the chieftainship, chieftainship
creates a situation of tension, giving rise to more elaborate myths among
those branches. Another reason for the difference between the "historical"
and genealogical knowledge of chiefly and nonchiefly branches is that this
type of knowledge may be used to distinguish the rights of royal branches to
scarce resources such as the chieftainship and participation on councils and
committees. The greater genealogical knowledge of members of chiefly
branches enables them to further their claims to valued posts and other
resources and, by defining the rights of members of other branches, to
restrict their access to them. All members of a chiefly branch have potential
access to what was traditionally the most powerful post within the chiefdom.
There is less reason for members of nonchiefly branches to possess a detailed
view of the internal organization of the royal clan. If numbers alone are
taken as an indication of the strength of a branch, the two nonchiefly
branches, Kaswanga and Vumbo, may be considered weak indeed; only 19%
of the adult males of the royal clan resident in Uyombe belong to them.

The stories told to me by senior members of branches were supposed to be
accurate accounts of past events. In fact, most of the accounts fail to
mention that in 1904 there was a dispute between Polomombo and
Vinkakanimba as to which was entitled to produce the chief. The Native
Commissioner of the time assembled the two sides and collected from them
a version of the myth to which they both agreed. It is likely that this
agreed-upon version was reached at the insistence of the Native Commissioner. Its value lies in the fact that it provides a point from which one may
begin to suggest the types of adjustments that have occurred in the charters
of branches and that these adjustments reflect changes in political relationships. It is probable that in 1904 Vinkakanimba lineage was less differentiated. This is suggested by the fact that Musenga's sons formed a single
council which considered such domestic matters as the marriage of sisters
and inheritance. That their descendants no longer share these domestic
rights is indicated by the different versions of the myth. The stories are used
to validate the claims of a branch to legitimate status within the royal clan

and its right to produce chiefs. Conversely, they are used to deny the rights of other branches. The struggle for power is carried on, not only at the level of political action, but also at the level of ideology.

The Account of 1904
In this discussion of the mythical charter I will first give the account contained in the *Isoka District Note Book* for 1910 and 1913, and then the variants told to me by members of the different branches. (The account has been edited slightly to enhance its clarity.)

Mughanga[2] (A) who was the last great chief of Uyombe . . . left two sons, Polomombo (P) and Winga Musenga ((B). There was an interregnum; Polomombo and Winga Musenga disputed the succession. Winga fled to the Nyika country and Polomombo became chief. Polomombo was a cruel tyrant who was so hated by the people that they appealed to Chungu (the chief of the Nkonde people, Kyungu) who recalled Winga. Chungu helped Winga to take the field against Polomombo and sent him to Uyombe as a chief of the country. Winga vanquished Polomombo, who was killed, it is said, by Winga himself. Winga became chief and was good and popular. At his death there arose another question of succession. Polomombo left a son, Kalechi, who was appointed by Chungu but would not accept the nomination because he was afraid of being killed like his father. Kalechi went to live near Karonga, taking with him his son, Kalinda, who was brought up there. Njera I, Winga's son, was then appointed by Chungu and became chief.
[The report of 1913 brings forward this account.] From Mughanga descend two branches of the family: the senior Polomombo and the junior Winga's, but Polomombo branch has forfeited the right to the succession, through cruelty and cowardice as tradition says, so that the Yombe people refuse to acknowledge as their chief any descendants of his.
Yombe recognize as their paramount chief the Wankonde chief Chungu. It is to him that they look to nominate their own chief.
There were two claimants to the chieftainship: Kalinda, son of Kalechi (elder branch), and Njera II,[3] son of Njera I (younger branch).
In 1903 Chungu sent Kalinda from Karonga to assume the chieftainship. He settled in the Yombe country, but the great majority of the people would not recognize him. . . . This being the state of affairs, Chungu was referred to early in 1904 and he then nominated Njera II in accordance with the wish of the people. But Kalinda did not waive his claim. He had, moreover, already become recognized by the Boma (government).
Native Commissioner Leyer visited the country and held a meeting at Kalinda's village . . . Then it was seen that Kalinda was greatly in the minority, notwithstanding that the gathering was taking place in his own village. As neither of the disputing parties would give in to the other it was referred to Chief Chungu, this time by the Boma.

The reply to this was that Chungu appointed Njera II. In September the
Yombe succession was referred to His Honor the Acting Administrator,
who suggested that Njera II and Kalinda should be appointed, each to be
chief of his own section of the people, with the boundaries to be fixed by
the Native Commissioner of the Division.

In July 1906, the Native Commissioner took a nominal census of the
section . . . and as Kalinda has only two villages in the midst of Njera's
country it does not seem practicable to fix any boundaries between Njera
II and Kalinda. Instead, it is suggested that Njera II be appointed District
Headman of the section, with the full allowance of five shillings per
month.

Three points in this account differ from the versions given by the Vinkakanimba branches. First, though Kyungu (or Chungu) is mentioned in their
accounts, his hegemony over Uyombe and his role in appointing or
confirming chiefs is not recognized. They consider Uyombe as having been
an independent area until British rule. Second, the two disputes over
chieftainship, one involving Polomombo and the other Kalinda are combined into one and projected into the mythical past. In other words, for Vinkakanimba there has been only one major dispute, that which resulted in the
defeat of Polomombo by Musenga. Finally, they have excluded from their
accounts the government's recognition of Kalinda as chief and the temporary division of Uyombe into two chiefdoms. Thus, they have reinterpreted
the past to fit their dominant political position in the present.

Njera and Chipanga
The "historical" charters of Njera and Chipanga were collected from the
senior members of these two branches. Though each informant made the
claim that his historical account was the correct one, he was in fact arguing a
political case. Therefore, I shall make no attempt to assess the historical
accuracy of the accounts given below.

I have put the charters of Njera and Chipanga together. Because their
senior members relied upon the same old man—a sister's son—to refresh
their memories of Yombe "history" and their respective genealogies, their
versions of the charter were always identical.

The myth of Vinkakanimba. The story of Vinkakanimba, as told by members
of Njera and Chipanga, is also the one accepted, with slight variations, by
other Vinkakanimba branches.

For members of these five branches their "history" begins with Vinkakanimba. Their version is as follows:

Vinkakanimba was an elephant hunter from Uganda. Following the
southward movements of elephant herds, he came to Ujiji in Tanganyika and from there to Manda Bay. In the company of four other hunters
Kaira, Gondwe, Chawinga I, and Chawinga II, he crossed Lake Nyasa

and landed at Deep Bay. These five hunters founded the royal clans of most of the Tumbuka chiefdoms.

Vinkakanimba went further north into the country of the Nkonde people ruled by Kyungu. He then came south to the country of Mwene Gamba, stayed for over a year, and married NyaGamba, who bore him his first son, Mughanga. When he left Mwene Gamba, he entered the country that is now Uyombe, where he found only the Bisa people living in small villages around Mt. Kalanga (the ritual center of the chiefdom).

The chief of the Bisa was Mwene Kalanga. Since Mwene Kalanga was the owner of the country, Vinkakanimba brought him ivory. Mwene Kalanga was angry because he did not want elephant bones, as he called them, but wanted meat. So Vinkakanimba brought him meat, and took the ivory to Kyungu. From Kyungu he received many wondrous things, *vizungu,* such as white beads and blue cloth. These things astonished and impressed the Bisa, who began to call Vinkakanimba their chief. But Vinkakanimba drove them from the country and established himself as the first chief of Uyombe. He moved away from Mt. Kalanga and built his capital at Zuzu, in the southern part of the chiefdom. Here two other sons were born to him, Kasololongo and Winga Musenga. Vinkakanimba then made war on the Chief of Kambombo in the Luangwa Valley; but he was defeated and fled alone into the bush, where he died of sadness. His men brought back his snuff box and his spirit in a branch of the Musolo tree. These were buried at Zuzu.

When Mughanga succeeded his father as chief, he left Zuzu and built his capital at Vumbo. He had two wives: the first bore him Mwene Vumbo,[4] a son, and NyaCungumira, a daughter; the second bore Mwene Kaswanga, Chimbwecilyenge, and Chilola. When Mughanga died, Kaswanga succeeded him and moved away to establish his own village.

The Myth of Polomombo. The daughter of Mughanga, NyaCungumira, married a man from Ntalire, Ghandira, who settled at Kaswanga. Polomombo was the only son of this marriage. As he grew up in the village of his maternal uncle, Kaswanga, he became jealous of him and wanted the chieftainship for himself. His father encouraged him in this ambition. Through witchcraft, he killed first Mwene Kaswanga and then Chimbwecilyenge. Kaswanga's sons and Vumbo and his sons then became afraid to rule, and permitted Polomombo to become chief. Polomombo left Kaswanga and built his capital in the southern part of the chiefdom.

Musenga was away fighting in Tanganyika. While there, he took two wives, NyaMbeye and NyaUpigu. When he heard that Polomombo had usurped the chieftainship, he returned to Uyombe.

Musenga, considering his men too few to defeat Polomombo, went to Kyungu, who supplied him with warriors. With these reinforcements he attacked Polomombo at night and slew him. Then Musenga went in search of Polomombo's father and his sons, Mengo, Kalechi, and Kalinda. Ghandira came out of his house, and Musenga slew him and two of his grandsons, Mengo and Kalechi. Kalinda escaped with his mother and went to live with her brothers.

Once Polomombo was defeated, Musenga burned his houses and took his four remaining wives as his own. These women were pregnant. The children they bore, Musenga raised as his own. They and their descendants form the branch of Chapyoka. Thus, the members of Chapyoka are not Wowo, but Ghandira.

Because the children and grandchildren of Mughanga permitted Polomombo, a sister's son, to become chief, Musenga told them that they were no longer eligible for the chieftainship.

This particular view of historical events has both a manifest and a latent function (Merton 1961, pp. 61–66). It is intended to account for the presence of Vinkakanimba Wowo in the chiefdom and to establish the claims of its living members to rights and status. In the story of Vinkakanimba there are a number of elements that support the claims of members of Vinkakanimba branches to be the rightful rulers of Uyombe. Vinkakanimba did not cross the lake alone but in the company of men who were destined, as he was, to become chiefs and founders of the royal dynasties of other Tumbuka chiefdoms. The crossing of the lake is itself significant because it distinguishes two categories of people, foreigners and autochthons, royals and commoners, or rulers and subjects. This distinction is made apparent in the praise name of the chief, Mulowoka ("he who crossed over"), and its use is a constant reminder to commoners of his origin and that of other members of the royal clan. Linking Vinkakanimba with the founders of royal dynasties of other chiefdoms supports the claims of members of the royal clan to be the rightful rulers.

Though other sources (Wilson 1939, p. 13, and *Isoka District Note Book*) indicate that Uyombe was part of Kyungu's "kingdom," most members of the royal clan deny this. The latter consider Mwene Kalanga as having forfeited his right to chieftainship by refusing tribute owed to a chief; he paid for his ignorance by losing his throne. For them, Vinkakanimba established his right to rule and that of his descendants by expelling the Bisa. They consider that with the expulsion of the Bisa, Vinkakanimba became the first settler in the chiefdom, since the ancestors of other descent groups presently residing in Uyombe found him living there when they arrived.[5]

The latent function of the Vinkakanimba story is that it emphasizes the identity of members of Vinkakanimba branches as a corporate group sharing descent from a common ancestor and their joint rights in a common estate. It expresses the vested interests shared by the Vinkakanimba lineage as a whole in contrast to those of Polomombo and the descent groups of commoners.

The story of Polomombo makes explicit the common assumptions of these charters and defines the type of fact which can be taken to validate a claim. The story of Polomombo emphasizes the principle of agnatic descent. Or, from another point of view, it establishes the rule that sisters' sons, in particular, and all persons related to the royal clan through females, in general, are not entitled to chieftainship. The important facts for the chiefly branches are (1) that NyaCungumira is the daughter of Mughanga; (2) that she married Ghandira; (3) that Polomombo was born of this marriage; and

(4) that he was killed by Musenga. As the outcome of these events the descendants of Mughanga were deprived of their rights to chieftainship but not their right to participate in the selection of the chief. In their attempt to gain power, members of Njera and Chipanga are covertly, and with considerable discretion, presenting a case against members of Chapyoka branch. The line of argument is similar to the one used to exclude Polomombo from chieftainship. The pivotal point of the argument is women: the wives Musenga is supposed to have captured from Polomombo. Since members of Njera and Chipanga consider the children of these women to belong to Polomombo and their descendants to comprise Chapyoka branch, they argue that members of Chapyoka are not Wowo but Ghandira. Thus, their argument does not contest the rules of agnatic descent but uses them to exclude their main competitor from the chieftainship.

The second part of the mythical charters, the genealogy, is no more than an extension into the present of the historical account. The historical account of Vinkakanimba and parts of that of Polomombo, the charter of Vinkakanimba lineage as a whole, dealt with the origins of this descent group and its claims to political authority. The political statement was made with reference to Polomombo and commoners. It did not concern the different claims and interests of branches and individuals with Vinkakanimba.

The genealogy, a branch's view of the internal arrangements of Vinkakanimba and itself, differs from the historical account only in that its reference points are internal to the lineage. At the same time that it expresses the unity of the lineage it divides it into its constituent branches and segments; it stresses their unity and also represents their interests. The different vested interests are expressed in arguments over crucial genealogical detail. Though these arguments are phrased in a genealogical idiom, they may refer to such basic issues as the status of branches and their entitlement to chieftainship and lineage headship.

Among the Yombe the characters and events of a genealogy are arranged and manipulated in terms of Yombe kinship rules. These rules provide the framework within which arguments occur, and to understand the implications of the arguments one must know the rules. The basic rule of Yombe kinship is that agnatic descent takes precedence over uterine descent; only the legitimate children of the male members of an agnatic descent group have rights in the lineage. A second rule is that men born of the same parents are ranked in birth order. The third rule is that the descendants of an elder brother are senior to those of a junior one and those of a first wife are senior to those of a second one. Thus, the branches and segments of Vinkakanimba are supposedly arranged in a hierarchical order with respect to the seniority of men and their wives. But in fact the seniority—the status and authority of branches—is the basis of argument. The position of seniority which one branch accords to other branches in their view of the genealogical arrangements of the lineage is usually related to political alliances.

Njera's view. To elucidate the view that members of Njera and Chipanga have of the internal organization of Vinkakanimba lineage, it is perhaps best to refer to the Wowo genealogy as given to me by Njera and Chipanga informants (see figure 2). In the genealogical plan I have made no attempt to include all members. It presents only the founders of branches and their component segments.

Mughanga (A) and Musenga (B) were the sons of the lineage founder, Vinkakanimba. A, the eldest son, took two wives, V and W. V bore Vumbo (av1) and W bore Kaswanga (aw2), Kaswanga (aw3), and Chilola (aw4). Vumbo (av1) is the eldest son of the senior wife, and all his descendants through males form the senior branch which bears his name. Kaswanga (aw2) is the eldest son of the junior wife, W. His descendants and those of his junior brothers form the next senior branch which bears his name, Kaswanga.

B (Musenga) is the younger son of the founder. He married Nyambeye (X) and Nyaupigu (Y). He also took the four pregnant wives of his classificatory grandson, Polomombo. X bore Njera (bx1), Mitanga (bx2) and Chimbilima (bx3). When the male descendants of bx1, bx2 and bx3 combine, they form the branch B1, which is Njera. Y bore Chipanga (by4) and Nkwanda (by5). The descendants of by4 and by5 form Chipanga branch, B4. The four wives (Z) taken from Polomombo are counted as one person, and their descendants are said to form Chapyoka branch, B6. Thus, not all ancestors are selected as the founders of royal branches. A royal branch carries the name of the eldest son of each wife. The order of seniority—in theory, the order of authority—of branches and their component major segments is shown by figure 2. It is as follows: Vumbo (A1), Kaswanga (A2), Njera (B1), Chipanga (B4), and Chapyoka (B6).

This is a segmentary lineage. A modification of the two principles of fusion and fission (Evans-Pritchard 1940) becomes apparent in the meetings of the Banangwa council and in other political situations where there is competition for power. When there is a political dispute involving members of bx1

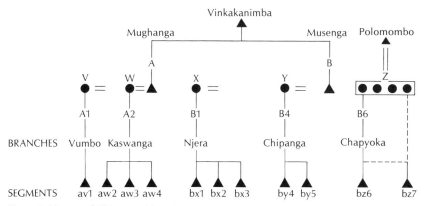

Figure 2. Njera and Chipanga Clan View

and bz6 (the segments of Deputy Chief Edwall and Chief Punyira, respectively), members of bx2 and bx3 come to the support and defense of bx1, forming the single royal branch B1. Members of by4 and by5 fuse to form B4 and attempt to arbitrate the dispute or support B1. However, because of recent conflict between the members of B6, its component units are never fully mobilized. When there is no outside threat, branches divide into their respective component segments.

Njera branch. Njera is one of the larger royal branches. From genealogical information collected on the royal clan, I estimate that roughly twenty-six (25%) of its adult male members living in Muyombe belong to Njera. To outsiders, Njera appear as an undifferentiated group. But to themselves they are divided into three major segments, which are arranged in a recognized order of seniority.

Their respective heads (as shown in figure 3) are: Fwira (K1), Unka (J6), and Bwana Samsalu (I6). The head of a segment is supposed to take a general interest in the affairs of its members, but in fact he may leave his responsibilities to a junior member. This is the situation in segment bx1. Fwira (K1) and his half brother Njera (K2) spent many years abroad. When they returned, they showed little interest in segment affairs. Because of his youth and frequent trips abroad, Left (K3) has not assumed the duties of segment head. They have been taken on by Fwasa (K4), who spends much of his time visiting members of the segment. He advises them, helps them to settle their disputes, reprimands them when they fail to fulfill obligations, and is generous with his maize and millet.

Because of the irregularities of birth and death and the rule of generational seniority, the head of segment bx1 is not the head of Njera branch. The head of Njera branch is Bwana Samsalu, the only living member of the senior generation. He is Unka's classificatory father and Fwira's "grandfather." Since he is a man of seventy-five or eighty, he has delegated most of his duties to his eldest son Esaw (Chimbilima, J7). He has, however, retained his ritual duties.

There have been serious disputes in Njera branch between Bwana Samsalu—in his capacity as headman of Njera's central village—and his classificatory sons, Unka of segment bx2 and Lamec (J4) of bx1. The sons of these two men told me that Bwana Samsalu accused their fathers of attempting to bewitch him and thus drove them from his village. In their opinion, their fathers were accused because each was a potential threat to Bwana Samsalu's authority. Unka has always been an ambitious man with aspirations to found his own village. As head of a segment he had a core of followers which he apparently sought to augment from among the residents of Samsalu. Lamec, on the other hand, though not ambitious, was a hunter noted for his skill and his generosity and, on this account, began to acquire a following. Bwana Samsalu was afraid that Lamec and Unka would leave and take most of his villagers with them. He also considered them and their sons

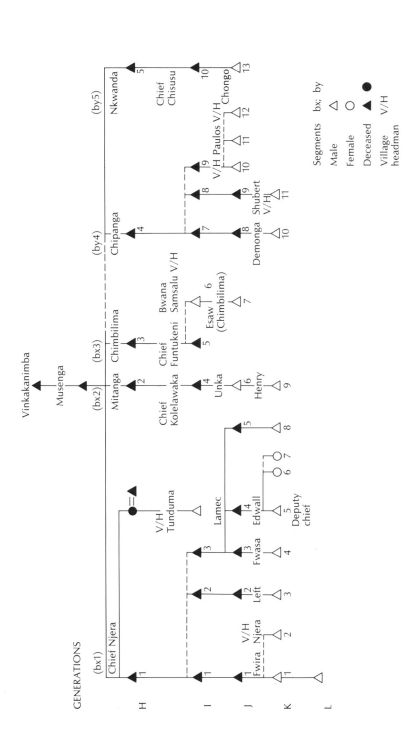

Figure 3. Njera and Chipanga Skeleton Genealogy

potential rivals for chieftainships. Lamec and Unka's sons thought that he had accused them in order to disqualify them and their sons and thus increase the chances of members of his own segment.

Deputy Chief Edwall (K5) has attempted to bring the segments of Njera closer together, since he needs a united political base in order to compete successfully with other political groups and to impose his policies on the Native Administration councils and the chiefdom. He does this by extending rights usually reserved for close agnatic kinsmen—men with a common father or grandfather—to more distant ones. For example, he has given Esaw (J7) sums of money received from offenses requiring compensation, with the understanding that it would be divided among all the senior men of Njera. He assists many of the members of segments bx2 and bx3 in small but important ways such as writing them letters of recommendation, giving them advice, and making small gifts of money and clothing. Though these gestures do not always have the intended result, Edwall has nonetheless secured the support of many senior members in the three segments. When his policies are challenged by members of other royal branches, these senior members are among his most vocal defenders. Thus, Njera presents a united public front when opposed by other political groups.

Members of Njera occupy important positions within the lineage and the Native Administration. Bwana Samsalu is the senior living member and, since he is also the head of the three chiefly branches, Punyira should discuss with him all important lineage and chiefdom matters. Moreover, Punyira, as a Christian, has assigned many of his ritual duties to Bwana Samsalu, who has become the de facto head of the chiefdom ancestor cult. At present, control of this cult is a point of controversy between Njera and Chapyoka.

Two members of Njera also hold important Native Administration posts. Edwall (K5) is the deputy chief and Esaw (J7) is a court assessor; the latter takes charge of the chiefdom when the former is ill or away. In this context Esaw is subordinate to Edwall. But in the lineage context he is Edwall's classificatory father. Much of the potential conflict in this situation has been avoided by the way in which Esaw has defined his role. He performs his job in a perfunctory manner when Edwall is in the chiefdom. As a result he is criticized by UNIP officials; he frequently threatens to resign and return to Tanzania, where he was formerly employed as a policeman. When he does in fact submit his resignation, Edwall sends for him and tells him that he depends upon his "father's" help and guidance. But when Edwall is away, Esaw takes control of the chiefdom and performs his duties efficiently.

Njera territorial support. A branch has territorial support, since some of its members are usually village headmen. Njera, for example, has control of two villages, Samsalu and Njera. The former is under Bwana Samsalu and the latter under Njera (K2).

Njera branch may claim allegiance from other villages whose headmen are related to them by close cognatic ties. These are usually the villages of "sisters' sons," and mothers' brothers, *mamarumi*. If these headmen do not give support, they may be threatened with punishment. An example is the case of headman Tunduma of Chigoma, a large village in the northeast. Tunduma's mother was the sister of Njera (H1). Chief Punyira appointed Tunduma to safeguard the northeastern boundary of the chiefdom from encroachment by a neighboring chief who sought to extend his boundaries. Punyira attempted to make Tunduma head of several adjacent villages, but Edwall told Tunduma that he must be satisfied with Chigoma. So Tunduma began actively to support Punyira against Edwall. Bwana Samsalu heard of this and sent for him. Though I was not permitted to attend this meeting, I was told that the substance of the rebuke was the reminder that Tunduma was a "sister's son" of Njera and not of Chapyoka. Tunduma was warned that if he did not support Edwall he might lose his post as village headman.

Other sisters' sons of Njera are Gombelima, Kambube, and Matendo. Njera can rely on these and call on them to arbitrate internal disputes. Finally, Edwall's personal kinship network gives him the support of four villages whose heads are his mother's brothers. Thus, Njera has a broad political base.

Chipanga branch. Chipanga, which includes roughly 28% of the adult males of the royal clan living in Uyombe, is divided into two major segments, Chipanga (by4) and Nkwanda (by5) (see figure 3). As the eldest son of Nyaupigu, Chipanga is regarded as the founder of the branch and his descendants as its senior segment. The head of this segment is Caira (J10), who is also the head of the whole branch and performs rituals to Chipanga in his dual capacity as segment and branch head. He is also the headman of Cika, the central village of Chipanga.

The other major segment was founded by Nkwanda (H5), who had only one son, Chisusu (I10). Whereas three chiefs have been selected from Njera and three from Chapyoka, Chisusu is the only member of Chipanga to have held the post. During his reign he married a large number of women and produced many children. But no one that I talked to was able to give me the names of his wives, the order in which he married them, and, thus, the order of seniority of his children. This indicates the disorganized state of Nkwanda, as a result of which Chipanga, numerous though it is as a group, is politically weak. Since Chisusu's death in 1901, Chipanga has lacked effective leadership and organization. Of Chisusu's sons, Chongo (J13), has come forward as the leader and senior member of Nkwanda. He has built near Chisusu's grave, and, although he is an officer of the local Watchtower Movement, he makes offerings to Chisusu and to Nkwanda. He has used his influence as a noted healer and diviner and his control of the rites to Chisusu to enhance his position in the branch. He attends most Banangwa council meetings, frequently speaking for members of his segment and branch. Many sisters' sons of the branch who are not headmen but who hold important posts in the chiefdom government or the Uyombe UNIP committee seek his support, and he has sometimes sought theirs. He has emerged as a prominent figure within Chipanga.

Chipanga territorial support. Members of Chipanga control three villages: Cika, Mayowa, and Shubert. Though the heads of these villages attend area committee and Banangwa council meetings, they do not take an active part in chiefdom politics. This responsibility has been assumed by Demonga (K10), Paulos (J11), and Chongo (J13). They hope to make a member of their branch the next chief. As a political group, however, Chipanga have access to power only through their close affiliation with Njera. In turn, members of Njera rely upon members of Chipanga for support in area committee and Banangwa council meetings.

Chapyoka
The last of the chiefly branches is Chapyoka. Punyira heads this branch, though not the whole lineage. As chief, he is the de jure head of the Native Administration, its staff, its councils and committees, and of the chiefdom. He is the source from which Edwall and the other chiefdom officers derive their authority. Here, however, we are concerned with the sources of his political support within Uyombe, i.e., Chapyoka branch.

The myth. Chapyoka's story of Vinkakanimba is similar to Njera's, except in one important point. According to my Chapyoka informants, Musenga (B) married three women who were, in order of seniority, Nyambeye (X), Nyamunthali (Z), and Nyanyiza (Y). In this version of the Polomombo story, Musenga did not marry Polomombo's wives but distributed them among his followers.

Chapyoka's clan view. Chapyoka's view of the internal arrangement of branches within the clan differs from that of Njera. Of Mughanga's (A) two sons, they say, Kaswanga (A2) is the elder son and Vumbo (A1) the younger. Musenga's first wife (X) bore two sons: Njera (bx1) and Nkwanda (by5). The second wife (Z) bore two sons: Chapyoka (bz6) and Nkukujeni (bz7). The third wife also bore two sons: Chimbilima (bx3) and Chipanga (by4). Mitanga (bx2) is absent from this inventory of ancestors. At this level, a segment of B1 appears to have been transferred to B4, and a segment of B4 to B1. However, the sons of bx2 and bx3 are included with the sons of bx1, and the sons of by5 are transferred to by4. Thus, B1 and B4 remain intact but internally undifferentiated. Figure 2 is altered in the following ways (see figure 4). With respect to the nonchiefly branches, which fuse to form A, Kaswanga (A2) has exchanged positions with Vumbo (A1) as the senior branch. In the case of the chiefly branches, Njera (B1) remains the senior, but Chapyoka (B6) changes places with Chipanga (B4), which becomes junior to all other branches.

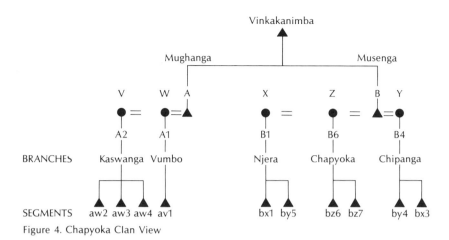

Figure 4. Chapyoka Clan View

Chapyoka branch. The members of Chapyoka are divided into two major segments: Chapyoka (bz6) and Nkukujeni (bz7). Chapyoka was Nyamunthali's (Z) eldest son; so he is considered as the founder of the branch and his descendants as the senior segment. Of the generation of his sons, Punyira is the only one still alive. Thus Punyira (I13) is the head of his segment and also of the branch (see figure 5). As such, he makes offerings to his father, Chapyoka (H6). But Donald (J18), Punyira's half brother's son, also performs rites to Chapyoka in his capacity as headman of Chapyoka's central village, Chifunda. As an indication of this he has taken the name of Chapyoka without the permission of Chief Punyira and Bwana Samsalu, who are responsible for redistributing the names of royal ancestors. These names are the property of the chiefly lineage, so that to take them, as many of the younger members have done, is a challenge to the authority of the heads of branches. Thus, by calling himself Chapyoka, Donald has assumed a right which is not his. He already appears to be making a bid for the headship of the segment and branch in anticipation of Punyira's death. As headman of Chifunda, he has a firm base of political support and ritual authority. None of Punyira's own sons is in a comparable position; his attempts to establish them in administrative villages of their own have been stopped by Edwall. Musantha, which was to be their village, was made part of Muyombe.

The position of Nkukujeni is ambiguous. Its head, Kaleb (J21), calls himself Njera. As has been seen, Njera claim that Nkukujeni was the father of Chief Vwalamawoko, Kaleb's father, and that he was of Chapyoka branch. But Kaleb is assigned to different branches in different contexts. At times of important area committee and Banangwa meetings, Njera may refer to him as one of them since they may need his support if there is a vote. But when Punyira proposes to set up small ad hoc bodies, which usually consist of two

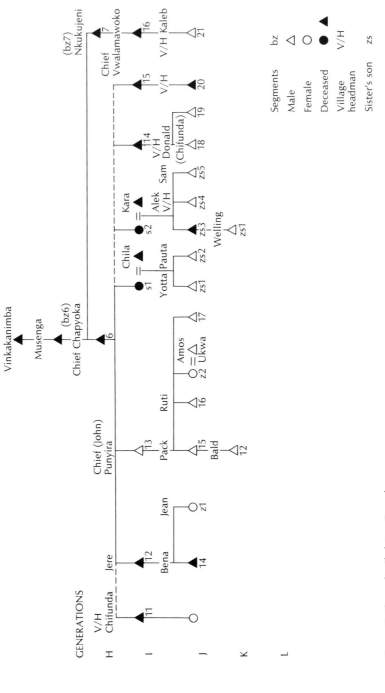

Figure 5. Chapyoka Skeleton Genealogy

representatives from Chapyoka and two from Njera, they insist on his being appointed in his capacity as a senior member of Chapyoka. Thus they can count on a majority if a matter should come to a vote.

Punyira agrees that Chief Vwalamawoko was a member of Chapyoka and that Kaleb is his son. But when asked about Nkukujeni, he sometimes lists him as Chapyoka's brother and sometimes not; he offers the tentative suggestion that not all of Polomombo's wives may have been distributed. He then says that he cannot be sure of this since he was not alive at the time. This confusion stems from the dispute already described relating to the founding of village B.

As Vwalamawoko's only son, Kaleb would in any case have sought the support of other branches. Gaining their support was facilitated by his father's generosity. Several senior members of Njera told me that Vwalama- woko had paid their school fees and had been generous to all members of the chiefly lineage. Moreover, when Unka and Lamec were driven out of Samsalu, they settled in Kaleb's village. Thus, Kaleb found allies in Njera. He is a potential ally in the enemy's camp. However, he is not always an active one, because he rarely attends public meetings. Nontheless, he and his sons are potential votes.

There is also a dispute within Chapyoka between Punyira (I13) and Donald (J18), who is not only the headman of Chifunda but also the chairman of the UNIP subregion committee. Punyira is supported by his sons and Donald by his brothers.

The dispute between Punyira and Donald reflects the unsettled political situation of the early 1960s in Zambia. As the local agent of the colonial government, Punyira was confronted with a dilemma. Either he could support colonial policies which opposed the founding of local UNIP branches and the disturbances and lose the allegiance of many of his subjects, or he could support his people against the government and jeopardize his tenure as an administrative officer. Punyira attempted to avoid this dilemma by redefining the situation. He claimed that the people of the chiefdom, particularly the members of the royal clan, were trying to bewitch him. In 1961 a meeting of the Banangwa council agreed to his proposal to invite Chikang'anga—a noted prophet (or witchfinder) living in Malawi—to the chiefdom to "search" his subjects. Orders were sent to all headmen to report with their villagers to the capital for Chikang'anga to identify and neutralize the "witches." Donald, who had taken an active part in founding UNIP branches and who had opposed the bringing in of Chikang'anga, was accused in public of being a witch and thereupon broke off relations with Punyira and his sons. This deprived Punyira of important political support not only on the Banangwa council but also in UNIP. He and his son, Ruti (J16)—Pack (J15) is teaching abroad—were left without support.

In 1964, through the mediation of the sisters' sons of Chapyoka branch living in Chifunda, important steps were taken toward settling this dispute.

Though Donald began to attend Banangwa council meetings, he rarely supported Punyira when personal attacks were made against him by members of Njera; he would only defend the interests of his branch. But within the Uyombe UNIP committee he often objects to Edwall's policies and is told by the committee secretary, Eric Enda, or the vice secretary, Ado Chila, not to introduce chieftainship disputes into party affairs.

Thus, we see that the component segments of Chapyoka do not automatically fuse when faced with opposition. Because the primary base of Punyira's support is his branch he is in a weak position with respect to Edwall, his main competitor.

Chapyoka's territorial support. Donald is the headman of Chifunda, the central village, and Samuel (J20) was, until his death in 1963, the headman of Cifwenge. Since Samuel's death Punyira has not appointed a new headman there. In theory, Muyombe is also a Chapyoka village; it belongs to Punyira. But it can hardly be considered as such now that Edwall and his supporters also live there. The ambiguity in Kaleb's allegiance has already been noted.

Only one of Punyira's sisters' sons is a village headman. This is Alek (Izs4), the headman of Chowa. Punyira's mother was from Nkamanga in Malawi, and none of her brothers is a village headman in Uyombe. There is, however, one other village whose headman often supported Punyira in the past. This is Jombo, where the headman is married to a Chapyoka woman. But he is an old man and does not take an active part in chiefdom politics. Thus, Punyira's territorial support is limited. Chapyoka is in disarray, divided by internal disputes. Because its adult male members living in Uyombe form only 14% of the royal clan, it is at a disadvantage in chiefdom meetings. Its strength lies in the fact that it controls the chieftainship. Because of its weak position Punyira has sought to form an alliance with the nonchiefly branches, specifically Kaswanga, a feature which is reflected in Chapyoka's view of the royal clan. In its turn, Njera has also sought alliances with the nonchiefly branches and with Polomombo. Though more than 50% of the adult male members of the royal clan in Uyombe belong to the three chiefly branches— which has helped to secure their claims—their rivalry and the fact that none of them form a majority has provided the basis for alliances with other branches.

Kaswanga

Zgoro, a man of about seventy, is the head of Kaswanga branch and of their central village, Kaswanga. Flywell, who is forty-two, is Zgoro's elder brother's son. He is Zgoro's heir apparent and the acting village headman. He represents Zgoro on the area committee and the Banangwa council. These two men supplied most of my data on Kaswanga (see figure 7, I21 and J24).

The myth. The Kaswanga story of Vinkakanimba is lacking in detail. They say that Vinkakanimba was a hunter who crossed Lake Nyasa with other chiefs

and came to reside in Uyombe, where he found the Bisa people. He drove
them out and established himself as chief. The Kaswanga version of the
Polomombo story is similar to other Vinkakanimba accounts, but those who
tell it are defensive. Zgoro agrees that Polomombo became chief but is not
convinced that it was through the fault of his kinsmen. He offered the
alternative suggestion that Polomombo became chief when lions forced his
kinsmen to flee. Flywell was also skeptical and offered another explanation
He put it this way: "We do not become chiefs because we are not educated.
Those of the south were the first to go to school and write down the history.
They made us lower and kept the chieftainship for themselves. Chief Punyira
has said that now we should become chiefs."

Kaswanga's clan view. Members of Kaswanga branch have a narrow view of
the arrangement of branches in the clan. They say that Vinkakanimba had
two sons, Mughanga (A) and Musenga (B) (see figure 6). Mughanga (A) had

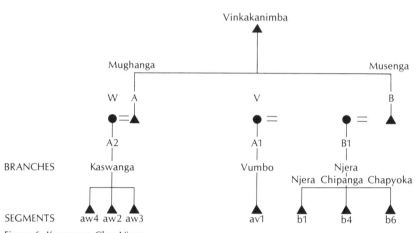

Figure 6. Kaswanga Clan View

three sons, Chilola (aw4), Kaswanga I (aw2), and Kaswanga II (aw3). Musenga
(B) took at least two wives. The first bore Vumbo (A1). One or other of his
wives bore Njera (b1), Chipanga (b2), and Chapyoka (b6), whose descendants
were considered by Zgoro and Flywell to form the single branch of Njera
(B1). Kaswanga's view of the internal ordering of branches is shown in figure
6. In this plan the descendants of Mughanga form the senior lineage, and
those of Musenga, including Vumbo, the junior one. In other words, there
are only three major branches, which are, in order of seniority, Kaswanga
(A2), Vumbo (A1), and Njera (B1)—the last consisting of three segments,
Njera (b1), Chipanga (b4), and Chapyoka (b6).

The three segments of the Kaswanga branch are descendants of, respectively, Chilola (H8), Kaswanga I (H9), and Chief Kaswanga II (H10) (see figure 7). Zgoro and Flywell were unsure of the order of seniority of these ancestors. To determine which was the elder led to an argument from kinship terminology. Zgoro contended that Chilola was the youngest while Flywell said that

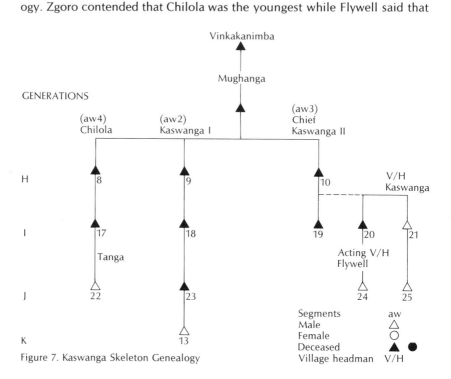

Figure 7. Kaswanga Skeleton Genealogy

he was the eldest. Flywell offered as proof that he called Chilola's grandson Tanga (J22), who is of the same generation as himself, elder brother (*mukuru*); thus making Chilola's descendants the senior segment.

Each of the three segments has its own head. The acting head of Chilola is Tanga, all of whose brothers are employed abroad. Living in Muyombe, he can take an active part in chiefdom politics. Though his grandfather left Kaswanga village and he has never lived there, he maintains relationships with Zgoro and Flywell by taking or sending gifts of clothes or maize and millet.

Tanga is the treasurer of the UNIP committee and an active party member. Though suspicious of Edwall, he supports his policies when they do not conflict with his own interests and UNIP committee policy.

Most members of Kaswanga I (aw2) are employed abroad. Bywell (K13), who is the head of this segment, only returned to Uyombe in 1964 after spending some twenty years away. Unlike Tanga, he takes no interest in chiefdom politics.

Zgoro is the head of Kaswanga II (aw3) and Kaswanga branch. Flywell, who represents him in chiefdom affairs, is chairman of the local UNIP branch of the area.

Kaswanga branch is weak as a political group. It does not form a cohesive unit, it does not have a wide territorial base, and it forms only 12% of the adult males of the royal clan living in Uyombe. The only village under the control of one of its members is Kaswanga, its central village.

Vumbo

The head of the Vumbo branch of Vinkakanimba is John (J29) (see figure 9), a man of about fifty. He was recently appointed by the Banangwa council as headman of Vumbo, the only village under a member of this branch. The Vumbo account of the Vinkakanimba myth is similar to the Kaswanga version but differs on one important point. Vumbo, and not Kaswanga, is considered to be the senior branch. This appears in Vumbo's view of the clan.

Vumbo's clan view. According to this view, the first wife of Vinkakanimba bore Mughanga (A) and Musenga (B) (see figure 8). She also bore Nyacungumira, the mother of Polomombo. Mughanga had two sons, Vumbo (A1) (the elder) and Kaswanga (A2). Musenga (B) died without leaving children. Vinkakanimba's junior wife bore only one son, Njera (B1) who was the founder of the three chiefly branches; the order of seniority of these was unknown. Members of Vumbo could not go further in describing the internal organization of branches other than their own.

Thus for members of Vumbo the three major branches are, in order of seniority, Vumbo (A1), Kaswanga (A2), and Njera (B1). Njera includes three segments—Njera (b1), Chipanga (b4), and Chapyoka (b6). They do not attempt to arrange these last three in any order of seniority.

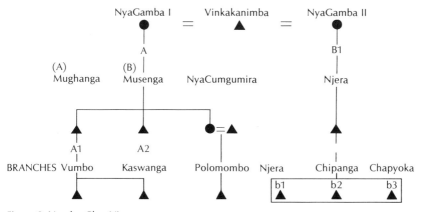

Figure 8. Vumbo Clan View

Vumbo branch. Vumbo is a single branch without any major internal divisions (see figure 9). It has few adult members; its adult men living in Uyombe form only 7% of the royal clan. Of these only three live in Vumbo village. John has three sons and three classificatory sons, but they are away. Though he rarely takes an active part in public discussion, the existence of his "sons" makes the branch a potential contender for power; other branches seek its support.

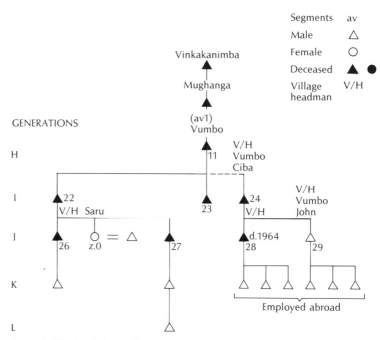

Figure 9. Vumbo Skeleton Genealogy

One way of attempting to gain the allegiance of another branch is to support its claims. This can be done with no loss to either party. As mentioned above, Chapyoka sought Kaswanga's allegiance by recognizing it as the senior branch and promising that in future it would be considered eligible to produce chiefs. In turn, Njera has sought Vumbo as an ally by supporting its claim to seniority. But neither Chapyoka nor Njera have benefited; Kaswanga usually supports Njera, and Vumbo is too weak.

The Excluded Branch: Polomombo
The remaining branch of the royal clan is Polomombo. Their version of the royal charter is closest to the account recorded in the *Isoka District Note Book* presented at the beginning of this chapter. Polomombo is the elder brother and Njera (or Vinkakanimba) is the younger.

The myth. Many of the same figures recur in the story told by members of Polomombo about their founding ancestor. In their version, Polomombo and his two younger brothers, Mughanga and Njera (or Vinkakanimba), are the central characters. It is as follows:

> Polomombo and his younger brother Mughanga were hunters from Tanganyika. They gradually moved southward until they reached Lake Nyasa, which they crossed in the company of such other hunters as Kaira and Gondwe. These hunters became chiefs of many of the Tumbuka chiefdoms. Polomombo and Mughanga, after leaving Kaira at Deep Bay, accompanied Gondwe as far as Nkamanga and then ascended to the country of the Phoka people. They crossed the Nyika plateau and entered the area which is now Uyombe. They built a village, Mavuvuma, and drove the local Bisa inhabitants out of the country. Polomombo became chief and founded his capital in the northwestern part of the chiefdom. He married NyaGhandira who bore him two sons, Mengo and Kalechi.
>
> Njera, the youngest brother, followed Polomombo and Mughanga and settled at Muvuvuma. Mughanga committed adultery with one of Polomombo's wives and fled for protection to Njera. He convinced Njera to make war on Polomombo. Njera attacked, defeated, and then slew Polomombo and his son Mengo. He took Polomombo's wives and children and made himself the chief of Uyombe.
>
> But Kalechi escaped and went to live in Karonga. Eventually he returned with his son Kalinda and fought Njera and defeated him. He did not kill him but told him they must now live in peace. He divided the chiefdom, established himself as Chief in the north, and assigned the south to Njera.
>
> But when the Europeans took control of the area they decided that there were too few people to be ruled by two chiefs. They recognized the children of Njera as Chiefs and told the children of Polomombo that they would no longer be permitted to have their own chiefdom.

According to this version there were two fights over the chieftainship. In the first, Musenga defeated Polomombo; in the second, Kalechi defeated Njera, his "father," but did not slay him. Instead he divided the chiefdom into two and permitted Njera and his children to rule the southern half. This arrangement was changed with the imposition of British rule. Though Kalinda lost his throne and his chiefdom, members of his branch still consider themselves to be the rightful rulers of the chiefdom.

Polomombo's clan view. The clan view of members of Polomombo differs in many respects from those of the other five branches. There is no named founding ancestor but three brothers, of whom Polomombo is the senior. Polomombo had seventeen wives, but only NyaGhandira is remembered; she bore two sons, Mengo and Kalechi. Polomombo's younger brother Mughanga had no children. Kaswanga (A2) and Vumbo (A1) were said not to be members of the royal clan but commoners who supported Njera (Vinkakanimba) against Polomombo and were rewarded for their services by being made headmen; they founded their villages near Kalinda. They also assumed the royal clan name. Musenga is left out of the account of members of Polomombo, and Vinkakanimba is considered to be the same person as Njera, the younger brother of Polomombo and Mughanga. Njera was the founder of the three sublineages, Njera (b1), Chipanga (b4), and Chapyoka (b6). These sublineages were not ranked in order of seniority, and no clear distinctions were made between their members. Figure 10 shows how the Polomombo view varies from that of Njera and Chipanga (figure 2).

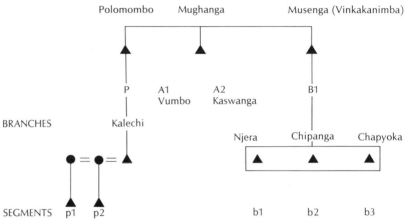

Figure 10. Polomombo Clan View

Thus for members of Polomombo branch there are only two major branches of the royal clan, Polomombo (P) and Njera (B1). Polomombo divides into one major segment with respect to Kalechi and two subsegments with respect to his wives. Njera branch consists of three segments, Njera, Chipanga, and Chapyoka. The descendants of Kaswanga and Vumbo no longer appear in the genealogical charter; consequently, their descendants are excluded from the royal clan.

Polomombo branch. The members of Polomombo are divided into two segments, p1 and p2, descended from Kalechi's two wives. Chief Kalinda (H11) is the founder of p1 and his younger half brother Muzula (H13), the founder of p2 (See figure 11).

Jeremiah (I27) is the head of segment p1 and of Polomombo branch. He is the head of the central village Kalinda; but since he is a very old man he has delegated most of his responsibilities to his elder brother's son, Anderson (J30), who is his heir apparent. Anderson is the acting headman of Kalinda and represents Jeremiah on the area committee and Banangwa council. He is active politically and attends council meetings when he thinks it is in his

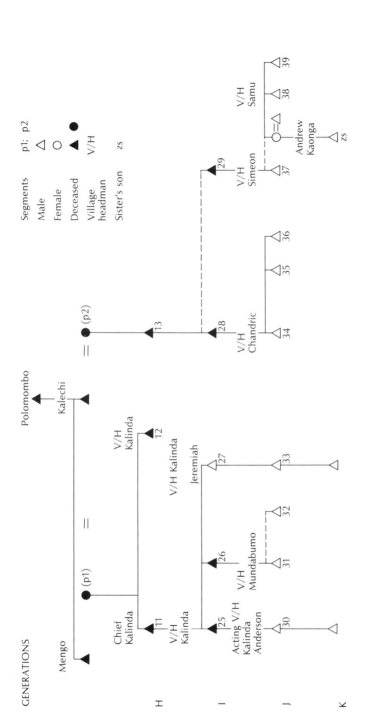

Figure 11. Polomombo Skeleton Genealogy

interest to do so; otherwise, he boycotts them. He is also chairman of the UNIP branch in his area, and his classificatory sister's son Andrew (Kzs1) is the branch secretary.

Chandric (J34) is the head of segment p2. Though he is a village head-man—and this applies to the other branch members who are headmen—he considers himself to be subordinate to Jeremiah, the headman of Kalinda. Polomombo headmen do not perform their village rites until Jeremiah has performed his. In other words, they consider Kalinda as their ritual and political center and look to its headman for leadership. Thus, when chiefdom ceremonies centering on Vinkakanimba are held in Muyombe, they do not attend them.

Polomombo's territorial support. Members of Polomombo branch are head-men in five villages: Kalinda, Lighton, Janakazi, Samu, and Mundobumo. But the headman of Mundobumo, along with his villagers, joined the Lenshina (Lumpa) camp and when he returned to Uyombe he was placed under Anderson's supervision. Polomombo also claims the allegiance of three other village headmen. These are the descendants of a slave who was given a village on Polomombo territory. They are not, however, entitled to attend the Banangwa Council.

Polomombo has a wide territorial power base that is expressed in action when its members boycott meetings concerned with such matters as the annual Vinkakanimba celebrations. Though they form only about 14% of the men of the royal clan, their strength lies in their unity, which stems from their exclusion from full rights as royals. Through Edwall they have regained some of those rights and, in return, have provided him with additional support against Chief Punyira and other branches.

Both the chief and the deputy chief can be removed from their posts only by the central government. This creates a situation in which neither can entirely remove the other from the game of politics. What is constantly at stake is the control of chiefdom affairs and the marshaling of political support to carry out policies. Polomombo support was crucial in the game in that members controlled a number of villages in the north and constituted a sizable block of votes on councils and committees. Their backing of the deputy chief was a loss for the chief but not a defeat. Moreover, individuals often shifted their allegiance depending on the issues involved.

Conclusion

The royal clan has been described in some detail because, until recently, its branches were the dominant political groups in Yombe society and the main contenders for power.

All branches claim that they have the right to provide the chief. These claims are supported by "historical accounts" which connect them to the conquerors (or founders) of the chiefdom. For the accounts to be accepted as authentic, they "must seem to the teller and the hearer to be exact, otherwise they will not serve as charters" (Richards 1960, p. 178). Thus they contain many of the same key figures and events. The difference between them is the way the key elements are combined (or manipulated), especially in the phase of the account concerned with the founders, Polomombo and Vinkakanimba, and their sons. It is to this early period (ibid.)[6] that members of Polomombo and Vinkakanimba lineages refer in order to invalidate each other's claims. The members of Vinkakanimba branches, on the other hand, manipulate Vinkakanimba's sons and their wives in order to establish their seniority and claims to chieftainship.

Genealogical knowledge is itself recognized as a resource; those who do not possess it must rely on others. The "historical charters" are considered by royal branches important for validating claims. The charters and their claims are sometimes recited on public occasions, usually disrupting the proceedings. They represent only one dimension of the political life of royal branches.

A more practical problem is to maintain political support. Though there are no marked differences in wealth, ambitious royals are generous with their goods and labor. They take every opportunity to help their fellow agnates. Their generosity is usually rewarded by political support. Thus, Fwasa of Njera was recognized as the leader of his segment, and Deputy Chief Edwall was able to gain the backing of the senior men of Njera.

From a more general perspective the segmentary character of the royal clan has helped to shape the nature of Yombe politics. Royal branches have their own central villages and spheres of influence. They form the core of political coalitions based upon kinship and clientship. Though colonial rule strengthened the authority of the chief and his men and further centralized authority, Uyombe has preserved many of the attributes of a segmentary state, in large part due to the persistence of the royal clan. Kinship and clientship remain important features of Yombe politics. Royal branches are still important political units. They compete on the councils and committees of chiefdom government and within the chiefdom for political support.

Because no branch forms a majority of the adult male members of the royal clan, branches seek alliances with others and also ally themselves with new potential sources of power, such as UNIP. The rivalry and cleavages within the royal clan has provided the UNIP committee with an opportunity to enhance its political power within the chiefdom.

5

The Structure of The New Men
Political Groups: and the Uyombe
UNIP Subregion Branch

The years preceding Zambian independence were marked by an increase in the intensity of political activity, not only in the urban areas but also in the countryside. From 1951 until 1958, the African National Congress (ANC), the first African political party to be founded in Northern Rhodesia, was the main nationalist political movement. ANC was, however, a loosely structured regional party which, under the leadership of Nkumbula, did not attempt to construct a well-organized, territory-wide political organization based upon urban and rural branches in all parts of the country (Mulford 1967, p. 62). In 1958 Dr. Kaunda split with Nkumbula and ANC and founded the Zambia African National Congress (ZANC); shortly thereafter ZANC was banned and Kaunda imprisoned by the government. Though the United National Independence Party (UNIP) was formed while Kaunda was still in prison, he became its president after his release in 1960. Under his leadership UNIP turned its attention to organizing a territory-wide party by founding local branches throughout Northern Rhodesia (Zambia), thus strengthening the political links between urban and rural centers, and providing UNIP with grass roots support (Mulford 1964, p. 40).

By 1962, UNIP had effectively displaced ANC as the principal African political party in Northern Rhodesia and had constructed an effective political organization which penetrated into most areas of the territory. It had developed into a mass party with its headquarters in Lusaka under a national committee. It was organized into twenty-four regions, each consisting of "constituencies" (subregion branches), which in turn were made up of local branches.

From 1960 through 1962, Northern Rhodesia saw a rapid spread of UNIP branches. The Northern Province, which had previously supported ZANC, became a UNIP stronghold. Within Isoka District, Uyombe became an important center of UNIP activity. The leading figures responsible for organizing branches of UNIP in Uyombe were a small number of men, most of whom had been active in politics in the areas where they were employed; they returned to Uyombe to help found UNIP branches. Unlike the chief and other royals, this new cluster of political leaders based its claims to leadership not on precedent but on the new order which the national party intended to establish. Although Punyira and the government considered their political activities illegal, they soon gained wide public support and were able to organize UNIP branches in Uyombe and in parts of the adjacent chiefdom of Ufungwe. By 1964 these local UNIP leaders were in control of a political organization in Uyombe which most Yombe had joined. They also had access to wealth accumulated from the sale of UNIP membership cards at two shillings and sixpence each. In other words, they had power (Bierstedt 1950, p. 737).[1] In addition, they had succeeded in occupying posts in chiefdom government and so could influence its policies—even the decisions of the Banangwa council—as well as make their own decisions within the context of the UNIP subregion branch; their decisions would be obeyed by most of the people of the chiefdom. Within Uyombe the authority and power of the UNIP subregion committee had come to rival that of the Native Administration. UNIP was the party of the people, its power based upon popular support.

The small core of men who were most active in founding local branches of UNIP in Uyombe represent a new element in the social and political life of the chiefdom. They are the "new men," as were the Livingstonia-educated men in their fathers' generation, and they form the growing edge of a new elite which, as Southall suggests (1966, p. 348), may either build new corporate groups to support itself or break into those which exist. The most active and the most powerful of the Yombe party leaders are all what the Yombe term "townmen." Although other prominent leaders are sometimes considered "townmen," they lack basic "western" skills and occupational experience. The special attributes of the true "townmen" set them apart from the average Yombe, thus demonstrating a gradual development of social distinctions. While royal status, based upon birth, had significance only within the context of the rural community, a Western education or training is accorded recognition in the wider Zambian society, where it increases opportunities for social and political mobility. Royal clan members form a corporate group in Yombe society, while the term "townmen" refers to social distinctions which form the basis for quasi-groups (Ginsberg 1934, pp. 40–41), a potential recruiting field for political cliques and coalitions (Harries-Jones 1969, pp. 301–2).[2]

The small town of Muyombe has formed the center for this growing core of the new local elite. Because it is the administrative and commercial center, its residents are more sensitive than are other Yombe to developments in other parts of Zambia. The first branch of UNIP was founded in Muyombe primarily through the efforts of the "new men," and it is here that their significance, their political activities, and their ability to found local UNIP branches may best be understood.

The New Men: "Townmen"

Residents of Muyombe distinguish three types of returned labor migrant: "villagemen," "minemen" and "townmen." Underlying the distinction are the criteria of education, type of employment abroad, and what may be described as a state of mind or orientation. The Yombe do not consider villagemen and minemen as having been part of the mainstream of urban life. Villagemen spend such short periods in urban areas that they are not regarded as having acquired an urban orientation. On their return to Uyombe chiefdom, most villagemen are considered to integrate easily into the established social and political fabric of village life. Minemen, on the other hand, because of their longer stay abroad, are thought to possess a more extensive understanding of urban ways. Their social contacts and experiences are thought to be less narrow. Yet the Yombe consider that the cultural and social experiences of minemen were gained mainly among fellow mine laborers or other unskilled workers. On their return to Uyombe, most minemen, it is thought, do not settle down to the normal routine of village life as easily as villagemen. They are no longer satisfied with the rural, peasant life of Uyombe, and many of them are concerned by the lack of amenities (electricity, running water, etc.) and basic services to which they have grown accustomed while abroad.

Intensive interviews with men living in Muyombe indicated that most of the villagemen and minemen had not taken an active part in political movements while abroad. Nonetheless, on their return to Uyombe they expressed their political awareness by their recognition of the contrast between village and town. They were dissatisfied with the chief, who had failed to explore means for improving the conditions of local life, and with the chiefdom administration, which did not include them in its deliberations. They formed a discontented section of the population, but one which lacked organization and leadership.

There are, however, men who regard themselves and are considered by others as forming a distinct group in Yombe society. They refer to themselves and are referred to by others as *bantu pa canya* (literally, "the people above"). They speak of themselves and are spoken of as "townmen," as opposed to villagemen or minemen. Townmen are men who attained a sufficient level of education beyond standard IV (six years of schooling) to allow them to acquire employment abroad as clerks and teachers. Some were union and political party organizers in the urban areas and were "repatriated" by the colonial government because of their political activities. It is they who tend to become poltical leaders in the rural area.

Townmen think of themselves as possessing an understanding of the range of African town ways, and, though they may lack the financial means, they attempt to emulate a town style of life. This subjective view of themselves is translated into objective reality in a variety of ways. The houses of these men are usually larger than others and furnished in an African urban style. Their dress and behavior also indicate their town orientation. Many of them put on coats and ties and may be seen hurrying about Muyombe, briefcase in hand, to attend this or that meeting. On special occasions such as Christmas they may organize dances at which men and women waltz and foxtrot together. They also form a "standard-setting group" for the young men and women of the community. As a local elite they are "looked up to and imitated, because they are credited with important gifts and desirable attributes" (Nadel 1956, p. 415).

But what is important here is that, because they aspire to reproduce the material and social conditions of the town in Uyombe, they take an active part in politics and have become an effective group within the rural community. Their activities have brought them into competition with the more conservative ruling elements: the chief, his immediate supporters, and many of the headmen. It is primarily among townmen that one finds political activists—the men who were able to harness rural discontent into an effective nationalist movement.

Material was collected on the education and employment abroad of 68 adult men living in Muyombe. Of the 68 men only 25 (37%) had received more than six years of schooling (English is not the language of instruction the first six years of lower primary school), and only 16 (21)% had been employed in professional or white-collar jobs while abroad.[3] Those who had completed their upper primary education and held jobs as primary school teachers, headmasters, and clerks, were the most active politically.

Some indication of the extent to which the 68 men participate in the formal political and commercial life of the chiefdom is suggested by the following figures. Of the 25 men with seven or more years of schooling, 5 hold Native Administration posts, 13 are members of chiefdom committees, and 7 hold neither type of post. Six of the 25 are store owners. In contrast, of the 43 men with six years of schooling or less, none holds a Native Administration post and only 4 are members of chiefdom committees. Two of the 43 men are owners of local stores. A similar pattern is apparent when one considers posts held within the local UNIP subregion. Of the 25 men with seven or more years of schooling, 5 hold important political party posts, whereas only 2 of the 43 men with six or fewer years of schooling hold such posts.

It is, then, primarily from the ranks of returned labor migrants with seven or more years of schooling that the new political leaders have been recruited. It was they who did most to found UNIP branches in Uyombe, and they are the ones who have most persistently contested the authority of the chief and even, on occasion, that of the deputy chief.

The New Men and the Founding of UNIP Branches

The penetration of urban-based political parties into the rural areas of Central Africa created new opportunities for leadership. In the case of the

Malawi Congress Party, as in UNIP, local educated commoners often provided the link between the national political party elite and villagers. Among the small numbers of such men in Uyombe, two types may be distinguished on the basis of their different educational achievements. The first were men between the ages of thirty and forty-five who had completed standard VI (eight years of schooling) at Lubwa Mission in Chinsali District. In 1961 they were former teachers and clerks who had lost their jobs because of their political activities. They represented the new townmen elite. The second type were educated in Uyombe and had completed standard III or IV (five or six years of schooling). While abroad, most had been employed in unskilled jobs. Many of them were asked to participate in the founding of local branches of UNIP because they were influential in the royal clan. Through their association with the more educated, they have taken on many of the superficial attributes of townmen. Because they lack the basic educational skills, however, the main organizing work in the UNIP branches has fallen to the more educated men.

One of the first political activists was Amos Ukwa, a standard VI Lubwa graduate, a former resident of Lusaka, labor organizer, and ANC member. While employed as clerk of the "Isoka Superior Native Authority" he used the opportunities of travel provided by this post to disseminate nationalist ideas. Before 1959 he distributed ANC membership cards but made no attempt to organize a party branch. These efforts, however, helped to clear the way for future UNIP party organizers. When, in 1959–60, the new national party, UNIP, was founded under the leadership of Dr. Kaunda, most of the Yombe young men who were active in politics dropped their membership of ANC and joined UNIP. They were vehemently opposed by those who remained ANC supporters. Amos did not join UNIP at once, and for this and other reasons he has been cold-shouldered by the party officials in Uyombe, who nevertheless recognize him as an extremely capable and thus potentially dangerous man. He is the chairman of the development committee, is consulted on all difficult problems in chiefdom dealings with the government, and is an active agent of change.

The principal founders of the first branch of UNIP in Uyombe, the Muyombe branch, were Ware Ntha, Eric Enda, Edwall Wowo, and Ado Chila. All these men had completed standard VI at Lubwa, taken additional courses, and gained employment as teachers and clerks. In 1961 they were in their early and mid-thirties.

During the late 1950s the government had reacted to the growing political unrest in the urban centers by returning political organizers to their home areas (Mulford 1967, p. 101). This policy naturally introduced a potentially disruptive element into the rural areas. In Uyombe, the returning activists mobilized their personal networks in support of UNIP. Financial assistance was obtained from local traders. Ware Ntha, who had been a teacher and party organizer on the Zambian copper belt, is an example. He was under close observation by Punyira, who was instructed to report him to the district commissioner if he attempted to organize a branch of UNIP. Ware had no power base or influence in Uyombe, but he secured the support of Eric Enda and Edwall Wowo, former pupils of Dr. Kaunda, who were head teachers of primary schools in the adjacent chiefdoms of Ufungwe in Zambia and Ntaliri in Malawi. Eric, whose elder half brother, Labe, was a prosperous local shop owner, resigned his teaching post and returned to Muyombe, where he began to organize. Labe not only helped him with money but also lent bicycles to party organizers. As the de facto head of his father's extended family cluster, he instructed its members to give Eric their assistance. Because their father, Isaac, was a loyal sister's son of Chipanga royal branch, Eric also found support among its senior members and other sisters' sons of Chipanga. Edwall Wowo, who relied upon his salary to provide for himself and his many dependents, did not leave his teaching post but made frequent trips to Muyombe. His status was an important asset to the movement in its early phases. Not only was he a member of Njera but several of his mother's brothers were the headmen of villages and one of these, Bwana Mbamba, was one of the three "traditional" councillors of the chief. Edwall advised all these people to support the founding of UNIP branches against the opposition of Punyira.

The final member of this standard VI Lubwa-educated political clique was Ado Chila, whose father was the chief's court assessor and loyal supporter. Ado, who had been a clerk in Asian stores on the Zambia copper belt, returned to Muyombe. He was employed as a clerk and driver by a successful trader whose wife was Katie Nyamkandawire, a standard VI Livingstonia-trained nurse. After the death of the trader, Ado and his brothers themselves opened a shop. Eric, who was Ado's intimate and trusted personal friend, recruited him into the movement to organize youth brigades for the new leaders to call into action when necessary. In his turn, Ado convinced his brothers to join and persuaded Katie to help organize women's leagues.

The policy of this core of young leaders was not to oppose Punyira directly but to induce his personal advisors (his sisters' sons) and his three traditional councillors to join them. The support of these powerful senior men was thought to be necessary to give the movement legitimacy. In addition to the men already mentioned, Tanga (a member of Kaswanga), and Donald (a member of Chapyoka), were active in recruiting. Though Tanga and Donald were less educated than the four founders, they were brought in because they were senior and influential members of their respective royal branches. Tanga's support for UNIP stemmed from his close relationship with Amos Ukwa, his mother's sister's son, while Donald was recruited by Ware, who had grown up with him in Chifunda village. The expanded core of the movement included important elements of the ruling stratum and even some of the chief's personal and traditional advisers. The reason why so many members of the ruling stratum were willing to respond to the claims made on them in the name of kinship and friendship by the founders of the movement and to give their support to UNIP was the widespread dissatisfaction with the chief's policies.

Many of the chief's personal and traditional advisers were standard VI graduates of Livingstonia, who had completed their courses in the 1920s. In their youth they had been schoolteachers, elders of the Free Church of Scotland, and the conveyers of Livingstonia ideals. They had been the progressive young men of their time, concerned with converting the people to Christianity, educating them, and improving their standard of living. Although they had lost much of the Livingstonia zeal, they were still deeply concerned to give their own children and grandchildren an education which would allow them to achieve high status and well-paying jobs. Like other former migrants, they wanted to improve the local standard of living. Punyira, who had become increasingly conservative, had done little for the development of schools and medical facilities. In addition he had alienated his "traditional" advisers and other important headmen by not consulting them. As the head of the Native Administration court he had given arbitrary and, at times, partial decisions which estranged many of his subjects. In 1960, he also alienated those of his personal advisers who were traders and shopowners by giving permission to an Asian to open a shop in Muyombe; he withdrew it only in the face of vehement protest. Thus, it was not difficult for the new leaders to persuade many of the chief's advisors to support the founding of a UNIP branch in Muyombe.

The local party leaders chose Donald as chairman of the branch; they hoped that, as Punyira's classificatory son, he could speak directly to the chief, and that Punyira would hesitate to arrest members of a body headed by a close kinsman. But they proved to be mistaken on both counts.

Meetings were subsequently held in the privacy of the bush to select persons for the remaining posts of secretary, treasurer, and their respective assistants. The choice for the post of secretary was considered to be an important one. The primary requirement was sufficient English to understand the party constitution, and to correspond with party and government officers. As an active party organizer and ex-teacher, Eric was selected and sent to Isoka District headquarters to register the newly formed branch. The qualifications set out for the post of treasurer were loyalty, honesty, and ability to handle party funds and keep accounts. Tanga Wowo was selected, although he had completed only standard IV. The vice-treasurer was also a locally educated standard IV man. The first vice-chairman proved to be unsatisfactory and was replaced by Simon Nyeka, a standard VI Lubwa graduate who had been dismissed from teaching because of his party activities.

The three village headmen who participated in the first meetings established branches in their villages. Other party officers began to tour the chiefdom on bicycles, holding meetings, selling UNIP membership cards, and founding branches.

The organization of youth brigades was assigned to Ado Chila. Once the youth brigade was well under way, Eric promoted him to vice-secretary of the subregion branch committee. His previous post was filled by a locally educated standard IV man, Sanford. The Women's League was established under the leadership of a forceful but illiterate woman, Agnes, with Katie as secretary. Other women were appointed as treasurer and vice-chairman, vice-secretary, and vice-treasurer. Ten other branches were founded in the chiefdom, nine of whose chairmen are also headmen or acting village headmen.

Ware and Edwall secured the recognition of the Muyombe branch as a subregion branch in charge of the other branches already established in the chiefdom, and its officers became the subregion branch committee. Ware was made publicity secretary, with a Nyika from Mulekatembo in Ufungwe as his assistant. The committee's activity in Ufungwe was actively opposed by the chief. Ufungwe chiefdom, however, is made up of two peoples antagonistic to each other, the Fungwe and the Nyika. The former, who provide the chief, live in the southern part, and the Nyika in the north around Mulekatembo. The subregion committee established branches among the Nyika, one of whom, Gala, was appointed to the committee. Gala, the assistant publicity secretary, received his earlier training in South Africa and later education in Kenya, where he says he first became aware of the possibility of Zambian independence.

In 1961 Dr. Kaunda introduced the "Master Plan" which led to disturbances in the Northern Province. During this period, local UNIP youth brigades burned schools and destroyed bridges and roads within the chiefdom (*An Account of the Disturbances . . .* 1961). Known as "Chacha-cha," these disturbances led to the arrest and imprisonment for periods of six to nine months of the subregion committee's vice-chairman and secretary, and members of the Muyombe youth brigade.

When these men returned, they lodged complaints against Punyira, claiming that he was incapable of performing his judicial and administrative duties. They did not present the complaints themselves but got prominent senior men to do so. Because of the political unrest in Uyombe, the district commissioner agreed that a deputy should be elected to assist Punyira, whereupon the salaried post of deputy chief was created. The district commissioner and the Banangwa Council decided that the salary of Chief Punyira should be divided with his deputy, who was expected to perform most of his administration duties. The deputy chief drew many of his personal advisers from the UNIP committee. Thus leaders of the party have become important figures in the political life of the chiefdom.

The Structure of the Uyombe Subregion Branch

The Uyombe subregion branch is an intermediate unit of UNIP party organization. Until 1965, it was one of the subordinate component units of Chinsali region. Chinsali, however, is over three hundred miles from Uyombe, which prevented regional officers from exercising direct supervision over subregion affairs.

After independence, a new region was created, consisting of all the subregion branches in Isoka District. Its salaried posts were filled by the appointment of loyal educated party men and women from the subregion branches. This had facilitated communication between the regional and subregional committees and is gradually leading to closer supervision by regional officers. However, these and other political appointments have deprived the subregion committee of its most competent party officers and organizers, the "townmen" element, and allowed men with parochial views and interests to dominate party affairs. Thus many of the present party leaders are concerned primarily with securing benefits for the Yombe as a people and for themselves as reward for previous loyal service. These are men who have not the qualifications for advancement in any wider system.

During the period of this study (1963–65) the Uyombe subregion branch included Uyombe and the adjacent chiefdom of Ufungwe. It consisted of twenty-one local branches, eleven of which were in Uyombe. The subregion branch was controlled and directed by a committee which included the eight officers of the subregion branch, the six officers of the subregion women's league, and two representatives of the youth brigade. In addition, there was a joint committee consisting of the committee and representatives from the executive committees of the branches. Beneath the subregion branch were the local branches, each with its executive committee consisting of the office holders. Affiliated with and subordinate to each branch were a woman's league and a youth brigade. Subordinate to the branch officers were the UNIP card-holding members.

Figure 12 illustrates the structure of the Uyombe subregion branch. It shows that party divisions do not coincide with administrative units. A local branch includes more than one village, and the subregion branch encompasses two chiefdoms, Uyombe and Ufungwe. The subregion committee supervises and directs the activities of local branches, links them to the region, and represents the local party to the Native Administration. The executive committees of these branches are responsible not for making decisions but for carrying out those of the subregion and regional executive committees.

Uyombe Local Branches

A UNIP branch may cover more than one village. For example, the Muyombe branch includes the administrative village of Muyombe and two others. Although I was unable to acquire exact membership figures, my impression was that most adult residents of the chiefdom are UNIP members. There is, in fact, some foundation for this impression. During the Lenshina (Lumpa) disturbances of August 1964, it was widely believed that persons without a UNIP membership card would be considered Lumpa church members, i.e., followers of prophetess Alice (Lenshina) Mulenga, and would be shot or imprisoned by the soldiers stationed in the chiefdom. Even in more normal times the card served as an identity card within Uyombe and a passport in crossing international check points.

Party divisions   Local administrative divisions

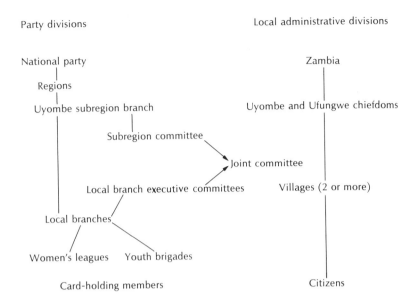

Figure 12. Uyombe UNIP Subregion

Local branch committee members are elected by the members of the branch. Thus, the founding of eleven branches provided sixty-six new political posts for ambitious men, with an equivalent number of posts for women as officers of the women's leagues and young men as officers in the youth brigade. This feature alone greatly expanded the participation of the local population in the political process and provided channels through which they could express their interests.

Few, if any, immediate financial rewards are derived from the party. Its officers do not receive salaries, and, for most, service to the party is not a full-time vocation. The main activities requiring money are financed from the sale of party membership cards and from the personal contributions of members and shopowners and traders. In contrast to many rural communities in East Africa, the commercial life of the chiefdom is in the hands of local Africans, not Asians. These African entrepreneurs are part of the society. They contribute to the party, and party leaders who are related to them expect and receive financial assistance for themselves and their families. Moreover, these African shop owners and traders are concerned with rural economic development and with improving African commercial opportunities which they think can be brought about only under an African government. Thus they have a stake in the success of the party and back its leaders. The alliance which has developed between them and the party's leadership has strengthened the position of the party. It is unlikely that this type of alliance would have been possible if the entrepreneurs had been non-Africans who were receiving economic advantages under colonial rule.

Because UNIP organizers in Uyombe were concerned with gaining legitimacy for their political activities, they encouraged headmen to join and found branches. This policy is reflected in the fact that nine branch chairmen are also village headmen. Of these, five are members of the royal clan and two are the chief's traditional councillors, i.e., headmen who participate in the selection of chiefs. The two chairmen who do not hold chiefdom posts are the heads of Muyombe branch and the adjacent one of Chidulika. The youth brigades of the two branches are used by the subregion committee to maintain order on such occasions as public meetings and chiefdom celebrations. Members of the two branches are expected to attend political rallies, especially when they are held by visiting party officials.

The chairman is the head of the branch and its executive committee, but the secretary holds the more important post. Most branch secretaries have completed standard V or VI (seven or eight years of schooling) and, unlike the chairmen, none is a headman. The branch secretary controls the sale of party cards and is expected to tour the branch. This brings him into intimate contact with the people of his area, allowing him to disseminate party information and to collect local views. He is thus in a better position than most to assess public opinion. It is usually the chairman and the secretary who represent the branch on the joint committee.

Branch officers are supposed to check on strangers making investigations in their area. Should such strangers prove to be smallpox vaccinators, agricultural assistants, or employees of government agencies supported by the UNIP committee, the officers are supposed to help them. Otherwise villagers may refuse to cooperate, and a stranger may have to explain his business to the youth brigade. Branch officers are supposed to hold public meetings to inform members of party policies, plans, and activities and are expected to raise funds to support local schemes. They also represent the interests of their members in the joint committee meetings of branch and subregion officers.

The branch youth brigade. Affiliated with and subordinate to each branch is a youth brigade, which consists of men under thirty. Each brigade has its own officers. It provides the branch with its messengers and "police." Its members are expected to obey party instructions and, if necessary, to impose them on members and nonmembers alike.

Members of the youth brigade perform a number of tasks. They give notice of public meetings held by the local branch, the subregion branch, or visiting party officers. They are expected to keep order at these meetings and to lead in the singing of party songs. They report on strangers in their area, see that the adult men and women have purchased or renewed their UNIP membership cards, and during elections they see that members register to vote.

During the period 1963–65 the activities of the youth brigade were closely watched by the subregion officers, who feared an abuse of power which could lead to popular disapproval and the loss of public support. Some of this caution came with Zambian independence, from observing and experiencing the activities of the Malawi Youth League. Branch officers were often warned against using the youth brigade for other than party business. The warning was specifically directed at branch chairmen, who were not always able to separate their party roles from their Native Administration roles. The control of a body of young men in one sphere was a temptation to use them in another, especially if one accepted the party slogan that "UNIP is government." An example of the inappropriate use of the youth brigade was the case of headman Jim, a branch chairman, who ordered members living in his village to drive out a man suspected of being a witch. Jim was summoned by Edwall and the court and threatened with dismissal by the Banangwa council. As he had no royal patron, he turned to the UNIP committee for support. However, he was strongly reprimanded by subregion officers and warned that he might be dismissed from his party post if he could not distinguish between party and government business.

The branch women's league. The women members are organized into a league with its own officers. They may be called upon to participate in such fundraising activities as agricultural work parties. They also are expected to keep the branch office in good repair by plastering it after the rains, helping to clear away the grass surrounding it, and contributing bundles of grass for reroofing. They must attend public meetings. If there is a branch choir, the younger women should join it along with members of the youth brigade. On the occasion of important meetings these choirs come marching into Muyombe carrying flags and banners, dancing, and singing songs, some of which tell the people to buy UNIP membership cards and praise the subregion chairman and other officers.

The officers of the women's league are expected to campaign among local women and to address them at public meetings of the branch, giving information on party policy concerning women—the present theme being "Educate a woman and you educate a family."

The Subregion Committee
The subregion committee directs, supervises, and coordinates the activities of the branches. Not only does it manage the affairs of the subregion branch, but it also links the local branches into the regional and national framework of UNIP. It is the UNIP committee which formulates policy on such matters as the relationship of the subregion branch to organs of chiefdom government. Because most Yombe belong to local UNIP branches, the UNIP committee's power rivals that of the Native Administration, so that its members are among the most powerful political figures in the chiefdom.

The officers of the subregion committee in 1963–65 were the small number of men who founded the Muyombe branch and laid the foundations of a mass political movement in Uyombe. At the practical level of substantive action they organized branches, youth brigades, and women's leagues. This has provided them with a chiefdom-wide political base. Through songs, flags, and slogans they received acclaim and were associated with national leaders and the nationalist movement. In 1962, the nationalist thrust of the local movement was recorded symbolically in the burial of an effigy of Roy Welensky in a grave dug near to the offices of the Native Administration. This grave and its marker were also symbolic of the growing power of the "new men." While power had once been the privilege of "royals," a new element of "highly" educated and progressive royals, commoners, and traders was preparing to assume many of the responsibilities of chiefdom government.

With the exception of subregion chairman Donald Wowo and the treasurer, Tanga Wowo, the officers represent a new elite which derives its status and power from the party and not from traditional obligations and loyalties. Their overriding allegiance is to the party. They offer the chiefdom an alternative leadership, with new political norms and values and with new channels through which local citizens may express their interests.

A variety of duties brings them into contact with the branches and the local community. They make periodic tours of the subregion. They may reorganize local branches which are no longer active, hear complaints, settle disputes, and, if necessary, dismiss branch officers and supervise the election of new ones. The secretary distributes party cards to branch secretaries, checks whether members have renewed their old cards, and whether the secretaries have kept minutes. The treasurer collects funds derived from the sale of party cards and reviews the branch's finances. The subregion officers may hold public meetings to explain party and government policies. Their talks may be summarized briefly in party slogans such as "one Zambia, one Nation, one Leader," "UNIP is government and government is UNIP," and "Freedom is work and work for Zambia is freedom."

Composition and cliques.[4] The subregion committee consists of sixteen members: eight committee officers, the six officers of the women's league, and the chairman and secretary of the youth brigade. The eight officers are: chairman, secretary, publicity secretary, treasurer, and their respective assistants. Of the eight men occupying these posts, six are commoners, five are standard VI graduates and five are ex-teachers or clerks. Chairman Donald Wowo, treasurer Tanga Wowo, and vice-treasurer Tisi Koko have completed only standard IV. Donald, the only subregion officer who is also a village headman, is the chairman of Chifunda branch. Only three of the eight subregion branch officers do not live in Muyombe; chairman Donald lives in Chifunda, in 1964 publicity secretary Ware was in Ireland on a special course, and vice-publicity secretary Gala lives in Mulekatembo in the neighboring chiefdom of Ufungwe.

The six officers of the women's league are: chairman, secretary, treasurer, and their respective assistants. The women who occupy these posts are all commoners and wives of commoners and all live in Muyombe. The secretary, Katie Nyamkandawire, is the most highly educated and skilled. None of the others speak, read, or write English. The chairman, Agnes, completed only standard B (two years of schooling); the vice-chairman, Sarah (who is the wife of Ado Chila, the subregion vice-secretary) completed standard IV; and the three others completed standard II. The two representatives of the subregion branch youth brigade are the chairman, Sanford, from Chidulika village, who has completed standard IV, and Tengo, from Muyombe, who has completed standard V.

The social distinctions found among the initial political party organizers form the basis of cliques and factions. On many issues considered by the subregion committee, members divide into two cliques or factions based upon informal personal networks of kinship and friendships and common educational achievements, social expectations, and shared interests. The core of one clique consists of the less educated members: Donald, Tanga, Tisi, Sanford, and Agnes. The four men who completed only standard IV at Uyombe schools share common interests and are linked by personal friendship through Tisi, the vice-treasurer. Tisi is the central point of the network; he and Sanford grew up in the same village and boy's house; he and Donald worked in South Africa together; and he and Tanga are intimate personal friends, who live in adjacent houses and cultivate adjacent gardens. A feature of this political clique is that it has no leader; Tisi has not been able to translate his personal friendship into a relationship of superiority. He is rather an intermediary between Tanga and Donald, both of whom are powerful "royals" and potential adversaries. All four have reached the age at which men no longer seek employment abroad. Hence their interests are orientated toward Yombe society. They are concerned with change insofar as they initiate it and it improves their own economic, social, and political position. But they are also concerned with developing Uyombe and providing opportunities for the Yombe, and they must consider UNIP interests as well.

The fifth member of this clique is the nearly illiterate Agnes. Because her husband is dead and the son with whom she lives has the reputation of being irresponsible, her social standing rests upon her post as chairman of the women's league. She has allied herself with the other less educated members of the committee.

The nucleus of the second clique consists of the more educated members including Eric Enda, Ado Chila, and Katie Nyamkandawire. The other three who have completed standard VI do not often attend meetings. Although they form a minority in most meetings, they can usually marshal support among the less educated; Ado is Sarah's husband, and Eric is the close kinsman of a standard VI Lubwa graduate who is the husband of another woman on the committee and an active UNIP supporter.

Eric, Katie, and Ado are all highly educated by rural Zambian standards and hold powerful posts. They are often in control of special information. Their recommendations are sought by local people in getting jobs as teachers and agricultural assistants, sometimes in other parts of Zambia. They have an extensive network of external contacts, both in the party and in the civil service. They participate in the wider social system, and their aspirations go beyond Yombe society.[5] They tend to take account of subregional, regional, and national interests. Although the distinction between the more and less educated members of the committee is one of degree, nonetheless it represents a cleavage within the committee which becomes apparent and assumes importance in meetings.

Subregion committee meetings. The committee is the principal decision-making body of the UNIP subregion branch. Its authority stems, on the one hand, from its position in the national party structure and on the other hand, from the rights which local UNIP members have accorded to it. It considers policies which affect the relations of the subregion branch, the local branches, the youth brigades, the women's leagues, and the average party member, to the Native Administration. This means that most chiefdom citizens are subject to the (sometimes conflicting) authority of both the UNIP committee and the Native Administration.

The subregion committee holds its meetings in its headquarters in Muyombe. Nonmembers may be invited to discuss particular topics, but they must leave once they have made their contribution. Unauthorized persons are prevented from entering the meetings by the two representatives of the youth brigade who place themselves where they can see outside and chase away anyone standing too near. The committee attempts to keep its deliberations secret. An exception was made in my case, however.

The items which the committee discussed while I was present throw light on its activities and interests and on the type of problems which confronted it during the period shortly before and after Zambian independence.

Table 4 sets out the business discussed at the eight meetings I attended over a period of several months in 1964 and 1965. The thirty-five major items discussed at these eight meetings have been classified under five general topics. The three topics most frequently discussed (see table 5) were subregion branch organization (thirty-six discussions), external relations (seventeen), and national government policies (eleven). The predominant concern with subregion branch organization and affairs is not surprising, because it is only through effective political organization that the subregion committee can command the support of chiefdom citizens and compete with the Native Administration, the royal clan, and village headmen for control of the chiefdom.

Tables 4 and 5 inevitably obscure any connection between the various topics and problems dealt with by the committee. They represent politics in its static and isolated form and fail to illustrate the flow of events which affected political relations within the chiefdom. I have selected three of the matters discussed at committee meetings to illustrate the actual working of the committee, its internal cleavages, and its relationship to other bodies.

Table 4. Business Transacted in Eight Subregion Committee Meetings

Subregion Organization	Special Items and Appeals	External Relations
Branch supervision	University of Zambia	Native Administration
Control of youth	National Conferences	Village headmen
Leadership: men	Independence	The region
Leadership: women	celebrations	Rural councillors
Participation of	Guns	African National Congress
women	Beer	Official visitors
Women's domestic		
courses	Local Chiefdom Services	National Government Policies
Women's clubs	Library	Loans
Husband/wife relations	Schools	Taxation
Membership cards	Dispensary	Labor migrants
Ufungwe branches	Civil servant salaries	Zambia Youth Camps
Cost of public meetings	Veterinary	Zambianization
Flag and anthem	Carpenter shop	Party and government

Table 5. Summary of Business Transacted at Eight Subregion Committee Meetings

	No. of Major Items	No. of Times Items Discussed
Subregion organization	12 (35%)	36 (47%)
Special items and appeals	5 (14%)	5 (6%)
Local chiefdom services	6 (17%)	8 (10%)
External relations	6 (17%)	17 (22%)
National government policies	6 (17%)	11 (15%)
Total	35 (100%)	77 (100%)

Case 1—women's clubs: the party and the deputy chief. A recurrent topic is the role of women in the party and in the life of the chiefdom as a whole. Most Yombe traditionally consider women political and jural minors. Although national UNIP policy has attempted to change their status, the subregion committee and the deputy chief have met with little response from the less educated officers of women's leagues and women members of the committee. This apparent apathy among women led the subregion officers to suggest that local branch officers, all of whom are men, should sit on the women's league committees and advise them on organization and development schemes for women. In his turn, Deputy Chief Edwall sought to organize women's clubs outside the party framework without first consulting the committee, in particular its more educated members. He considered this to be a concern of the Native Administration. His intention was that the clubs should be formed in each village, electing their own officers from among the members. Those who had special skills were to teach others to read and write, to cook and sew, to make clay pots, and instruct them in other domestic arts as well as in hygiene and sanitation. Goods produced by

members of these clubs, Edwall suggested, could be sold within the village or in other villages, or marketed in Muyombe. The money thus raised was to be divided. The larger portion would be used by the club to purchase needles, thread, and cloth. The remainder would be kept by the individual producer to buy such small items as soap and salt for her family.

Edwall held a meeting of the women of Muyombe, outlined his scheme, and appointed temporary officeholders, all women who had completed standard V or VI. Many of them had attended courses in domestic science and were former teachers. At this point most of the women, led by Agnes, chairman of the women's league, walked out of the meeting. The leaders of the walkout regarded Edwall's scheme and his choice of officers as a threat to their control of the women and as questioning their educational qualifications for leadership.

At the next meeting of the subregion committee, the women explained that they had left Edwall's meeting because they had had to get home to cook for their families. This explanation was not accepted by the men, who told them that the party and government must cooperate. If the women had complaints, they should have presented them at Edwall's meeting instead of walking out.

Edwall was then invited to the subregion committee meeting to explain his scheme. He did this, and apologized for not having consulted the committee before. Most members of the committee agreed that his scheme was a good one. They saw in it a means of increasing the participation of women in the party and, at the same time, of strengthening its control of chiefdom affairs. After he left, the women were instructed to cooperate with him but to see that the posts of officers of the clubs were filled by officers of the women's leagues. The subregion committee would then gain control of the clubs and credit for the scheme.

This case indicates the forces which operate against change within the subregion branch. The less educated women have derived authority and prestige from holding posts within the party, and view any attempts at further change as a threat to their standing. Apathy in the women's league is due to their inadequate leadership, but the present incumbents value their posts too much to be easily removed.

Another factor in this case was the attitude of the chairman. Donald considers the subregion branch to be his sphere of jurisdiction and opposes any attempt at interference in party matters by Edwall. Hence he opposed the scheme. But both Eric and Ado argued in support of it. They are men who do not derive their status from the "traditional" order and thus are not dependent upon it. They continually criticize Donald for attempting to introduce royal clan rivalries into the affairs of the party.

The way in which decisions are reached often depends on the issues. Noncontroversial matters are usually settled by discussion leading to compromise and agreement or by a decision of the chairman. Decisions on some matters may in fact be taken outside the committee meeting. For example,

many of the committee members have received outside political appointments and have left their posts vacant. Donald and Eric (the ex-secretary,
now the local credit supervisor) did not wait for proposals from the
committee to fill the vacancies. They decided that qualfied persons should
be chosen from the branches. Thus, they selected a secretary and presented
his name to the committee as the most likely candidate. A choice backed by
one less and one more educated member was readily accepted.

Voting is one possibility, though rarely employed. When an issue involves
a matter of principle, and the committee cannot agree, it may refer the
matter to the regional committee.

Case 2—government loans. In 1965 the Zambian government initiated a
policy of granting loans to Africans through the Land Bank of Zambia in an
attempt to stimulate economic growth in the rural areas and reduce the rate
of labor migration. Credit supervisors (or officers) were appointed to
administer the loans and advise the local population. In Isoka District these
were educated local men who had demonstrated their loyalty to UNIP. Eric
Enda was appointed from Uyombe. Although he was obliged, on becoming a
civil servant, to resign his post as UNIP subregion secretary, he continued to
serve the party and attend committee meetings.

Within the committee the less educated, led by Tanga Wowo, the
treasurer, argued that subregion officials should have special preference and
that other applicants must have letters of recommendation from thier local
party branches before their applications could be considered. The more
educated argued that all qualified and capable persons should be granted
loans on the basis of the merits of their applications, regardless of their party
affiliation. They also supported the applications of former Lenshina (Lumpa)
followers and Watchtower members. The disagreement was serious, since it
concerned the possibility for local party men to translate their political
status and party loyalty into economic advantages. The less educated
considered that loans should be a reward for service rendered to the party.

The less educated, led by Tanga, refused to apply for loans except on their
own terms, and began to discourage other people from doing so. Eric sought
the aid of Edwall and Amos Ukwa, Tanga's mother's sister's son, who was one
of the first political activists in Uyombe and chairman of the development
committee. Because the distribution of loans was mainly a Zambian government policy, under the direction of the Land Bank of Zambia, the Native
Administration was concerned that it should be implemented without subregion branch opposition.

The main local government body concerned with this scheme was the
development committee, most of whose members sought to encourage
Yombe to apply for loans. Since Tanga and his friend Tisi were also members
of this committee, it too had reached an impasse.

Edwall, Eric, and Amos attempted, without success, to convince Tanga
that loans were for the benefit of all and not the privilege of a few. Supported

by the less educated, Tanga had the matter referred to the regional committee, which decided that all persons applying for loans must get testimonials from their local branch and approval from the subregion branch before their applications would be considered. Eric was instructed to put aside applications not meeting these criteria. This meant that the party was controlling the implementation of government policy. Though Eric accepted the decision, he continued to argue that those who were in the greatest need were being excluded. In particular, to exclude Lumpa members deprived them of the possibility of reintegration into Yombe society and would lead to problems in the future.

Because, in the first months after independence, the spheres of competence of UNIP and of the chiefdom government were not clearly defined, Tanga and the less educated were able to achieve their goal at the expense of those who supported national government policy. In this situation Tanga considered party membership and service more important than being a Yombe.

The disagreement over loans was referred to the region because it could not be settled in the development committee by the chairman, by discussion, by compromise, or by vote. It involved control of and access to new sources of wealth introduced into Yombe society. The region's decision strengthened the position of the local party and of the less educated members within it. Not only did this decision go against the policies of the Zambian government, but it also enhanced the powers of a local element which attached greater value to its own and local interests than to regional and national party interests. The debate over loans transcended the bounds of the party and entered the more inclusive political arenas of chiefdom government. It produced a confrontation between the less and the more educated members of chiefdom councils and committees. In support of their position the less educated members of the subregion committee, under Tanga's leadership, turned to the region for support. Because Eric holds a political appointment and is loyal to the party, he did not contest the decision of the region.

Case 3—rural council elections. When the interests of the party are attacked, members tend to drop their differences. A situation of this type arose over the selection of Uyombe representatives on the Isoka Rural Council. It shows how the more educated members may manipulate cleavages to gain support.

The Isoka rural council deals with such matters as the allocation of district funds for the construction and maintenance of schools and roads within the six chiefdoms of the district. It consists of "twelve elected and twelve appointed members. Of the latter, six are chiefs, and there is one other member from each chief's area; most of these are the former petty chiefs" (Hudson 1965, p. 50).

Uyombe has four rural councillors—two appointed and two elected. It is divided into two electoral wards, Uyombe east and Uyombe west. Though these posts are supposedly elective, subregion committee policy had been to choose suitable party members. Up to 1965 these had been Eric and Ado.

In the 1965 elections Edwall expressed the opinion that candidates should be publicly nominated and should campaign throughout the chiefdom. As Eric did not intend to stand, he proposed to nominate Amos, the chairman of the development committee.

Eric opposed all these proposals.

"I do not want to organize against the deputy chief," he said. He then paused. Other members immediately responded by saying that this was the party and he could say what he thought. He continued, "The deputy chief says the people must choose whom they want. But we are UNIP. We must work with the deputy chief. We must call him to this meeting and tell him whom we are nominating. We and the deputy chief must argue this out in private. The deputy chief has in mind educated people. But Chapyoka's [chairman Donald's] committee wants someone of the party. We want a party man who knows the problems of the people." This opening speech met with the approval of the committee. Eric had emphasized the two areas of conflict, (1) the more educated versus the less educated, and (2), by referring to Donald as Chapyoka, Chapyoka branch versus Njera. He stood up again, this time speaking in the name of the party's leader: "Dr. Kaunda would be surprised if there were many candidates." The other members then shifted to the position that there was no need to consult the deputy chief. But Ado had said that the party and Edwall must work together. In this way the more educated members achieved immediate control of the situation. Eric then nominated Ado and Tanga. When Tanga expressed some reluctance, Eric suggested Andrew—the branch secretary of Kakoma, one of the highly educated—as a possible alternative. This done, the committee sent for Edwall. As soon as Edwall had explained the government system for electing rural councillors, Donald told him that the candidates of the party were Ado and Tanga. However, Tanga decided to withdraw. Edwall than proposed Amos, arguing that he would need intelligent support on the rural council in order to gain development projects for Uyombe. Eric, in his turn, again suggested Andrew, who proved to be acceptable to Edwall. Since the committee and Edwall had selected the two elected rural councillors, they agreed that there was now little point in holding elections.

In this case, the lines of cleavage were between the party and the Native Administration. Eric used a number of devices to secure the support of members of the committee. By claiming that Edwall wanted only educated people as rural councillors, he identified himself with the less educated and gained their backing for his candidates. By referring to the committee as Chapyoka's committee, he introduced royal rivalries as a means of controlling the situation, again in support of his own candidates. The consistent policy of the more educated has been to see that when civil service posts fall vacant, educated party men are selected to fill them. Though Amos is highly educated, he is not considered to be a reliable party member. Thus, his candidature for most posts is opposed by the party; it is only because of Edwall's backing that he is chairman of the development committee. Amos occupies an ambiguous position; he has taken wives from both Chapyoka, (his senior wife is Chief Punyira's daughter) and Chipanga royal branches; yet he is descended from a Njera woman. Though he is an affine of Chapyoka and Chipanga, he is often claimed as a sister's son by Njera and is supported by its members. Thus Eric's reference to Chapyoka's committee identified Amos with Edwall and Njera. Andrew, on the other hand, is a sister's son of Polomombo, the royal branch that stands in opposition to other royal branches. His selection not only gave recognition to the Polomombo Wowo and the northwestern region of Uyombe but also put an educated loyal party man in an important political post. His loyalty would be not to Edwall but to the more educated members of the UNIP committee.

The Joint Committee

The subregion committee is the principal decision-making body of the subregion branch. It is not insulated from its public, for it periodically confronts their representatives in the joint committee. The latter includes the subregion committee and local branch officers. It is supposed to meet once a month, but meetings are actually held once every two to three months, and even less frequently during the rainy season when travel is difficult and members are actively engaged in agricultural tasks. Meetings are held in the Muyombe subregion branch headquarters. Most local branches are represented by at least one officer.

While the subregion committee is, in Bailey's terms, an "elite committee," which considers itself a ruling oligarchy confronting its public, the joint committee is an "arena committee," in which members pursue the interests of the groups they represent (Bailey 1965, p. 10). Officers seek to gain benefits for their own branch against the claims of other branches. Though the subregion committee forms the elite element in joint committee meetings, it too pursues its own interests, as well as those of the region and the national party.

The meetings of the joint committee give the subregion committee an opportunity to discuss with local branch officers such matters as regional and local party and government policies, and branch problems, and to assess public opinion. Local branch officers are enabled to question the activities of the subregion committee and air any grievances. They present demands for such things as footballs, carpentry shops, schools, adult night schools, and higher prices for crops.

Conclusion

The founding of UNIP branches in Uyombe provided new opportunities for ambitious men and women to gain political influence, power, and status. It allowed for an increase in popular participation in chiefdom affairs. Yet, at the same time, control of the party apparatus was being centralized in the hands of a few men and women. These were the organizers of the first branches and consisted of two elements. There were the more educated, who not only sought to gain positions of power within Uyombe but also aspired to enter the regional and national arenas of politics. Because they possessed special skills, they were potentially mobile in the wider social system. In party and chiefdom affairs they represented regional and national party interests. The second element included men and women who lacked the necessary education and skills for social advancement in an independent Zambian society. Their interests lay solely in Uyombe and in securing control of the local party and the new sources of wealth introduced by the central government. They constituted a conservative element, which sought to entrench itself and stabilize political relationships in its own favor by reducing public participation in both party and chiefdom affairs. In 1965, when many of the more educated were appointed to regional party posts or to jobs in the Zambian civil service, the less educated conservatives assumed control. Neglecting to hold elections for party posts, the party was gradually losing contact with its grass roots.

6

Politics in Chiefdom Government: The Chief, the Deputy Chief, and the Banangwa Council

In the precolonial era, the political system of Uyombe represented a type of petty state organization which, in varying degrees, was based upon those three key institutions, royal kinship, rulership, and clientship, which Fallers (1956) identifies in his study of the small Soga states of Uganda. These institutions persisted through the colonial phase and were significant in the preindependence arrangements of local government. Within the formal context of local government, they formed a framework of informal relationships for political coalitions and brought a particularistic or personal element into the Native Administration system.

The Northern Rhodesian Native Authorities ordinance of 1936 introduced a uniform system of local government in Zambia. Within Uyombe the Native Administration system regularized administrative procedures, reinforced centralized authority, and imposed a potentially more representative body than the Banangwa council. Under this new system the chief became a minor officer in the colonial administration with a staff and an advisory body, the chief's council, consisting of village headmen and other prominent persons of the chiefdom.[1] His main duties were to maintain law and order, collect taxes, promulgate minor laws, and gain compliance with government policies. If he performed his duties to the district commissioner's satisfaction and the chiefdom's account books and records were in order, his position was secure. Though he was recognized and paid by the colonial administration, neither he nor his staff were accorded the status of career officers; they were not eligible for promotion.

The chief was the Native Authority. His authority and powers, his duties and responsibilities as well as his income stemmed from his new post as an officer of the colonial administration. Though he lost many of his traditional powers and much of his income, the new system buttressed his position and insulated him from many of the demands of his subjects. He could disregard the traditional checks on his authority and pursue a more personal management of chiefdom affairs.

Under the new system, the Banangwa council also became part of the Native Administration. Most of its activities, however, were taken over by the chief, who ruled with the assistance of his cognatic kinsmen and his educated clients. The Native Administration system has remained substantially intact with minor but significant changes. The Native Authorities ordinance of 1960 provided for the retirement of elderly, infirm, or incompetent Native Authorities through the creation of the new post of deputy chief. But the imposition of the ordinance was left to the discretion of the district commissioner. It was he who decided whether a chief was capable of performing his duties. In 1961, the tempo of the nationalists' struggle for independence increased; in the Northern Province there was widespread violence. Within Isoka District, Uyombe was an important center of this form of anticolonial expression; schools were burned and roads and bridges destroyed. It became apparent to the district commissioner that the Yombe chief could no longer maintain law and order, and, fearing further violence, he introduced the post of deputy chief in Uyombe. Elections for the new post were held in 1962, resulting in Edwall's taking office. During the same period the chief's council was reconstituted as the area committee, and within this larger body a standing committee was established, the development committee, to be specifically concerned with meeting public demands for building schools, roads, bridges, dispensaries, and dams. The chief's rule was directly affected by these changes, which introduced new "collegiate" principles, based upon rule by committee, into local government. There was the potential for a more bureaucratic and representative system of local government to develop. But there was also the potential for conflict between the chief and his ruling clique on one side and the deputy chief and the new men on the other.

The Deputy Chief: Edwall's Election

With increasing years, Punyira's efficiency as a Native Administration officer had declined. He neglected his duties, abused his powers, and restricted the membership of the Banangwa council to the three chiefly branches. He rarely summoned meetings and consulted individual members. He rarely held meetings of the chief's council, and, when he did, it was usually to rubber-stamp his decisions. As the head of the Native Administration court he decided cases in favor of his supporters. He was also accused of accepting bribes. Thus, by the late 1950s Punyira had both concentrated power in his own hands and lost the support of most of his subjects.

The founding of branches of UNIP in Uyombe crystallized the opposition against the chief and provided a channel through which popular discontent could be expressed. Punyira failed to suppress opposition by accusing its leaders of witchcraft. Even the imprisonment of party leaders during the 1961 disturbances of the Northern Province did not subdue them. On their return to Uyombe they sent a delegation of respected older men to protest to the district commissioner. In an attempt to forestall the district commissioner's intervention, the chief appointed as his assistants first his son Ruti and then his sister's son Pauta Chila. These two appointments were vehemently opposed, mainly because the men were close kinsmen of the chief. The district commissioner then proposed the creation of the formal post of deputy chief.

The deputy chief was supposed to assume most of Punyira's administrative duties, and Punyira's salary was to be divided between them (see chapter 2). The post was open to members of the chiefly branches and was to be filled by election. The franchise was restricted to male members of the royal clan including Polomombo. Though these proposals were opposed by Punyira, they were approved by the Banangwa council.

Before the election there were extensive negotiations between royal branches, and between their segments, and with party officers. Within Njera there were three prospective candidates: Edwall of Njera segment, Esaw of Chimbilima, and Krist of Mitanga. Each was supported by his own segment, and negotiations were undertaken by the senior members. Edwall was in the strongest position. He was supported by the more educated officers of the UNIP subregion committee, who attempted to have Njera branch put him forward as their only candidate. This was not acceptable to Bwana Samsalu, the head of Njera branch, who wanted his son Esaw to be elected, nor to Esaw himself. The compromise reached was that both Edwall and Esaw should stand but that Bwana Samsalu should not instruct the members of his segment for whom they should vote. Should Edwall win the election, it was understood that he would keep Esaw as court assessor and appoint him second-in-command. In other words, Esaw was to be Edwall's deputy and take charge of the chiefdom when Edwall was absent. Bwana Samsalu then agreed that he would not oppose Edwall as a candidate and would support him if he were elected. Once it was clear that Krist would be supported only by his own segment, Mitanga backed Edwall.

The only candidate of Chapyoka was Pack, Punyira's eldest son, who, like Edwall, was abroad working as a teacher. Though Chipanga branch put up candidates, none of them was sufficiently qualified to assume the post. Thus the three main contenders were Edwall and Esaw of Njera and Pack of Chapyoka. But only Edwall had the support of the UNIP committee, and many of its officers used their influence to gain him the backing of members of the nonchiefly branches and of Polomombo. Edwall won the election with a substantial majority.

After the election, Bwana Samsalu sent for Edwall, and required him to go through ceremonies which traditionally preceded the installation of a chief; the three traditional councillors—Bwana Mbamba, Zumbe, and Mpemba—and the Banangwa seized him and abused and beat him until he fell to the ground unconscious. He was then secluded in his house and instructed in the arts of ruling.

Deputy Chief Edwall and Chief Punyira

The election of Edwall to the post of deputy chief produced a new source of political conflict. Edwall expected that chief Punyira would henceforth deal only with traditional and spiritual matters. But Punyira was reluctant to relinquish any of his authority.

Edwall had been elected through the support of the subregion committee of UNIP, most of the royal clan, and his mother's brothers, who were influential village headmen. For Edwall to retain the support of these three elements against Punyira and his supporters, he had to meet at least some of their demands. But he had to avoid being dominated by any one of them, in particular Njera and the UNIP committee, both of which groups considered him to be their man. Thus, he had to manipulate his supporters and to adjust their demands from one situation to the next.

After he was installed in office, Edwall took a number of steps to consolidate his position. By making Esaw his second-in-command, he met his obligation to Njera royal branch. When Matt Chila, the second court assessor, retired, Edwall appointed his son, Eddi Chila, to the post. Eddi was Ado's brother and the chairman of Muyombe UNIP branch. This appointment fulfilled Edwall's obligation to the UNIP committee. Next he made a village-by-village tour of the chiefdom to publicize his plans for developing the chiefdom. This brought him into contact with villagers and headmen and helped to show them that authority and power were shifting from Punyira to himself.

The recognition of this shift in authority and power has become increasingly apparent in the behavior of subjects. When subjects meet the chief, they are supposed to show him respect by kneeling, averting their eyes, and clapping their hands. But now it is not unusual for them to pass Punyira as if they do not see him. It is far more common to see them approach Edwall in a respectful manner, even though he usually reminds them that they must not behave toward him as if he were the chief. If ever he does assume the traditional behavior of a chief, UNIP committee officers object, since they helped to get him elected because they thought he would be a "modern" chief and put aside traditional practices.

What is more important is that Punyira can no longer expect his subjects to obey him. In 1964 and 1965, when he summoned the villagers for work, only the members of his family and a few of his affines appeared. Punyira is barely able to maintain his very large household. The full responsibility for meeting public commitments has fallen to Edwall. Though this places a heavy burden on Edwall's resources, it helps to establish him as the de facto head of the chiefdom. And for the villagers it is another indication of Punyira's loss in power.

On his village tour Edwall announced his intention of establishing a special day of celebration to commemorate the founding of the chiefdom by Vinkaka-nimba. Although the UNIP committee had supported his election, he saw them as a potential threat to his authority and that of the royal clan. Such a celebration would reaffirm the position of Vinkakanimba as the rightful ruling stratum.

As deputy chief, Edwall introduced changes within the chiefdom government. He extended membership on the Banangwa council to all members of the royal clan and appointed UNIP committee officers and many of the more educated men of his own generation to the area committee. He also saw to it that his supporters made up the core of the development committee, the executive and planning body of the area committee. Finally, he began to make wide use of ad hoc committees. On all these bodies Punyira and his supporters were in the minority.

Punyira's and Edwall's respective duties have never been clearly defined. For some months after Edwall became deputy chief, Punyira continued to use his office in the Native Administration building and dealt with Native Administration business. When it was explained to Punyira that he was no longer supposed to deal with these affairs, he stopped going to his office, which was now occupied by Edwall. But he continued to use chiefdom messengers to carry orders to village headmen and would stamp written orders with the Native Administration seal. Headmen would frequently receive conflicting orders and not know which to obey. Edwall told the chiefdom messengers that they were responsible only to him. In 1965, he complained to the district commissioner of Punyira's misuse of the Native Administration seal, with the result that Punyira was forbidden to use it.

In general it may be said that Edwall now performs most Native Administration duties. He is the president of the councils and committees of chiefdom government. One of his major duties is to organize and supervise the actual carrying out of development schemes approved by the development and area committees, and most of the arrangements are left to him and his staff. They decide, for example, on which days headmen and their villagers should perform such tasks as site clearing and brickmaking. Edwall usually visits any site where villagers are working and makes a special point of joining in. Anyone who goes with him must be prepared to hoe, cut trees, make bricks, or participate in whatever activity the villagers are engaged in. Edwall believes that he must set an example for his subjects to follow; if he does not, the villagers may refuse to help when there is another self-help scheme.

With the assistance of his staff, Edwall administers regulations affecting health and sanitation, seasonal settlement patterns, and maximum prices for fruits and vegetables. Edwall handles Native Administration correspondence and sees that government circulars are posted. He writes letters of recommendation for men seeking employment abroad or wanting to buy shotguns. He also makes frequent trips to different parts of the chiefdom to inform villagers of his and the government's policies.

Though Edwall is the head of the Native Administration court, he has made a point of not attending all its sessions. He gives two reasons for this. The first is that he is primarily concerned with administration and development. The second is that, foreseeing the day when the government will appoint magistrates, he feels that he must prepare his subjects for the time when their cases will be settled by an ordinary civil servant. It has become not unusual for a case to be heard by the court clerk and the two court assessors, although, if it proves to be a difficult one, Edwall is consulted. Toward the end of 1965 the central government introduced court magistrates.

In general it may be said that the area of Punyira's authority was effectively restricted to spiritual and traditional matters. But even here he had to compete with Bwana Samsalu, who attempted to gain control of the chiefdom ancestor cult. Punyira, as mentioned earlier, was able to exercise some control through the use of dreams, since many Yombe believe that potential disasters may be revealed to the chief in dreams. In 1964 Edwall banned all prophets from the chiefdom, but two headmen who supported Punyira allowed prophets to enter their areas. Edwall intended to hold a meeting of the people of these villages to gather sufficient evidence to dismiss them. For more than two months, however, he had to postpone his trip, since Punyira's dreams indicated that he and the chiefdom would experience misfortunes if he undertook the journey. Eventually the matter was brought before the Banangwa council and one of the headmen was dismissed from his post.

Punyira may also be called upon to settle boundary disputes between village headmen. These are usually disputes requiring a knowledge of chiefdom history. He may reprimand elderly headmen for neglecting to perform their duties, and he also hears cases involving witchcraft accusations in his compound. These cases are heard in secret because the Native Administration is not supposed to know about them. But in practice they may even be referred to Punyira by members of the Native Administration.

Finally, Punyira deals with moral problems and the use of magic. For example, in 1965 there were a number of cases of adultery within Muyombe. So Punyira held a meeting in his compound of all the men of the village. He told them that his dreams had revealed to him all the persons commiting adultery in the village and that, if they continued, either he would have them brought to court or they would suffer misfortunes.

One of the traditional ways for a chief to secure support was by appointing followers to headmanships. While Punyira is alive, it is difficult for Edwall to do this. But the problem has been overcome through the use of ad hoc committees. When a headman dies, Edwall appoints a committee to select a new one. It usually consists of Edwall, Punyira, and two other members of each chiefly branch (or sometimes only one from Chipanga). The other person from Chapyoka branch is Kaleb, who sometimes considers himself Njera. Thus Edwall is always assured of a majority. This was what happened when the headman of Mpemba died during the smallpox epidemic of 1965. Before meeting with Punyira to decide which one of his sons should be appointed, Edwall discussed the matter with his informal personal advisers. They decided that Jonas was the most suitable candidate, since he was highly educated, for many years had been the court clerk, and held a UNIP post. Edwall then appointed a selection committee which consisted of himself, Punyira, Kaleb, one member of Chipanga, and one other from Njera. Jonas was selected. Although Edwall is able to extend his power by appointing headmen, the process is a slow one.

It should now be apparent that although Punyira is still the de jure head of the Native Administration, Edwall effectively controls the chiefdom. In order to accomplish this, Edwall has relied increasingly on the support of the more educated members of the UNIP committee and development committee. He seeks their advice on most matters and expects their backing on councils and committees. Their support enables him to overlook some of the demands of his own branch.

An example is the case of Edwall's former court clerk Joe Kaonga, a classificatory son of the headman of Sanga village. In June 1964 the Banangwa council expelled the headman of Sanga and his agnatic kin from the chiefdom. Punyira and senior members of Njera wanted Edwall to dismiss Joe from his post and replace him with an educated "royal." Bwana Samsalu wanted the successor to be from Njera and Punyira wanted somebody from Chapyoka. Edwall argued that as long as Joe performed his duties efficiently there was no reason to dismiss him. Eric, the secretary of the UNIP committee, agreed. With their support, Edwall refused the particularistic demands of his own royal branch and thus met the expectations of his post as a civil servant. But when Joe was killed in a hunting accident, the problem arose again. Eric nominated Elto Mbamba, who was a standard VI graduate of Livingstonia, an ex-teacher, and the secretary of Muyombe UNIP branch. Against the wishes of Punyira and Bwana Samsalu, Edwall recommended Elto to the district commissioner. As a civil servant Elto could no longer take an active part in party affairs; nonetheless he discussed most Native Administration affairs with Eric, who is his classificatory mother's brother; both are "sister's sons" of Chipanga branch. Elto's appointment in fact strengthened Edwall's position; Edwall had rendered a service to the UNIP committee and at the same time, gained the backing of a sister's son of Chipanga.

The Banangwa Council

The Banangwa council consists of the male adult members of the royal clan. There is, however, another category of persons who in some situations are allowed to sit as members. These are the sons and sometimes the grandsons of Bakamba—female members of the royal clan—who stand in the recognized relationship of "sisters' sons" to a particular royal branch, at one level, and to the royal clan, as a whole, at another. They act sometimes as mediators arranging compromises and at other times as referees, upholding or modifying existing rules in order to preserve the structure of the arena and order within the course of a political contest (Bailey 1969, pp. 63, 153). They are expected to intervene in disputes between members and segments of the branch to which they are attached and attempt to bring them together. This has political implications in the contest for power. A branch that cannot mobilize its members is in a weak position. Moreover, if a branch is politically weak, its sisters' sons have only a minimal amount of prestige and influence in directing chiefdom affairs. Thus the sisters' sons of a branch have an interest in maintaining cooperation within it. The stronger the branch, the more prestige, influence, and indirect power accrues to its sisters' sons.

The role of sisters' sons on the Banangwa council is a complicated one. They are expected to advise, defend, and support their branch, but they must be careful not to go too far or members of other branches will attempt to exclude them. When such an attempt is made, sisters' sons of the different branches rally as an interest group to protect their special privileges. The senior ones remind the members of the royal clan that their "mothers" were Bakamba and that they have been its defenders, its "spears" and "guns." By taking this position they have shifted their loyalty from particular branches to the clan as a whole. At this level, they may act as mediators. They begin to maneuver for a compromise—usually one which favors the branch that they support. Thus their inclusion on the council operates to regulate conflict between branches.

The Banangwa council derives its character from the traditional position occupied by its royal members as the "free people," *Banangwa*, of the chiefdom. The Banangwa are the rulers and owners of Uyombe. Because its other inhabitants are commoners, their right to live in Uyombe and use chiefdom land are subordinate to those of the royal clan, which, sitting as a council, can expel them if they are guilty of serious offenses. If a person who has been expelled wishes to return, he must apply to the Banangwa council. Since he cannot himself attend its meetings, he goes to a council member, who may or may not speak on his behalf. Some council members belong to other interest groups and may represent them in the council. This is especially true of officers of the UNIP committee.

Thus, in their capacity as rulers, Banangwa council members are concerned with matters related to chieftainship. They are the body primarily concerned with selecting the chief and the heads of the six royal clan villages. They arbitrate disputes between members occupying posts in chiefdom government and may review the way in which they conduct public affairs. They may arbitrate village boundary disputes and those arising between royal and commoner headmen. They may also review the conduct of headmen. Finally, they are concerned with maintaining chiefdom boundaries against encroachment.

The Banangwa council has only two officers. As de facto head of the Native Administration, Edwall serves as chairman; and the Native Administration court clerk as secretary. Edwall convenes meetings when he thinks a sufficient number of items have accumulated or when special problems arise.

Many of the heads of branches are now old men, who have delegated most of their political responsibilities to their potential successors. It is the latter who attend meetings, but the former may do so if they consider an issue of sufficient importance. Many junior members of the clan are not concerned with chiefdom affairs, attending meetings only when there is a major issue to be discussed or when they are directly concerned; besides, in most discussions their opinions carry little weight. Thus the most important members of the council—who also attend most frequently—are the acting heads of branches and the senior men within them. These senior men are usually the heads of segments.

Attendance depends upon the agenda. Members do not attend if they consider that some items concern branches other than their own or entail responsibilities which they are unwilling to assume, if they are likely to be subjected to criticism.

Banangwa council meetings are held in the Native Administration building in Muyombe. Senior members sit on benches arranged along the walls. The seniority of members is indicated by the way in which they enter a meeting and address their fellows. When a junior member comes in, he may fall on his knees, clap his hands, and address the chair by using the chief's praise name, "Yewo Mulowoka" ("Greetings, he who crossed over"). In speaking to the meeting he indicates his subordinate position by behaving in a respectful way. He leans slightly forward, clasping his hands before him, tilts his head to one side and directs his gaze away from the chairman and other elder men. He speaks slowly and clearly. Most of these forms of respect are not usually followed by senior members, but when one of them feels that he has been wronged or seeks moral support he may take on the mannerisms of a junior member. Moreover, changes in the behavior of a speaker may indicate to the audience that he has shifted roles; at one moment he may be a son addressing his "fathers" and, at another, a leader of one branch opposing the views of leaders of others.

The Case of the Chief's Salary

The way in which the Banangwa council handles problems may best be seen by examining the dispute over the chief's salary. This dispute was only one of the issues in the continuous power struggle between Punyira and Edwall. The division of the chief's salary is the concern not just of two men but also of their respective groups.

Background

In 1962, when Chief Punyira's responsibilities were taken over by Edwall, the district commissioner summoned a meeting of the Banangwa council to decide what remuneration each should receive. He made two proposals: either Punyira should receive a lump sum of £400, with Edwall drawing the whole salary due to the chief; or the salary should be divided (unevenly) between them with Punyira receiving only £ 7 a month and Edwall £ 17. Edwall supported the latter proposal because he believed that if Punyira received a lump sum it would soon be spent, and Punyira would become dependent upon his kinsmen for financial support. The Banangwa council voted in favor of the divided salary proposal which was accepted reluctantly by Punyira. The monthly salary voucher would be sent to the Native Administration and both Punyira's and Edwall's signatures would be required to cash it. There would then be no question that each would receive his share.

In 1965, owing to mistakes at the district headquarters in Isoka, Edwall received a single payment of £ 144, while for several months Punyira received nothing. Readily observing Edwall's sudden prosperity, Punyira suspected him of having stolen his salary. The scene was now set for a dispute.

The Setting

Controversy between men in high office is of interest to royals and commoners alike. The whole society becomes the arena in which the disputants compete. The controversy forms a topic of discussion for commoners, who may take sides and bring pressure upon royals. Besides its intrinsic interest for them, commoners are aware that its outcome may change power relationships.

Punyira derived both moral and political support from the Free Church and therefore turned to the Reverend Chavura for help. He wanted Chavura to write a letter to the district commissioner accusing Edwall of stealing his salary. When the minister refused, Punyira asked his sister's sons Pauta Chila and Sam Kara, both Free Church elders. A letter was eventually sent to Tyson, Punyira's son who was working in Isoka.

Rumors began to circulate in the town of Muyombe and outside. Whether Edwall had stolen the money became a regular topic for discussion at "beer drinks." In a short time Edwall himself heard of the gossip, but there was little he could do, since there had been no direct accusation.

The more educated members of the UNIP committee supporting Edwall watched the situation closely. If he were known as a thief, it would reflect poorly on them for they had backed him for the post of deputy chief and were associated with his policies. But they too felt that they could not interfere, since this was basically a dispute among Banangwa, the "free people." They advised him to wait for the rumors to exhaust themselves or for a concrete public accusation.

Allies and Disputants

A letter that Edwall received from Bald provided him with the necessary material to give the dispute a public hearing. Bald is Punyira's grandson. Though he is employed in Livingstone, a distance of several hundred miles from Muyombe, he maintains contact with his kinsmen. In his letter, he accused Edwall of forging Punyira's signature on the salary voucher and advised him that, if Punyira did not receive his salary immediately, Bald would consult a solicitor and bring a suit against him.

Edwall sent the letter to the district commissioner, inviting him to attend a meeting of the Banangwa council and explain the misunderstanding. He arranged for a special meeting composed of representatives from the chiefly branches, their close cognatic kin, and the chairman and vice-chairman of the development committee. He invited Native Administration officers and also the Reverend Chavura.

Edwall selected five persons to represent each branch. Table 6 lists the representatives and summarizes their positions and relationships.

The Chapyoka group includes three branch members and two sister's sons. Punyira is the leader and head of this branch. Ruti is the eldest son living in Uyombe and represents him in public affairs. Attacks made by members of other branches are usually directed at Ruti. Donald is the head of a segment of Chapyoka branch and Punyira's classificatory son. Since 1961 their relationship has been strained, and cooperation between them minimal. Punyira failed to intervene on Donald's behalf when Chikang'anga accused him of being a witch. Yotta Chila, as one of the senior sisters' sons, has sought to bring them together, thus strengthening Chapyoka as a political group. Though he is loyal to Punyira, Yotta's primary concern has been to protect Chapyoka. Thus he may attack an individual member if he considers the interests of the group are threatened.

Since Chipanga branch was not directly involved in this dispute, Edwall selected representatives who were his allies. They are not the only persons who are Chongo's close cognatic kin. As a group, they include two senior Chipanga branch members and three "sister's sons": Elto is the son of a Chipanga woman, and Labe and Eric are the grandsons of one; these three men are part of the more educated elite that supports Edwall.

The members of Chipanga consider themselves more closely related to Njera than to Chapyoka, as their genealogical charter indicates. Chongo and Demonga usually support Njera against Chapyoka, but they may also attempt to reconcile them.

The political allegiance of the three sister's sons is more clearly defined. Their emergence as important leaders in chiefdom politics was partly due to the election of Edwall as deputy chief. They were instrumental in getting him elected and have since been his advisers and supporters in opposing Punyira. Thus, representatives of Chapyoka formed a political minority unable to command support from other groups.

Office holders in the same interest group may belong to opposed royal branches. UNIP subregion branch chairman Donald, for example, belongs to Chapyoka, while his secretary Eric is aligned with Chipanga. These cross-cutting ties operate to regulate conflict and to direct its flow. If individuals are political allies in one sphere, they may be reluctant to criticize severely

Table 6. Edwall's Choice of Representatives for Salary Dispute Meeting

Name	Relationship	Political Post	Chiefdom Post	Church Post
From Chapyoka				
1. Punyira		chief		
2. Ruti	son to Punyira			
3. Donald	"son" to Punyira	UNIP subregion chairman	village headman	
4. Yotta	sister's son to Punyira			Free Church elder
5. Pauta	sister's son to Punyira (younger brother of Yotta)			Free Church elder
From Njera				
1. Edwall			deputy chief	
2. Esaw	"father" to Edwall		court assessor	preacher of Jordan church
3. Bishop	"father" to Edwall (Esaw's younger brother)			
4. Nelson	"elder brother" to Edwall			Free Church elder
5. James	mother's sister's son to Edwall			
From Chipanga				
1. Chongo				head of Watchtower
2. Demonga	"son" to Chongo			preacher of National church
3. Elto	sister's son to Chongo	UNIP branch secretary	court clerk	
4. Labe	sister's son to Chongo			
5. Eric	sister's son to Chongo (Labe's younger brother)	UNIP subregion secretary		
From Kaswanga				
1. Tanga		UNIP subregion branch treasurer		

each other's competence in another, especially in public (Bailey 1969, p. 32). Such criticism would generate ill-feeling between them and thereby reduce public confidence in the interest group to which they belong. Thus, Eric does not in public cast aspersions on Donald's competence, but instead attacks others of Chapyoka group.

The one person from Kaswanga that Edwall invited, Tanga, is active in chiefdom politics and is one of Edwall's supporters on the Banangwa council.

Two further points must be made here. The first concerns Esaw and his younger brother Bishop. Esaw and Bishop are Edwall's classificatory fathers, and so are expected to support and defend him when he is opposed by members of other branches. Hence their criticism of Punyira and others of Chapyoka is direct and vehement.

The second concerns the use of kin terms. In disputes of this sort, such terms as *citwazi, sekulu/muzukulu, mudala* are used by and to refer to Punyira and Edwall. The use of these terms denotes relationships based on permissiveness and affection, but also implies rights and obligations. *Citwazi* is used by men who have latent rights in each other's wives. It may be translated as brother. *Sekulu* and *muzukulu* mean grandfather and grandson (or elder and younger brother). Their use also indicates joint rights in property and women. A person may freely use the property of his grandfather because it is also considered his. *Mudala* is a term used by men to refer to two categories of person, their small sons (frequently including their potential heir) and old men, for example their fathers and grandfathers. In public discussions these terms may be used in different ways. At times Punyira uses them to show his goodwill toward Edwall and his willingness to accept a reconciliation. He appeals to those values that define the royal clan as an undifferentiated corporate group. He attempts to create a bond of solidarity. On the other hand, Edwall and his supporters may use the same terms to emphasize the boundaries between the branches. They use them to indicate Punyira's failure to fulfill the expectations of his kinship role. By accusing Edwall, Punyira failed to behave as a grandfather and to demonstrate the affective permissiveness implied in the relationship. Both Punyira and Edwall attach a moral evaluation to the behavior of the other with respect to the values and norms derived from kinship. In a segmentary system boundaries may be fluid, and for a reconciliation the boundaries must be pushed to the outer limit, to the most inclusive level of agnatic kinship and not that of the branch. To do this one must establish the primacy of the values underlying common agnatic descent. To prevent this maneuver, adversaries may attempt to redefine the situation by using other titles such as chief, deputy chief, church elder, or subregion secretary. The dispute remains the same, but the attempt is made to place it in a different framework, particularly if it is to the advantage of an opponent to do so, and to mobilize support on a different basis.

Interests
The main two issues that Chapyoka and Njera attempted to pursue at the meeting were (1) Did Edwall in fact steal Punyira's salary? and (2) Who were the local people involved in making the accusation? Because there was some doubt as to the validity of the charge, the primary aim of members of Chapyoka was to have the dispute settled in private. This was not surprising if Punyira's actions were considered to have gone against Yombe standards of proper behavior. By settling the dispute in private, members of Chapyoka would be able to protect Punyira from loss in prestige. Moreover, they also sought to avoid a direct confrontation or an encounter which would reveal the weakness of their political support. But this was exactly what Edwall wanted. He sought a public exoneration because he thought that the accusation of theft had damaged his own position as a public figure and the trust which the chiefdom people had in him. Therefore, he and his supporters attempted to block all moves to remove the dispute from a public to a private setting. He wanted an apology and a written retraction of the charges made against him. Much of the discussion during this meeting was concerned with the pursuit of these aims.

The Meeting
During the previous months, interest in the dispute had gradually built up, and on the day of the meeting a large crowd assembled at the court to await the main participants. When the district commissioner arrived, a messenger was sent to inform Punyira and Donald.

Edwall called upon the district commissioner to explain the whole affair. He explained that the matter did not concern Punyira at all, that Edwall was paid the money as the result of an error, and it was not back pay. He assured Punyira that in future he would receive a separate salary voucher. Punyira replied that it was in fact other people who were responsible for the dispute. He also said that "people have separated me from my *citwazi* (Edwall) and it is best that I receive my own voucher." In this way Punyira tried to shift the cause of this dispute from himself to others and to establish a basis for reconciliation.

Esaw immediately objected to Punyira's assertion that the dispute was not his fault. He said, "It is the *themba* (chief) alone who has caused this dispute and accused his *muzukulu* (Edwall) of theft. No, it is not because of other people. It is the themba (chief)."

Edwall got to his feet to address the meeting and as he spoke his voice began to quaver and tears filled his eyes. He said: "The district commissioner said let *sekulu* (Punyira) receive £400 gratuity. We refused because we knew the money would not last. Get all the records and you will find I have never stolen from the *themba* (chief) or anyone else."

Although he began to cry, he continued "The truth must be found. To begin to write outside has made me very sad." Edwall left the meeting sobbing. Whether intended or not, this performance had a dramatic effect on the meeting. For several minutes there was silence. Esaw then rose, assuming the posture of a junior man speaking to his seniors, he began: "That the person (Punyira) who has borne him (Edwall) should accuse him falsely is very sad. That old people should lie about their children makes me very sad." Then Tanga and several other supporters of Edwall began to repeat "Let the district commissioner go." A break was called while the district commissioner talked to Edwall and prepared to depart.

Punyira's goal was to disengage himself from the dispute as rapidly as he could without losing prestige and revealing the weakness of his own position. He attempted to make others responsible for the dispute and to have the matter settled in privacy. By referring to Edwall as grandson, *muzukulu,* he appealed to the norms of kinship. Esaw, who was the senior representative of Njera present, was Punyira's principal adversary and spokesman for the opposition. Although he is Punyira's classificatory son, in this phase of the dispute he referred to Punyira as chief, *themba,* not as father, *badada.* On the other hand, he did not refer to Edwall by his administrative title but used the term grandson, *muzukulu,* thereby stressing the kinship relationship which Punyira had broken by accusing Edwall of theft. He also wanted a direct confrontation, an encounter, which would reveal Njera's strength and Chapyoka's weakness. Both Esaw and Edwall were concerned about the indirect participation in the dispute of Yombe working outside the chiefdom. They feared that serious damage would be done to Edwall's reputation if he were known as a thief and that Yombe working abroad might refuse to contribute to local development schemes. Another danger was that pressure would be brought to bear on the district commissioner to have Edwall dismissed from his post. As this particular political drama or episode unfolded, different individuals and groups with their respective "repertories of resources, values, and rules" (Swartz 1968, p. 15) were brought into the struggle. The district commissioner, though not Edwall's ally, was a resource, a source of power and authority, a referee, who was brought in by Edwall to buttress his position. Thus, Punyira had to confront not only his local adversaries and equals, the Banangwa, but also his administrative superior.

Punyira Withdraws
In meetings of the Banangwa council, Chief Punyira, unlike Bemba kings and many other African rulers (Richards 1971, p. 7), may be publicly criticized and opposed. One way of avoiding this is to withdraw. So Punyira retired to his compound and refused to come back. Yotta Chila then proposed that the disputants meet privately. But members of Njera wanted not only a public apology but also letters written to Yombe living outside Uyombe retracting the charges made against Edwall.

Punyira refused to return, but there were a sufficient number of the Chapyoka group remaining to continue the meeting. Ruti, as the senior member present, became the focal point of criticism, but since he is a weak and ineffectual leader, Yotta and Donald became the main spokesmen for Chapyoka. Yotta attempted to explain Punyira's actions by saying the chief was old. His point was that it is not a person's fault that he grows old and at times behaves unwisely.

The desire for reconciliation was growing. Chongo of Chipanga royal branch followed Yotta's lead by saying that everyone knew the chief was now an old man.

In the meantime Edwall had returned to the meeting and again put his case. He spoke of the personal sacrifice he had made when he became deputy chief, and implied that he could easily return to his previous occupation (Michels 1959, p. 46).[2] Edwall then suggested that the Banangwa should meet again to discuss the dispute.

At this first meeting Edwall established that he did not steal money from Punyira. During the break he put it to the district commissioner that if Punyira did not use the Native Administration seal (or stamp), such issues would not arise. The district commissioner agreed and a further limitation on Punyira's authority was imposed by the decision that his written communications to the chiefdom would no longer be official unless approved and stamped by Edwall.

The Meeting of Reconciliation

At the next meeting, Edwall's vindication permitted him to pursue two issues. The first was to establish who the people were who started the dispute, and the second one was to have those who had accused him apologize in public. A reconciliation was brought about by associating the dissension between royal clan members with recent chiefdom misfortunes.

Dissension as an explanation. The first phase of this meeting was concerned with inducing Punyira to attend. Most members viewed the dissension between royal clan members, in particular between Punyira and Edwall, as an explanation of the recent misfortunes that had plagued the chiefdom—more than 120 people had died in two and a half months and the rains had been late—and as a potential cause of further misfortunes. Because the Banangwa are the rulers and owners of Uyombe, Yombe believe that a serious breakdown in their social relationships might well have adverse consequences for the well-being of their subjects and the chiefdom. But this was only one aspect. Another was that members of the Banangwa council might use beliefs to control disputes and to pressure important members to set aside their differences. Beliefs influence men's actions, but men manipulate and use those beliefs. And I consider that both these elements were present in this situation.

The dispute had also weakened the royal clan, which was now faced with a strong rival force, the UNIP committee. Senior members of the royal clan therefore began to work for a reconciliation, which they thought required Punyira's presence.

When Punyira finally arrived, his opening remarks related public misfortunes to dissensions within the royal clan. He told the meeting that he had written letters explaining that there was a mistake and that this should end the dispute. He also related the following story, which was supported by witnesses:

> One of my children came and said "I want £ 5." I am very poor. I did not have £ 5. My child said that a letter containing money came from the Boma. He asked why then I had no money. I was shamed and thought that my *muzukulu* (Edwall) was taking my money. I wrote to him telling him I had not received any.
> My child asked me for a plank. I said to myself I will sell this plank and give my child £5. This child was Esaw.

Although this story brought angry denials from Esaw, it aroused the sympathy of Council members. It pointed to Punyira's actual situation as an old man whom his real and classificatory children neglected but continued to make demands on his limited resources. It indicated his willingness to meet his obligations, even though he lacked the means to do so. On the other hand, Esaw was presented as having intentionally shamed his "father."

The dispute was concluded when the chief and his son Ruti agreed to write letters to important Yombe living abroad explaining that Edwall had not stolen the chief's salary and that the entire dispute had been an unfortunate mistake.

The dispute illustrates how individuals and groups in the Banangwa council pursue political interests. The arena was a traditional one, but the underlying issues concerned the authority and power of local government officers. The Native Administration had encapsulated many of the particularistic elements of the precolonial political system. Kinship and clientship provided the basis for mobilizing political support, so that the main contestants relied upon their cognates, clients, and friends in this struggle for power. The dispute was phrased primarily in the idiom of kinship and the resolution, in the idiom of ritual. But what had brought it about was a change in colonial policy. The new post of deputy chief was a serious threat to the authority, power, and income of the chief and of his ruling clique.

The dispute may be seen also as a "social drama" in which the main contending social groups, the mechanisms for regulating disputes, and the enduring relationships of social structure are revealed. Turner (1964, p. 92) has suggested that social dramas may be divided into four phases: breach, crisis, redressive action, and reintegration. These four phases are apparent here. Phase one began when Punyira did not receive his share of the salary and turned for advice to his sons, sisters' sons, and other important villagers who he thought would support him. He broke norms of kinship—which permit free interchange between grandfather and grandson—by accusing Edwall of stealing. This was done through gossip. A second phase began when Punyira's and Edwall's respective followers rallied to their support so that dominant cleavages became visible. Bald's letter brought the dispute into the open and permitted the operation of redressive mechanisms. Edwall assembled important members of the three chiefly branches in order to settle the matter. There then followed the final phase of reconciliation. But Yombe recognize that the very nature of the social situation makes this reconciliation a temporary one.

Throughout the episode, norms and values were invoked for different purposes. Edwall at first used them to maintain the boundaries between branches. But Punyira phrased his arguments in terms of common descent, thereby attempting to remove these boundaries. This was achieved in the final phase when beliefs associated with the ancestor cult were appealed to and reconciliation was seen as essential in order to prevent misfortunes befalling the chiefdom.

7

Politics in   The Development
Chiefdom   and Area
Government: Committees

Although the central government of Zambia has been concerned with promoting rural development, it has not always possessed the resources to provide the rural populations of remote regions with extensive basic services and thus to meet their growing demands and expectations. Much of the responsibility for initiating local development schemes has fallen upon the shoulders of local government officers and community leaders who are faced with the difficult task of generating popular support. After independence, villagers often expected an immediate improvement in their living conditions, but they were not always willing to contribute their own money, labor, and services, especially when they saw no direct benefits for themselves. Yet their support for local government officers and community leaders largely depended upon an improvement in the conditions of rural life.

In Uyombe Chiefdom, responsibility for originating local development schemes does not lie with the Banangwa council, but with the area committee and, in particular, its executive body, the development committee.

After more than thirty years in office, Punyira had appointed most of the headmen and restricted the activities of the Banangwa council and the chief's council. But both headmen and "royals" had grown dissatisfied with his rule. With the intensification of the struggle for independence, and the founding of branches of UNIP, they began to shift their support to the new party leaders.

Edwall's Reforms

During his 1962 tour of the chiefdom, Edwall told headmen that they were expected to attend area committee meetings and play their part in its deliberations. He nominated a number of UNIP officers and more educated men of his generation from the capital and the chiefdom. He introduced new offices. He became president, and the court clerk acted as secretary. The posts of chairman, vice-chairman, treasurer, and vice-treasurer were supposed to be elected annually. At first the chairmanship was open only to headmen, but before the February 1964 elections the UNIP committee officers on the area committee proposed this restriction be removed; their motion was carried by 37 votes to 29. Kenon Mbamba,[1] a former schoolteacher who had taught most of the younger political leaders, was elected chairman, and Andrew Kaonga, a UNIP branch secretary, vice-chairman. The two other posts, those of treasurer and vice-treasurer, were filled by Labe Enda, a prosperous store owner, and Samson Mbamba, a carpenter and former teacher.

The election of these men, though by a narrow margin, demonstrated the growing power of the UNIP committee, support for Edwall, and the rise of the "new men" to positions of authority. None of these four elected officers was a village headman or a "royal," and their primary allegiance was to UNIP or Edwall, not to Punyira. They had supported the founding of branches of UNIP. Kenon and his younger brother Samson were Edwall's mother's sister's sons, Labe was Eric Enda's elder brother, and Andrew was a sister's son of Polomombo branch of the royal clan. These four men had completed standard VI at either Livingstonia or Lubwa missions. Only Andrew was not a former teacher and only he was not from Muyombe.

Edwall and the UNIP committee expected the area committee to originate development policies. They thought that if headmen participated in making decisions, they would cooperate in development schemes. Development was intended in four major areas: health, education, agriculture, and communications. But the headmen depended on the support of villagers whose unpaid labor would be used for these schemes; those headmen who failed to take into account the interests of their villagers might lose them to another headman. When villagers began to complain, the headmen in their turn grew increasingly reluctant to initiate and support general development. They wanted development in their own areas and were not interested in schemes in other parts of the chiefdom. Most of the initial schemes were to be in Muyombe, so that a conflict of interests arose between villagers and the new elite in the capital. In 1962 this conflict became explicit over the construction of a dispensary and a dam in Muyombe.

The Dispensary and the Dam
One of the first major development schemes brought before the area committee was the construction of brick buildings for the chiefdom dispensary, to replace the small wattle and daub huts which had previously housed patients. Though the new buildings were to be in Muyombe, they were supposed to serve the whole chiefdom. This scheme was approved by the area committee, which also agreed that chiefdom labor should be used to

make bricks, lay the foundations, and perform any other such tasks. Letters were sent to Yombe living abroad,[2] mainly on the Copperbelt, and by 1963 the sum of £102 had been collected. The building was part of a larger plan, the next phase of which was the construction of a dam to supply water to the dispensary, to schools, and to the residents of Muyombe, who were expected to build new houses of sun-baked brick. This was a first step toward making Muyombe the center of local basic services and development. Initially, the area committee voted in favor of this plan, but villagers soon began to complain that their labor was used to benefit only Muyombe. Headmen responded to their complaints and began to oppose the use of chiefdom labor to build a dam in Muyombe. Because popular opposition was widespread, UNIP officers, who are always sensitive to public opinion, sided with the headmen and told Edwall that he was going too fast. Some headmen now said they could see no point in the schemes. They refused to embark on new ones and began to raise objections to proposals in the initial stages of discussion.

In this, as in other cases, headmen and villagers are not opposed to development as such but want the schemes to be located in their part of the chiefdom, so that they will receive immediate and tangible rewards from their unpaid labor. Without such rewards, they want to be paid. Headmen of adjacent villages often form a block in pursuit of their common interests. The dispute over the dam also gave the more conservative elements a reason for opposing any form of development. Conservative headmen could oppose the demands of their villagers to those of the Native Administration. The UNIP committee recognizes that its authority and power stem from popular support, and so had to side with the headmen and oppose the dam scheme.

Edwall and the UNIP committee recognized that the area committee was essentially an unmanageable and conservative body, ill-suited for an active part in planning development. Hence they began to make more extensive use of smaller committees, the most important of which is the development committee. This is in theory subordinate to the area committee, but it has a considerable degree of autonomy and at times makes decisions on its own. Development committee members may hold secret meetings before those of the area committee to work out their tactics.

The success of the development committee has led to the extensive use of ad hoc committees. The most important have been the Uyombe Lenshina (or Lumpa) rehabilitation committee, the Vinkakanimba Day committee, and the adult night school committee. Most of the members of all these are drawn from the development committee. They are subordinate to it and it in turn is responsible to the area committee.

It is the area committee which has official government recognition. Its approval of development schemes is required. It is a useful sounding board of public opinion. But its size makes it a body that usually rubber-stamps the decisions of others (Bailey 1965, p. 2).

The Development Committee and the New Men

The development committee has provided Edwall with a means of avoiding many of the problems he initially confronted with the area committee. It has brought together a number of highly skilled and like-minded individuals whose primary aim is to develop Uyombe as rapidly as social and financial conditions will permit. It consists of three types of members: elected, nominated (or trustees, as Edwall calls them), and ex officio (the local representatives of government departments). The fifteen elected members are elected by the area committee from among their members and hold their seats for a year, after which new elections are supposedly held.

In February 1964 the Native Administration convened a special meeting of the area committee to choose development committee members. Edwall opened the meeting by explaining the purpose of the development committee and the qualities expected of members. He said that they should be concerned with developing Uyombe, should represent the different segments of the society, and should include persons from different parts of the chiefdom. Members then nominated candidates, and when the number reached twenty, Edwall closed the nominations. Any member was allowed to vote for as many candidates as he liked. The fifteen persons receiving the most votes were elected.

Once the election was completed, the Native Authority presented a list of eight nominees who are appointed for a year. Their numbers may be augmented by additional appointments of persons considered to possess special skills and be particularly concerned with chiefdom development. Such persons are usually men who have recently returned from abroad.

The ex officio members are the local heads—or their representatives—of government institutions such as schools, the dispensary, and the agricultural station. Edwall expects these men, most of whom are from other parts of Zambia, to take an active interest in improving local conditions. As he frequently tells them, "We are all Zambians, and by helping us you are helping Zambia." There are, however, more practical reasons for their inclusion. Membership of the development committee provides them with the opportunity to present their policies to local leaders, to gain their support and cooperation in carrying them out. It also creates a situation in which they can complain of such things as local working conditions and present the problems they confront in dealing with villagers. At the same time, it enables local leaders to acquire new ideas, to complain to the heads of these institutions about their failure to perform their duties, and to inform them of various development schemes.

Election of Officers
The development committee has a chairman, secretary, treasurer, vice-chairman, vice-secretary, and vice-treasurer. These posts are filled annually

by election; the electoral body consists of the newly chosen elected and nominated members. The committee also has a president—a post held by the Native Authority.

In March 1964 the development committee held a meeting to elect new officers. The main issue was whether the existing chairman, Amos Ukwa, should be reelected. Members of the UNIP committee opposed him because of his previous political affiliations and for other reasons. But his candidacy was supported by Edwall and Esaw, who argued that his originality, knowledge, experience, and competence qualified him to be chairman. The UNIP subregion officers, who valued party loyalty more than these attributes, only reluctantly agreed to withdraw their opposition, and Amos was elected.

The "New Men" and the "Traditional" Order

Many development committee members represent the gradual development of a new social stratum in Yombe society, which derives its position not from the "traditional" social order but from a new "Western" one. The traditional order is for the most part based on ascribed status. There is an important distinction between royal clan members, *Banangwa*, and chiefdom people, *Bantu ba caru*. The Banangwa are the owners and rulers of the chiefdom and the latter are commoners. Commoners may be divided into headmen, "village owners," and villagers. Men are also ordered with respect to their status within the lineage. The heads and elder men are superior to younger ones, whose services they may command. Next to the headman they play a leading part in village affairs. They are shown respect not only by members of their own lineages but also by villagers at large. Thus Yombe are stratified with respect to the positions they occupy in the lineage and territorial frameworks. The traditional order does not, however, extend beyond the chief.

The backgrounds of development committee members indicate the increasing importance of new standards. In some rural areas, such as Uyombe, acceptance of new standards—namely, those associated with town dwellers —can be an important dimension of prestige. The more closely one's behavior and local life style conforms to Yombe impressions of the style of life of the African urban elite, the more "civilized" one is thought to be.

Elected Members

Among the ranks of the elected members one may distinguish committee officers and committee members. Though there is no restriction on nominated members holding these posts, they have been filled by elected ones.

In order to indicate the social position held by development committee officers in the "traditional" order, I have used two criteria—lineage position and chiefdom post. An additional aspect, which will be considered below, is the type of cognatic and marriage ties which committee members generally have with the royal clan.

Table 7 lists the officers of the committee and gives relevant information about them. None of the committee officers is a member of the royal clan; they are all commoners. In their descent groups, three occupy senior positions as heads of segments above the "minimal lineage" level (Fortes 1957, p. 7). This means that they are not only elders of their lineages but also senior men of their community—a status that is not, however, combined with territorial office. Development committee officers, therefore, seem not to have come from the "traditional" ruling elite but to have been incorporated into it on other criteria.

Three types may be identified in terms of their place of education. Type 1 includes men who were the first to be educated at Livingstonia. Many of these were the local agents of Livingstonia mission, employed as evangelists and teachers. They built the first schools, staffed them, and prepared the next generation, as Mair puts it (1963, p. 22), "to make their way in the western world before government had taken much responsibility for this." The second type includes locally educated men.[3] They completed only standard III or IV, which has restricted their occupational careers. They are primarily oriented toward Uyombe, because they may not easily find skilled jobs abroad. Third, there are the Lubwa-trained men who have completed standard V or VI. They have been employed abroad as clerks, teachers, and in other similar jobs. Since independence, many anticipate leaving Uyombe to take up new posts such as teachers and directors in the Zambia Youth Service or as credit officers. Within Uyombe they represent a new elite which is gradually displacing the old one.

Officers' education and occupation. Though all the officers of the development committee went to schools in Uyombe, the vice-chairman, Darius Sukwa, is the only one who did not attend Lubwa, having been educated at Livingstonia. As is shown in table 8, they completed standard VI, three of them taking further courses in teacher training. They were able to gain employment in jobs which are considered locally as having high status but in a wider context would place them on the lower rungs of the new Zambian elite (Kilson 1966, p. 69).[4] Four were teachers and two were employed as clerks.

At present all the officers engage in farming, but Labe is also a prosperous store owner, Elto is the court clerk, and Samson is a carpenter.

The development committee officers, then, all possess special skills and experience which are not derived from the "traditional" sphere. They have sought to introduce change not only in the area of chiefdom government but in others as well. Amos, for example, was one of the first to practice irrigation and to organize his wives into a single work group. He has continually attempted to introduce new crops by the use of control and experimental plots. In the area of sanitation he has frequently argued against certain burial customs. Eric, in his turn, has attempted to convince the elder women of the community of the convenience and efficiency of using piped

Table 7. Development Committee Officers

	Lineage	Post		Occupation		Education
		Chiefdom	Political	Previous	Present	
Chairman						
Amos Ukwa	Elder			Clerk	Farmer	Lubwa VI
Vice-chairman:						
Darius Sukwa	Junior			Clerk	Farmer	Livingstonia VI
Secretary:						
Eric Enda	Junior		UNIP subregion secretary	Teacher	Farmer	Lubwa VI +
Vice-secretary:						
Elto Mbamba	Elder	Court clerk	UNIP branch secretary	Teacher	Farmer	Lubwa VI
Treasurer:						
Labe Enda	Elder			Teacher	Store owner/ farmer	Lubwa VI +
Vice-treasurer:						
Samson Mbamba	Junior			Teacher	Carpenter/ farmer	Lubwa VI +

VI + indicates that the person has completed standard six and has had additional training.

Table 8. Elected Members of Development Committee

	Lineage	Post		Occupation		Education
		Chiefdom	Political	Previous	Present	
Ado Chila	Junior		UNIP subregion vice-secretary	Clerk	Store owner/farmer	Lubwa VI
Andrew Kaonga	Junior		UNIP branch secretary	Carpenter	Carpenter/farmer	Livingstonia VI
Katie Nyamkandawire	Junior		UNIP subregion women's brigade secretary	Storekeeper	Store owner	Livingstonia VI
Tanga Wowo	Junior		UNIP subregion treasurer	Storekeeper	Store owner	Livingstonia VI
Tisi Koko	Elder		UNIP subregion vice-treasurer	Farmer	Farmer	Muyombe IV
John Kaluba	Junior			Bakery "boy"	Farmer	Muyombe IV
Tuduma Simbeye	Elder	Village headman		Bus "boy"	Farmer	Muyombe III
Jake Wowo	Elder	Village headman		Chauffeur	Farmer	Muyombe III
Gindo Nyondo	Elder			Prophet	Farmer/store owner	Muyombe III

Levels of education: standards—III, IV, and VI

water, which would cost them a minimal monthly sum, instead of fetching water from the river. Their reply has been that water has always been a free commodity and that, in any case, God made it to run in rivers and not in pipes. Development committee officers are constantly confronted with this kind of popular resistance to change.

It is apparent that development committee officers do not belong to that group of Yombe who were the first to receive an education at Livingstonia. While the latter were concerned with conversion to Christianity and education, the former have attempted to convert the people to their ideas of "nationalism" and to gain popular support for their development schemes. They tour the chiefdom advocating new schools, roads, bridges, and the use of the dispensary. They also discuss amongst themselves the problems created by labor migration.

Other elected members. Table 8 indicates the position of the other elected members in Yombe society and their educational qualifications and occupations as well as their party posts. In contrast to the office holders, only three out of the nine elected members have completed eight years or more of schooling, though five out of the nine are UNIP committee or branch officers. The office holders represent the more educated elements of Yombe society. They possess valuable technical skills, useful for originating and planning development schemes and for convincing district officers to contribute materials and financial assistance. The regular elected members represent the less educated elements of the society. As party officers they are useful in gaining the backing of the party and the cooperation of the commonfolk in actually carrying out new development schemes.

Nominated Members
The nominated members of the committee are appointed by the Native Administration. They have the same rights as elected members and are expected to participate fully in its affairs. Their position in Yombe society and their educational qualifications and occupation are shown in table 9.

Though one might expect that Edwall would have appointed a number of UNIP officers or his personal supporters, only two nominated members are UNIP branch chairmen. Altogether, 25% of the nominated and 46% of the elected members are UNIP officers. Of the eight persons whom Edwall has appointed, only three are his own supporters. The four who oppose him are linked with the Chapyoka branch of the royal clan. One is neutral.

It was found that only six of the twenty-three committee members are royal clan members and/or village headmen. This suggests that individuals are not chosen solely on the basis of their positions in the "traditional" status and administrative hierarchy. Many committee members have achieved a high level of education and possess occupational experiences that enable them to plan local development schemes and deal with the complex issues considered by the committee. Fourteen members were educated abroad at

Table 9. Nominated Members of Development Committee

	Lineage	Post		Occupation		Education
		Chiefdom	Political	Previous	Present	
Yotta Chila	Elder			Teacher	Store owner/farmer	Livingstonia VI
Pauta Chila	Junior			Teacher	Store owner/farmer	Livingstonia VI
Ruti Wowo	Junior	Ex-deputy chief		Clerk	Farmer	Lubwa VI
Sam Kara	Junior	Ex-kapaso		Kapaso	Store owner/farmer	Muyombe III
Unka Wowo	Elder	Ex-court clerk		Teacher	Farmer	Livingstonia VI
Joe Vwalika	Junior	Act. village headman		Mine laborer	Farmer	Muyombe III
Ezek Mbamba	Elder	Village headman	Branch chairman UNIP	Teacher	Farmer	Livingstonia VI
Noah Zimba	Junior		Branch chairman UNIP	Mine laborer	Farmer	Muyombe III

Livingstonia or Lubwa and worked as teachers, clerks, carpenters, and storekeepers. The nine other members were educated in Uyombe and completed only standard III or IV. Consequently, they have been restricted to such unskilled occupations as laborer and baker "boy." An interesting feature of the committee is that about 40% of the owners of local shops in Uyombe are members, and they make up 30% of the committee membership. Their predominance suggests the concern of shop owners and traders in development and their political importance in rural community life.

Many committee members were also UNIP officers. Of the nine (or 39%) members holding UNIP posts, five are subregion committee officers, and four hold posts in UNIP branches. The development committee might appear to be a meeting ground of the "new men"—shop owners and traders—and the party. But in its discussions, occupancy of UNIP posts forms one major basis for alignment and kinship another.

Hence the kinship links of committee members with the chiefly branches must be considered. These links are of two types. One is based on the personal kinship network of an individual and the other on the relationship of an individual to a branch. For example, some committee members are related as mother's brothers or as mother's sister's sons to Edwall, but not directly to other members of his descent group. Accordingly they will support Edwall but not necessarily his descent group. On the other hand, some members are "sister's sons" of Njera branch and are expected to support its members.

Njera. On the basis of kin and affinal ties, Edwall may expect support from three elected and three nominated members. Figure 13 shows that, of the elected members, Samson Mbamba is his mother's brother's son (*kavyara*). John Kaluba is married to his eldest sister, and Tunduma Simbeye is a Njera sister's son. Of the nominated members, Unka Wowo is head of Kolelawaka segment of Njera branch, Ezek Mbamba (Bwana Mbamba) is Edwall's mother's brother, and Joe Vwalika is considered an Njera sister's son. In addition, James Gonde and Henry Nyondo, who are Edwall's mother's sister's sons, are, as local teachers, ex officio members of the development committee. Though James may be relied upon to support Edwall, Henry, who is not from Uyombe, has his own views on most issues and frequently opposes him. Amos Ukwa is also a Njera sister's son. But members of Njera do not always look to him for support, because he has married two of Punyira's daughters and two women of Chipanga branch.

Chapyoka. Punyira may expect to have his interests represented on the development committee by four nominated members led by Ruti. Ruti is his son, and Yotta, Pauta, and Sam are his sister's sons (see figure 14). Thus he may command the support of four members against Edwall's six or more.

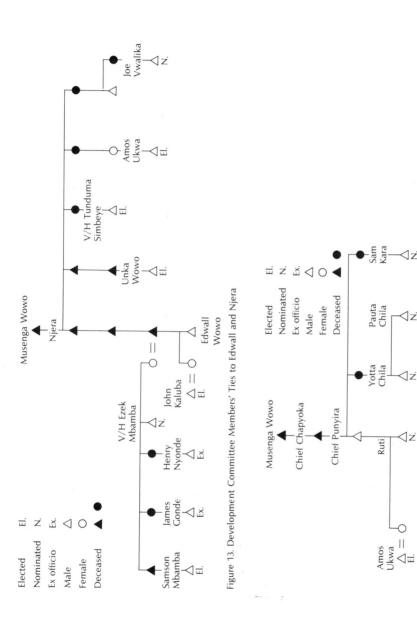

Elected — El.
Nominated — N.
Ex officio — Ex.
Male — △
Female — ○
Deceased — ▲

Musenga Wowo

Njera

V/H Tunduma
Simbeye
El.

Unka
Wowo
El.

Amos
Ukwa
El.

Joe
Vwalika
N.

V/H Ezek
Mbamba

Samson
Mbamba
El.

James
Gonde
Ex.

Henry
Nyonde
Ex.

John
Kaluba
El.

Edwall
Wowo

Figure 13. Development Committee Members' Ties to Edwall and Njera

Elected — El.
Nominated — N.
Ex officio — Ex.
Male — △
Female — ○
Deceased — ▲

Musenga Wowo

Chief Chapyoka

Chief Punyira

Ruti

Amos
Ukwa
El.

Yotta
Chila

Pauta
Chila

Sam
Kara
N.

Figure 14. Development Committee Members' Ties to Ruti and Chapyoka

Chipanga. Nobody from Chipanga branch is at present on the development committee. But three of the elected members are sometimes considered Chipanga sisters' sons, and one is married to a Chipanga woman. Elto's mother and the grandmother of Labe and Eric Enda were sisters of the late Chief Chisusu—a classificatory brother of Punyira. These three men frequently consult on the policies they should pursue in meetings. But on most issues they support Edwall, because he usually discusses them with Eric in his capacity as UNIP committee secretary before they are brought before the committee. Darius Sukwa is married to a Chipanga woman, but he does not ally himself with members of Chipanga.

Other members. Two of the other eight committee members belong to branches of the royal clan. Jake Wowo is the head of Vumbo branch and Tanga Wowo represents Kaswanga. Tanga usually aligns himself with Edwall or Eric, depending on the issue. But in any independent stand he takes he relies on the support of his intimate friend Tisi Koko. With the exception of Andrew Kaonga, who is a sister's son of Polomombo branch, Tisi and the other four members are not related to the royal clan. Tisi, Katie, and Noah are, however, UNIP officers and support UNIP policies. Andrew and Gindo did not attend any of the sixteen meetings at which I was present.

The Development Committee and Chiefdom Affairs

During 1964 and 1965 I attended sixteen meetings of the development committee. At most meetings the same general topics and problems were discussed, which may be divided under four main headings: education, health, agriculture, and roads and bridges. Other items were also discussed, such as communication within the chiefdom, taxation, credit, the Lenshina movement (or the Lumpa church), and cooperation between the Native Administration and the local political party. The case of the building of a teaching block will show how the committee works.

Education: The Musantha Teaching Block
Education is of special interest to the development committee. It is valued not as an end in itself but as a means of social and financial mobility in the wider Zambian society. The development committee has sought to provide better education for children and has also been concerned with opening adult night schools to allow school leavers and adults to complete primary school and attain a standard VI certificate. The committee also deals with such things as constructing new schools, upgrading old ones, standards of teaching, the behavior of teachers, and the maintenance of school buildings and houses for teachers.

Most Yombe share the committee's interest in improving educational opportunities and thus readily accept its policy of having more schools. A number of problems arise, however, over the location of the new school buildings and the contribution of money and labor.

As part of its educational program, the development committee instructed the four of its members who were rural councillors (Edwall Wowo, Tanga Wowo, Eric Enda, and Ado Chila) to ask the Isoka rural council for funds to build a new lower primary school in Uyombe. The Isoka rural council refused to finance a new school. Instead, it agreed to supply materials such as cement, zinc roofing, and steel window frames. The actual construction was to be by "self-help"; Yombe were to supply the labor, skills, and materials such as sand and rocks. Bricks would also have to be made locally.

In September 1964 the development committee decided that the new building should be built at Musantha, one of the component settlements of Muyombe. The entire scheme was presented to the area committee for its approval, since the people of the whole chiefdom would be required to contribute money and labor. Because the scheme had the backing of all the members of the development committee, who represented leading political factions, it was not difficult to get the area committee to approve it. However, some headmen argued that there were already two lower primary schools in Muyombe and that the interests of the chiefdom would best be served by constructing the building at a more distant school. These headmen also argued that the development committee was primarily concerned with improving Muyombe and not the rest of the chiefdom. Thus, there was controversy at the outset over the interests of Muyombe versus those of other villages.

The first stage of constructing the new building entailed organizing the residents of the chiefdom to make bricks. The development committee divided the chiefdom into twenty-five groups, each consisting of several villages. The headmen of these groups were expected to see that the able-bodied residents of their villages came to Muyombe on an assigned day and made four thousand bricks. The first group to make bricks were to be the people of Muyombe, who were supposed to set the example. Absentees were summoned to the court to explain their absence. If they could not give a valid reason, they were fined two shillings and sent to make bricks.

Members of the development committee were supposed not only to help headmen supervise but also to participate. Most complained that they had other responsibilities, so that this task was assumed by Native Administration officers. Carpenters from different parts of the chiefdom were assigned the task of making forms for bricks. The construction of an open-air kiln was left to the residents of Muyombe.

Opposition soon arose from those villages that did not have schools near them. The residents of some villages came but left before they had completed their quota; others did not come at all. The Native Administration sent messages to the headmen of these villages instructing them to come to Muyombe with their villagers and make bricks. A headman's refusal to comply to such an order may form the basis for removing him from his post.

Because headmen value their posts, the ones who had been delinquent came to Muyombe with their villagers and performed their duty. Thus, though the development committee may not directly impose sanctions, it may rely upon other bodies of chiefdom government to do so.

Because of these difficulties the development committee thought it best to hold an area committee meeting. Summoning such meetings, however, must be done by the Native Authority. So Edwall called for a meeting of the area committee to discuss the second stage of building the teaching block. This stage entailed transporting sand and rocks to Musantha. The discussion at this meeting concerned whether the rocks and sand should be transported by head-load or by truck. The first alternative would require considerable labor, whereas the second would involve imposing a money levy. When the proposals were put to a vote, sixty members voted in favor of hiring a truck and forty opposed it. The area committee then agreed that women would be expected to contribute one shilling and men one shilling and sixpence. Edwall closed the discussion by informing members that "persons who do not give will have to collect sand for six days."

The final stage involved the actual building of the teaching block. This was primarily the responsibility of the residents of Muyombe and of carpenters and bricklayers from different villages, such as Samsalu's and Kaleb's. Though Muyombe carpenters and bricklayers cooperated, many of those from other villages refused, arguing that they had already done their duty by making bricks and contributing money for hiring a truck. Their leaders were important members of chiefly branches, and they were supported by Bwana Samsalu, the head of Njera; two of the leaders were his sons. Hence Edwall was reluctant to impose sanctions on them. Instead, he summoned the leaders to Muyombe to discuss the matter. Once it was decided that carpenters and bricklayers would in future be exempted from chiefdom labor, they agreed to help complete the building of the teaching block.

This case indicates the type of problems that confront the development committee and how it attempts to overcome them. The committee makes constant use of those members who belong to the Isoka rural council to gain district assistance for its own schemes. Although the Uyombe rural councillors were not successful in getting money for a new school, they did get financial backing for a new school block. The Isoka rural council agreed to provide the basic building material. The location and the actual construction of the new school block was left to the Yombe. The development committee was in favor of having the new school block built in Muyombe and used its influence on the area committee to get its proposal approved. Nonetheless, the development committee met with opposition from two quarters, headmen and villagers on the one hand, and carpenters and bricklayers on the other.

The refusal of carpenters and bricklayers to work on the project came as a surprise to the committee. Because these workmen were led and supported by important members of chiefly lineages without whom Edwall would find it difficult to rule, they were able to force Edwall and the development committee to meet most of their demands. This meant that in future the committee would have not only to consider what schemes villagers would be willing to accept but also to secure the agreement of carpenters and bricklayers. When the block was completed in July 1965, the development committee decided that it would be unwise for it to undertake another project for a few months. After a short time, however, headman Donald of Chifunda village informed them that his and neighboring villages had begun to make bricks for the construction of a school. Donald sought the development committee's assistance in gaining Isoka rural council financial aid and assurance that the school would be recognized, a teacher provided, and the development committee would supply chiefdom labor. In August 1965 the committee received a similar demand from another group of headmen. What these two instances suggest is that the headmen of neighboring villages are beginning to come together to make demands on the development committee in pursuit of common interests. It will mean that the labor and money of the people of the chiefdom will be directed toward developing not only Muyombe but also other parts of the chiefdom.

This chapter has indicated the success of the UNIP committee and the "new men" in gaining power in chiefdom government. They are now in a position to manage the affairs of local government and to influence the course of change within Uyombe, although not the rate at which change will occur. Paradoxically, the very social conditions and political processes which have enabled them to rise to prominence have also generated new forces over which they have only moderate control. These new political elements have impeded the attempts of the new leaders to implement local development schemes and to centralize basic services in Muyombe. Sectional interests and those of persons sharing common skills must now be taken into account. Headmen and their villagers are beginning to come together to get basic services in their parts of the chiefdom, and bricklayers and carpenters are starting to protect their interests. The interests of headmen, villagers, carpenters, and bricklayers are now poised against those of the new elite, the growing alliance of store owners and traders, the more educated members of the UNIP committee, and other educated "new men." The royal clan still persists as an important feature of the political landscape, but as a political body it has not concerned itself with development. Though Punyira has lost much of his ability to control political events and the direction of chiefdom development, nonetheless he remains a powerful and an astute political adversary. This will become apparent in the drama of Vinkakanimba Day, a series of related events and episodes which will indicate the operation of the different political elements of Yombe society.

8
Vinkakanimba Day

This chapter will describe what may be termed a political drama in the social life of the chiefdom—the events leading up to the celebration of Vinkakanimba Day in 1965. The issues surrounding Vinkakanimba Day flowed across the political landscape, penetrated different structures and groups, and brought into play the various political interests of the people of Uyombe. The planning of Vinkakanimba Day created a series of related episodes in which one may observe the working arrangements of Yombe political life (Firth 1964, p. 45), the meshing of political arenas, and the maneuverings of individuals and groups as they pursue their interests in different contexts. The drama illustrates how norms are being shaped and transformed by choices and decisions, by the struggle for power between different sections of Yombe society, and by the flow of events.

Events like those found in this drama generate their own field of political activity, which may not be constrained by the boundaries of groups or structures. As an event unfolds, it may expand outward into society, bringing into play a progressively larger number of individuals and groups, all with their respective resources, values, norms, and demands. It may develop to the point where society itself becomes the principal context in which diverse political and para-political units of the community are engaged. The central actors may begin to lose control of the stream of events as participants respond to the pull of various demands, obligations, and relationships. The actions of individuals and groups structure the course of events, and events themselves structure the actions of the participants. The central actors must always look to their support and consider demands which may impose constraints on decisions and choices and restrict options.

Through Vinkakanimba Day one may observe the operation of the significant features of political arrangements as well as the inconsistencies in the performances of the same individuals as they align themselves with different interests and groups. Vinkakanimba Day is itself new and as yet has not become entirely rooted in Yombe life. It is still in that precarious, experimental phase, a feature so pronounced in Yombe political affairs, and for this reason it illustrates political process during this transitional period.

The Significance of Vinkakanimba Day

Edwall's Dilemma

Because the more educated members of the UNIP committee were Edwall's personal friends and their goals tended to coincide with his, they usually supported him and his policies whenever these were opposed by Punyira or by the less educated and more conservative members of the UNIP committee. This placed Edwall in a dilemma. Having given Edwall its support, the UNIP committee was gradually increasing its power within Muyombe and the chiefdom at his expense, since he could not implement decisions without its backing. In an attempt, inter alia, to control this process, Edwall saw to it that the Banangwa council, the area committee, and its executive body, the development committee, would accept his proposal to set aside August 1st of each year as a day to commemorate Vinkakanimba. This emphasized the status of the royal clan as the rightful rulers of the chiefdom, since Vinkakanimba was considered by members of five royal clan branches to be the founder of the royal clan and of the chiefdom of Uyombe. The members of the sixth royal branch, Polomombo, did not recognize Vinkakanimba as their founder or as the founder of the chiefdom; hence they did not take part in the arrangements, in the political struggle, or in the Vinkakanimba Day celebrations of August 1st, 1964 or 1965.

The deputy chief intended Vinkakanimba Day to be a purely secular occasion in which all the chiefdom people would participate. For many Yombe, however, it also acquired a ritual significance, since it was to be held at the time when chiefs traditionally performed rites after the annual harvest of maize and millet. Because Punyira professed to be a Christian, he had discontinued all public performances associated with the chiefdom ancestor cult, though in private he and Bwana Samsalu, the head of Musenga lineage, discussed when the chiefdom priest should undertake rites at the graves of former chiefs.

For the celebrations following the commemoration ceremonies the royal clan was supposed to provide one or more large bulls, while headmen and their villagers were to supply large quantities of food and drink. On August 1st the chiefdom people were expected to come to Muyombe for the festivities.

The introduction of this new ceremony had several aims. One was to make the inhabitants of the chiefdom aware of the transfer of duties from the chief to the deputy chief and to gain popularity for the latter. In the face of a party that sought the full allegiance of the populace, Vinkakanimba Day would emphasize the position of the royal clan as the rightful rulers vis-à-vis the new politicians, most of whom were based in Muyombe. Within the framework of the royal clan it would reinforce the claims of the descendants of Vinkakanimba, and it would bring the residents of the chiefdom to the capital, emphasizing it as the political and, for many, the religious center of the chiefdom. Through his own efforts Edwall had created a new public occasion, which would place him and the royal clan at the center of community life, if only for a short period each year.

Interpretations

There were several interpretations of the significance of Vinkakanimba Day. The official one given by the development committee, which in 1964 and 1965 was mainly concerned with organizing the event, was that it was a purely secular occasion. In fact, different committee members offered three interpretations. Any one of the three could be expressed by the same person, depending on the group he was representing, the role he was playing, and the context in which he was performing. The first was that Vinkakanimba Day was simply Yombe founder's day; the second that it was both founder's day and the time for the chief's ancestor rites; and the third was that it was the time Punyira performed ancestor rites and was a purely religious occasion.

One committee member who expressed different views on different occasions was Elto Mbamba. In development committee meetings, in his role as committee member, Elto expressed the view that Vinkakanimba Day was a secular occasion, unrelated to ancestor worship. But he was also an elder of the Free Church of Scotland, which condemned it as ancestor worship. So, in discussions with other Free Church elders, Elto condemned Vinkakanimba Day as ancestor worship and agreed with them that any church members who celebrated it should be suspended. The church also forbade its members to participate in any arrangements associated with Vinkakanimba Day. For two reasons this was awkward for Elto. The first reason was that as the head of Mughanga segment of Mbamba lineage he hoped to have the Banangwa council and the development committee incorporate the Mbamba version of Yombe history into the official "historical" account; he and his agnates claimed that their ancestors were the original inhabitants of the chiefdom. Many of the senior men of Mbamba lineage were the deputy chief's cognatic kinsmen, and in 1964 Elto had supported the inclusion of part of their version of Yombe "history" in the official account presented on Vinkakanimba Day. After the 1964 celebrations most "royals" were opposed to including the Mbamba version, which was subsequently deleted from the official account, in 1965. As a senior member of Mbamba, Elto had to defend Mbamba interests, so that for a while he was involved in making arrangements for the celebration. Moreover, the deputy chief expected him not only to take an active part in arranging Vinkakanimba Day but also to support it in Free Church kirk sessions. Elto owed his position as court and chiefdom clerk to the deputy chief, who had appointed him in the face of strong opposition from Punyira and Bwana Samsalu. He readily and easily changed roles as he aligned himself with different groups and relationships in different situations.

Another variable was the impression which a person wanted to project of himself or the committee or group to which he belonged. Most members of the development committee were, or had previously been, clerks, school-teachers, and local businessmen. Considering themselves to be the progressive, or more town-oriented, element of the community, in development committee meetings they usually denied any ritual significance to Vinkakanimba Day. However, when this same body merged with the area committee of village headmen, those development committee members who supported the deputy chief and wanted the larger body's approval stressed both its secular and ritual aspects. In this way they sought to manipulate others in support of their goal.

The differences in interpretation suggest flexibility in employing norms and values as well as inconsistencies of individual participants as they acted now within one set of interests, now within another, in pursuit of their own and their groups' goals. Vinkakanimba Day did in fact have an underlying ritual component, one which involved Punyira and Bwana Samsalu in a struggle for control of the chiefdom ancestor cult. Bwana Samsalu considered it a ritual occasion on which offerings should be made to Vinkakanimba; so he performed the proper rituals himself without consulting and gaining the permission of Punyira. Punyira, however, could make no public protest, since he claimed to be a Christian for whom traditional rituals were obsolete. Even so, the fact that Bwana Samsalu performed the offerings and then publicized the fact meant that Punyira had suffered a further loss of control over the remnants of his "traditional" authority and power.

Vinkakanimba Day 1965

As the capital and political center of Uyombe chiefdom, the small town of Muyombe provided the physical and social setting for Vinkakanimba Day. Although many of the principal figures were Muyombe residents, this particular event in one way or another involved, directly or indirectly, most of the people of the chiefdom and made apparent many of the basic cleavages within Yombe society. It involved the Banangwa council, the area committee and its executive body the development committee, the UNIP joint committee and its executive body the UNIP committee, and the Free Church of Scotland.

The series of events leading up to and surrounding the Vinkakanimba Day celebrations of 1965 became the focus for the on-going struggle for power between Punyira and Edwall. Both men sought to control Muyombe and the chiefdom; the chief's goal was to retain what was left of his power, and the aim of the deputy chief and senior members of Njera was to seize that remnant.

Planning
The first phases of planning Vinkakanimba Day began some weeks prior to the actual celebration on August 1st. At the end of June, Edwall summoned the Banangwa to Muyombe to begin discussing arrangements. An important item of the agenda was the payment for a bull that the Banangwa council had purchased on credit for the previous year's celebration. The £ 2. 10s. already paid had been contributed by members of Njera and Chipanga, but there remained a debt of £ 5. Edwall asked for further contributions, saying that if they were not forthcoming, no one would give the council credit in future, and subjects would lose confidence in it for not honoring debts. Members of Chapyoka agreed to contribute, but those of Kaswanga and Vumbo complained that they were only recognized as kinsmen in times of need. Members of Polomombo branch refused to give anything at all, claiming that Vinkakanimba Day did not concern them. For them to accept Vinkakanimba as the founder of the chiefdom would have seriously compromised their position in the chiefdom by making them subordinate to other royal branches. The meeting ended on this note; members of Polomombo did not attend other Banangwa council and area committee meetings dealing with Vinkakanimba Day arrangements.

Edwall then called a meeting of the area committee to discuss the part headmen were expected to play. The headmen of Kalinda, Kaswanga, and Vumbo villages were absent. The last two told me that the Native Administration messenger had failed to arrive in time; otherwise they would have come. But they also commented that Vinkakanimba Day was mainly the concern of the chiefly branches and expressed their resentment at having been excluded from the previous year's march from Punyira's compound to the Native Administration building. They told me they intended to attend future meetings.

Edwall's assistant, Esaw of Njera, who is Bwana Samsalu's son and apparent heir, opened the meeting by reviewing the history of Vinkakanimba Day, reminding headmen that they had approved of its introduction, and adding that because there were differences between the Banangwa they would probably not provide the usual bull. But each headman would be expected to contribute four calabashes of millet beer, one of chidongwa, a nonalcoholic drink, and an as yet undecided quantity of maize and millet. The headmen responded by pointing out that in the previous year many of them and their fellow villagers had received nothing to eat, since most of the food was given to visitors invited by the Banangwa (neighboring chiefs with their entourages, teams of dancers, and local royals). Edwall brought the lengthy discussion to a close by telling them that the number of visitors, including dancers, would be reduced and that another meeting would be held in the near future. This concluded the first phase. Now began the process of maneuvering to gain support before the next meeting. This occurred in private over meals and in informal discussions.

Maneuvering: Opposition and Support

Opposition to Vinkakanimba Day in 1965 came from three principal sources: headmen, Punyira, and the Free Church of Scotland. Many headmen and villagers had felt exploited for the reasons just given. Hence the villagers were not prepared to make large contributions in 1965, especially if the Banangwa were not going to meet their obligation to contribute meat. The issue was a serious one. Villagers complained to headmen who, in their turn, brought their objections not only to the area committee but also to UNIP branch officers and before the UNIP joint committee. Although the subregion branch committee did not allow a lengthy discussion of all the issues, it was made aware of growing public resentment. Its members recognized that part of its power stemmed from popular support. Although some had claimed that Vinkakanimba Day fell within the sphere of the Native Administration, nonetheless they would speak on behalf of villagers at Banangwa council and area and development committee meetings. In late June and early July the members of the UNIP committee had not yet formulated a clear policy toward Vinkakanimba Day. They were, however, being pushed by headmen and villagers to represent and support their demands. The founding of the UNIP subregion branch had provided headmen and villagers with a new channel through which they could express their political interests and pressure not only party leaders but also the Banangwa and the Native Administration to consider their interests.

The other principal sources of opposition to the celebration were Punyira and the Free Church. Because the deputy chief was the main instigator of Vinkakanimba Day, Punyira sought to disrupt it or to have it canceled. In 1965, he had two excuses for public opposition to it. The first was the decision of the Free Church to forbid its members to participate. In 1964, the Reverend Chavura, who had been sent by the Livingstonia Synod in 1963 to take charge of the Uyombe Free Church congregation, had not realized the underlying ritual significance of Vinkakanimba Day. When, however, he was made aware of its significance for many Yombe as ancestor worship, he forbade church members to participate. Though Punyira was a suspended member, for more than thirty-five years the Free Church had provided him with a base of political and ritual support. Since his selection as chief in 1927 the majority of the Free Church elders had been either his personal friends or his kinsmen. These were the men on whom he had relied to stand with him against his opponents. They included men such as Yotta and Pauta Chila, and Sam Kara. Although younger men who belonged to or supported other branches of the royal clan had become elders of the Free Church, many other "royals" were leading figures in the National and Jordan churches and the Watchtower movement. The Free Church, however, remained the church of the educated and socially aspiring. Most of these attended Free Church Sunday services at the central church in Muyombe or in village churches.

The second reason for opposing the celebration was that, in 1965, August 1st fell on a Sunday, and, given the fundamentalist creed of the Free Church, to hold any celebration other than those of Sunday prayer would be sacrilege indeed. Even Free Church supporters of the deputy chief had difficulty in arguing for this. Instead, they attempted to have it postponed until the Monday, a position eventually taken up by Punyira.

The scene was now set for a major political struggle between Punyira and Edwall. Neither man could be sure of the nature and duration of his support within the various contexts of Yombe political life.

As the struggle took shape, the residents of Muyombe began to arrange themselves into two camps. The key to both the town and the chiefdom lay with the development committee—in particular, those members who were also officers of the UNIP committee. Nine development committee members belonged to the deputy chief's effective political support base; eight were linked to him through women, and one was his agnate, a senior member of Njera. Amos Ukwa is included as part of Edwall's supporters, since during the unfolding of this event he backed Edwall and was an outspoken supporter of Vinkakanimba Day as both a secular and a ritual occasion. Of the four men who supported the chief, one was his son and the other three were his sisters' sons and prominent members of the Free Church. Of the remaining ten members, five were UNIP committee officers and two were UNIP branch officers. Eric Enda and Ado Chila were the key to their support and that of the UNIP committee, and, though they often backed the deputy chief, on this occasion Eric and Ado did not commit themselves.

Although Edwall, Eric, and Ado were intimate friends who had worked together in founding branches of UNIP in Uyombe and were part of the more educated elite, in this situation they represented potentially conflicting interests. The main reason Eric and Ado did not commit themselves was the headmen's complaints, which they had to take seriously because they needed the villagers' support for their party.

A number of options were open to them. They could let village discontent run its own course; they could back the villagers against the wishes of Edwall and the royal clan; or they could negotiate a compromise by asking the deputy chief to lower the amount of food and drink expected of villagers. As Edwall's personal friends, Eric and Ado used the informal context of meals to inform him of the growing discontent in the villages. Without their backing Edwall might seriously jeopardize an important source of his political support on the development committee and within the UNIP subregion branch. Accordingly, he agreed to reduce the contributions asked from the villages, to cut down the number of dignitaries invited from other chiefdoms, and to get the Banangwa council to purchase a bull to provide meat. Eric and Ado, in their turn, persuaded the other members of the UNIP committee to support Vinkakanimba Day. Edwall was also assured of the backing of most shop owners, who would benefit from the purchase of goods at their shops.

Now the struggle shifted to the Banangwa council. The issue was whether it would agree to reduce the contribution expected from villages and to provide a bull for meat as Edwall had promised. Edwall had already set about securing "royal" support. He was assured of the backing of Bwana Samsalu and other senior members of Njera who saw Vinkakanimba Day as an opportunity to increase their power, since they would assume the ritual functions. Without consulting the chief, Bwana Samsalu had already begun to prepare millet for the ritual offering to Vinkakanimba. Elto Mbamba, the court clerk and a trusted sister's son of Chipanga, and Labe Enda, the owner of two stores (one of which was the only bottle store where bottled beer was sold), who could also claim to be a Chipanga sister's son, had sounded out the senior members of this royal branch. Most senior members of Chipanga who were not Free Church elders agreed to back Edwall's proposals. Tanga Wowo, the UNIP committee secretary and an important member of Kaswanga branch of the royal clan, used his influence with other senior Kaswanga members to gain support for Edwall. Vumbo remained uncertain. In theory, the two contending royal branches, Chapyoka and Njera, were those of the chief and the deputy chief, but the segments of royal branches do not fuse automatically. Their heads and other important members may pursue their own interests or those of the other groups to which they belong. For example, the chairman of the UNIP committee was also the head of a segment of Chapyoka, and members of segments of Njera and Chipanga were Free Church elders or members of other religious groups which opposed Vinkakanimba Day as ancestor worship. Hence their behavior was not always predictable. But once the UNIP committee had agreed to back the deputy chief, its chairman supported Vinkakanimba Day as well as Edwall's proposal to reduce the contributions of villages and to provide a bull within the Banangwa council, thus weakening the position of the chief. A similar position was taken by other members holding posts within the UNIP subregion branch. On this particular occasion the interests of the party overrode other allegiances.

It may also be argued that the behavior of Banangwa council members holding party posts was consistent with royal clan norms and values. They supported Vinkakanimba Day, a day honoring the founder of their descent groups, while the chief opposed it, acting within the interests of his personal political relationships based within the Free Church. Though the behavior of the UNIP committee chairman was consistent with royal clan norms and values and with the interests of the party, he acted against the interests of his own branch. He had in fact lent support to the deputy chief and Njera and had opposed the interests of the chief, who was the head of his royal branch, Chapyoka. Thus, the Banangwa council not only accepted Edwall's proposal but also agreed that Vinkakanimba Day should be held on August 1st, a Sunday.

In this particular encounter, then, Edwall had successfully mobilized support against Punyira. Through the use of his personal contacts among the more educated members of the UNIP committee and with his fellow "royals" or their sister's sons, he had succeeded in gaining the approval of the UNIP committee and the Banangwa council. There now remained the area committee. If Edwall and Njera could gain the unambiguous and unqualified backing of this body against Punyira, it would reveal the weakness of Punyira and Chapyoka and the absence of support for them within the chiefdom. It would constitute a major victory for Edwall and Njera. Thus, more than Vinkakanimba Day was involved.

The Development Committee
Before the area committee meeting was held, Edwall called a meeting of the development committee, in theory to prepare the agenda to be discussed by the larger body. The main topic was Vinkakanimba Day. There were two important issues: whether the celebration should be held on a Sunday and whether it should be discussed by the area committee at all. Many senior "royals" considered it the concern of the Banangwa council and not of commoners. They felt that headmen and villagers should accept the decision of the royal clan council, which represented the view of the "owners" of Vinkakanimba, the rulers of the chiefdom. They saw little need for further discussion. These conservative "royals" had failed to grasp the fact that commoners were now an intimate part of the political process.

Although the UNIP committee and many members of the development committee rejected the idea that discussion of Vinkakanimba Day should be confined to members of the royal clan, Punyira's sisters' sons, Pauta Chila and Sam Kara (both development committee members) said it was solely a royal concern. This would mean that all the arrangements would be settled in private. In taking this stand, they were acting not only in their capacity as development committee members but also in their roles as Punyira's sisters' sons and as elders of the local Free Church congregation.

Once the chairman of the development committee had made his opening address in support of Vinkakanimba Day, arguing that it did concern the area committee and that it should be held on August 1st, Pauta made the following appeal: "On the 29th our people [officers from the Livingstonia Synod] are coming from Kandowe [Livingstonia] to Muyombe. Why do we not postpone Vinkakanimba Day until Monday?" He was immediately supported by Sam, who made the following proposal: "Why do not the *sekulu* [grandfather, Punyira] and the *muzukulu* [grandson, Edwall] meet and settle this matter in private? It concerns only the Banangwa."

These two statements represented the interests of both Punyira and the Free Church. Pauta spoke as a church elder and demonstrated his willingness to compromise. His appeal was not lost on those other committee members who were also Free Church elders though for the most part already committed to the UNIP committee. In this context Pauta was part of the opposition. They had to support Edwall, though they also felt that they should attempt a compromise. Tisi Koko, the UNIP committee vice-treasurer and himself a Free Church elder, was the one who replied to Pauta and Sam.

He said: "We must settle this here and now. Vinkakanimba Day is not a Banangwa matter but concerns the chiefdom. The celebrations should begin in the afternoon and not in the morning when people are in church." Once Tisi had made this statement, Pauta and Sam could no longer act as the sole spokesmen for the Free Church. Nor could Sam prevent the inclusion of Vinkakanimba Day in the business of the area committee, where the final decision as to the day would be taken by headmen. That the chief's decisions were brought before the development committee at all was an indication of his loss of power; commoners were debating chiefly and royal concerns. If his decision was rejected by the headmen, even his remaining rights over "traditional" and spiritual matters would have been taken over by commoners.

Tanga Wowo and Labe Enda reminded the committee that not all Yombe were members of the Free Church and that Vinkakanimba Day was a special day for those who prayed to the ancestors. Elto Mbamba replied to them as a Free Church elder, but also criticized Punyira. He said, "The laws of the Free Church are against Vinkakanimba Day, and we church members are against it." He paused. "If the chief were only interested, all would go well and we would not have problems with planning Vinkakanimba Day." In the space of a few moments he had both opposed and supported the celebrations, speaking now as a church elder and now as a supporter of Edwall and the party.

The above detail demonstrates the types of maneuver made by committee members. The Free Church elders wanted the celebrations postponed, either until after the morning service or until Monday. They recognized that they could not prevent them altogether, but they were divided by their membership of and obligations to other groups, and by their affiliations to opposing factions. Those Free Church elders who were party men had to conform to party policy and support Edwall, while those who were Punyira's sisters' sons had to pursue his interests. But the important point was that Edwall, supported by the UNIP committee, was able to impose his policies on the development committee. Most members approved of his plans and agreed that Vinkakanimba Day should be brought before the area committee. A major public encounter was now about to take place. It seemed clear that Edwall would emerge with an unequivocal victory.

The Area Committee Meeting
The meeting of the area committee was well attended by headmen, important "royals," and members of the development committee. The problem of the contributions expected from villages and the Banangwa council had already been settled. The main issue to be considered was whether to accept Punyira's proposal to change Vinkakanimba Day from Sunday to Monday. In a sense this was Punyira's last stand, after being overruled by the Banangwa council and the development committee. Though both he and Edwall had rallied support, they were unprepared for what in

fact happened. The Reverend Chavura of the Free Church came to the meeting, and the views that he expressed redefined the situation. Political commitments became secondary to religious ones, so that members regrouped along lines of religious affiliation. Edwall's and Eric's allies who identified themselves with the Free Church supported its policy of changing the date. Area committee members who belonged to the Jordan and National churches rallied against the Free Church. The political issue was submerged in interchurch rivalries. The Free Church was the oldest church, many of its members belonging to the old and new educated elite and the socially aspiring. It was not the church of the common villager.

Once the meeting was called to order, the chairman of the area committee put the question whether Vinkakanimba Day should be held on Sunday or postponed to Monday as proposed by the chief. To everyone's surprise—the Free Church elders had not been consulted—the Reverend Chavura asked to be heard. His speech was short and to the point. He argued that God had set Sunday aside for prayer, not festivities involving drum beating, dancing, beer drinking, and drunkenness. To hold Vinkakanimba Day on a Sunday would be sacrilege.

The speech made by Chavura antagonized the leaders of the National and Jordan churches. Many of them were prominent "royals" and village headmen. With the exception of Eddi Chila, a court assessor and former Free Church elder, the initial confrontation was one between men of equal social rank; they were Banangwa in the truest sense. They were prominent members of the royal clan and classificatory brothers of the same generation, i.e., Punyira's sons. Esaw Wowo—Bwana Samsalu's eldest son and Edwall's second-in-command—set the course of the discussion by attacking Chavura on two levels. He indicated his own religious affiliation and competence to interpret God's words as a preacher of the Jordan church, reminding the Reverend Chavura that he was a foreigner, subordinate to the descendants of Vinkakanimba, the rulers of the country. Other Banangwa who were Free Church elders rallied to Chavura's defense. The argument was phrased no longer in terms of the struggle between Njera and Chapyoka, or that between Edwall and Punyira, but in terms of the rivalry between the Free Church and the Jordan and National churches. In this context Elto Mbamba and Tisi Koko assumed their roles as Free Church elders, rejected their previous positions, and publicly supported a change of date for Vinkakanimba Day. Most other elders followed suit, including the head of Edwall's own minor segment of Njera.

Though members of Njera and Chipanga usually united against Punyira and his branch, they were now divided. The division was based on religious affiliation, not kinship or political allegiance. Acting as leaders of their respective churches, one member of Njera (or Chipanga) would speak in favor of Vinkakanimba Day's being held on Sunday, while another suggested that it should be changed to Monday. Headmen followed suit. Thus members of the area committee divided into two religious camps, the one supporting the Free Church and the other the Jordan and National churches. It was clear that most members were in favor of having Vinkakanimba Day on Sunday.

Although Edwall's proposal was approved by the area committee, he had by no means won a clear victory. The proposal was approved because it became a focus for religious differences, themselves indicative of basic cleavages within Yombe society. The leading political figures recognized that the headmen were not expressing support for Edwall but simply their hostility toward the Free Church. Nonetheless, the decision was that Vinkakanimba Day should be held on August 1st. Edwall could proceed with making the practical arrangements, among which was an invitation to the Minister of the Northern Province.

This meeting revealed many of the basic tensions which produce the unpredictable contingencies of Yombe political life. During Punyira's long rule, the Free Church, despite all changes, had remained the church of the elite and of those who aspired to join it. It had been the first Christian organization to take root in Uyombe. Punyira had used it as a source of moral, religious, and political support. Over time, educated commoners and royals from branches other than Chapyoka became prominent within it. This affected its value as support for Punyira but emphasized its role as the church of the more educated and the socially aspiring. For those with social aspirations along "Western" or African "town" lines, the Free Church was the church to belong to and attend.

The Jordan and National churches are predominently the churches of villagers. Many of their officers are prominent royals and headmen, but very few have completed standards V or VI. It may be said that, to a large extent, less educated villagers, both commoners and royals, belong to the Jordan and National churches. Punyira, however, backed by many of the prominent leaders of Muyombe, has forbidden churches other than the Free Church to establish congregations and build in Muyombe and thus has sought to preserve the town as the center of the Free Church. The dispute that developed in the area committee meeting, though expressed in religious terms, had a political foundation. It was not between royal branches or between the party and the Native Administration, but between Muyombe— the center of the old and new educated elites—and the more traditionally oriented villagers. Paradoxically, it could be argued that Edwall won the support of the area committee while most members were in fact expressing their opposition to the social attributes which he represented.

Vinkakanimba Day was held on a Sunday. Throughout the event there was no indication of the antagonisms which had preceded it. True, none of the Polomombo Wowo attended, and most members of the Free Church did not take an active part in the festivities; nonetheless, they made no attempt to disrupt it, and some of them even assisted in inconspicuous ways. The principal political figures cooperated in coordinating and supervising the activities. The UNIP youth brigade helped the Native Administration staff in maintaining order among the hundreds of villagers who attended the celebrations. Speeches were made by the chief, the deputy chief, and other senior members of the royal clan, honoring Vinkakanimba as the founder of the chiefdom and proclaiming the royal clan as the only rightful rulers of Uyombe. The Native Administration staff made a special effort to see that all village headmen had food and drink and that the more important ones received a portion of meat. Thus, on the actual day of celebrations there was no sign of hostility between the main political adversaries. But the struggle for power was by no means resolved, and the chief was to have the last word.

While the celebrations were being planned, Edwall and Eric had sent a telegram to the Minister of the Northern Province, inviting him to the Vinkakanimba Day celebrations of August 1st. Though the Minister was unable to attend himself, on Monday, August 2d, a Zambian government land rover arrived to inform the Native Administration that the government was sending a special team of photographers to take moving pictures of Vinkakanimba Day as representative of "traditional" Zambian culture. The chief lost little time in reminding the deputy chief, the UNIP committee, headmen, and villagers that he was the one who had opposed holding the celebrations on Sunday and that it was within the chief's spiritual powers to know about such things. By not accepting his authority the young political leaders had lost an important opportunity to widely publicize Vinkakanimba, the royal clan, and the chiefdom of Uyombe.

9
Conclusion

My analysis of Yombe political life has been concerned not only with social movement within a continuing structural frame but also with movements which acted upon and effected changes in the structural frame itself. These gradual movements and social forces are cumulative and eventually produce a move toward a new continuity, a new set of factors which in their turn will alter political arrangements. The significant feature of rural societies in Africa is the rate at which change is now occurring and the fact that they are part of larger political systems. There is more to social change than just the changes in the rules that govern social relationships, as Mair contends (1965, p. 21). Social life involves constant interplay between behavior and rules: the rules may persist while the realities of behavior may depart from, be contrary to, and even subvert the rules, in response to different forces. Firth (1964, p.11) suggests that the identification of social forces is as important a part of dynamic analysis as is the charting and description of social movements. The foregoing has been an attempt to identify those social forces which are operating not only in Uyombe but also in other rural communities in Zambia.

The social forces which are producing movement and change in Uyombe are based upon the interaction of potentially opposing units and interests. This interaction generates spheres of political activity which structure political behavior, choices, and decisions. The principal relationships are briefly discussed below.

The Local Community and the Central Government

Few, if any, local communities in Central Africa are unaffected by the policies of central governments and by the economic and political arrangements of the wider society. Central African rural communities are, to use Redfield's term, part societies (1961, p. 24), related to people and institutions outside them and locked into national state systems which impinge upon their social, political, and economic arrangements. This does not mean, however, that local and central government interests always coincide; local communities compete with one another and with the central government for scarce resources. The residents of Uyombe chiefdom have demanded of the central government things such as a direct road to Isoka, improved local roads, a hospital, and a secondary school. But the priorities of the central government not necessarily being those of the Yombe, the government has not always met Yombe demands. Because the Yombe are very few in number, lacking wealth and power, they cannot enforce compliance. They are, however, adjacent to Malawi. Local leaders have often considered using the threat of joining Malawi (or another district of Zambia) to get what they want. Fully aware of the risk involved in such a threat, these leaders also recognize that to get basic services and, at the same time, to maintain some degree of local autonomy they must take dramatic steps.

The power of the central government was made apparent to the Yombe during the period of religious strife between the Lumpa church (a prophetic movement led by Alice Lenshina Mulenga, a Bemba woman) and government troops. During 1963 and 1964, Lumpa congregations in the Northern and Eastern provinces of Northern Rhodesia founded independent religious communities and disregarded the authority of the central government. In August 1964, violence broke out between Lumpa and non-Lumpa. The Lumpa were defeated by Northern Rhodesian troops and placed in special detention camps. When members of the Uyombe Lumpa congregation were returned to Uyombe for resettlement, the development committee, reconstituted as the Lenshina rehabilitation committee, proposed to the Banangwa council that prominent Lumpa leaders who had not been born in Uyombe should be expelled from the chiefdom. The central government threatened with arrest anyone who molested or attempted to expel Lumpa members. It made explicit that only the government had the authority to decide rights of residence. Thus the Banangwa were deprived of their most valued right, privilege, and sanction. They were no longer the owners of the land and its people. Through a single decision the central government had removed the primary source of the Banangwa's authority and power: it had reduced local autonomy, had increased centralized authority, and had strengthened its control over the periphery. It had created a residue of discontent among a powerful segment of Yombe society by making them rulers in name only. But it had the power to appoint qualified local men to posts within the Zambian civil service and the national party. Through such appointments it could reward loyalty and maintain support at the local level. After independence, many qualified Yombe were appointed to important posts within the civil service and UNIP. Although this furthered the Yombe's integration into the national community, it did not satisfy Yombe demands for improved basic services.

The Small Town and Lesser Communities

Within Zambia and other African territories, small towns in the rural areas are important links between the wider society and lesser settlements of the countryside. The principal impetus for development comes of course from the urban areas, which are the main centers of authority, power, and wealth. Yet small towns, embedded in the fabric of rural life, are important centers for rural development. It is through them that new links are forged between rural communities and national organizations and it is also through them that changes are introduced which, after being molded and tempered by the local rural elite, are disseminated into the more rural areas. These small towns are the social middle grounds in which the skills and behavior, the customs and practices, the norms and values of the wider society gain significance for rural life.

It is within these small towns that local elites tend to cluster, in order to pursue their economic and political interests. Smaller rural settlements look to them for development and change. They are important for national and local integration but they may also become centers of political unrest. The local elites living in these small towns are easily disillusioned. They may become dissatisfied and provide leadership for those resisting central government policies.

The significance of these small rural towns for economic and political change and for establishing new patterns of leadership and ethnic relations in the rural areas of Africa has been demonstrated in the studies made by Vincent (1971) of Gondo in Uganda, by Owusu (1970) of Swerdu in Ghana, and by Hopkins (1972) of Kita in Mali. These three small towns are all marked by economic and occupational differentiation and specialization, and, as centers of commercial activity and transport, they have attracted people of diverse ethnic identities. Muyombe has not yet attained this order of importance. It is more intimately tied to its agricultural subsistence base. Nonetheless, its stores and basic services provide for lesser village communities, and it is over the allocation and distribution of basic services, the way in which limited community resources are to be used, that competition has arisen between Muyombe and the villages of the chiefdom. This competition over the use of community resources and unpaid chiefdom labor and skills has become a source of political controversy. The local elite living in Muyombe has sought to develop the capital by centralizing basic services, while village headmen have argued for development in their areas. This has produced a number of pressures and has led to the development of potential interest groups.

The Old Guard and the New Men

Within Uyombe the ruling elite—which based its authority on precedent, the control of basic resources such as land, and the colonial order—has had to contend with a small cluster of political leaders who derive their authority from the possession of special Western skills, popular support, and from their control of the local branches of UNIP. The ruling elite had manned the composite authority structures which were developed under colonial rule and which had dominated the political life of the chiefdom. Kilson (1966, p.

284) suggests, for former British colonial Africa, that traditional authority structures were utilized to mediate change in local societies and that the rural masses experienced much of colonial change through these traditional structures. The peoples of the Northern provinces of Zambia and Malawi were also subjected to change from two other sources. The first was early contact with Christian mission stations such as Livingstonia, Mwenzo, and Lubwa. Large numbers of Yombe attended these missions at one time. They received an education and acquired skills which enabled them to obtain skilled jobs in the growing urban/industrial centers of Central and Southern Africa. The missions themselves provided jobs for the new, educated, Christian elite, which staffed mission schools, founded local congregations, and used the church as a base for political, religious, and moral support. The second source of change was labor migration. The Yombe labor migrant was exposed to new economic and technological processes. He was neither urban nor rural but possessed a repertory of both urban and rural experiences, skills, and practices which he could draw upon as the situation dictated. Through labor migration and contact with Christian missions, many Yombe had experiences of European and Western ways at home and abroad. Like other Tumbuka-speaking peoples of the region, they took an active part in religious, union, and political movements in the urban area. The returned labor migrant had two reference groups, the one urban and the other rural. The discrepancy between the living conditions of the two no doubt contributed to the growth of political awareness and consciousness in rural communities like Uyombe. The labor migrant was deprived, not in comparison to other villagers, but when his rural standard of living was measured against that of his urban fellows. Dissatisfied with their present living conditions, returned labor migrants formed a potential source of political discontent. They wanted changes in their material condition of life.

Some indication of the growing dissatisfaction among rural Africans in the Northern Province was provided by the numbers who joined movements which promised a new spiritual order, in which Africans would assume power and gain both an improved standard of living and protection against traditional misfortunes. Another indication of widespread political discontent with local rule was the rapid acceptance of local branches of national political movements which held the promise of Zambian independence and economic opportunities for Africans.

Within Uyombe, the "old guard"—the chief and his ruling clique—controlled the apparatus of government. They had systematically consolidated power by excluding rival branches of the royal clan and the younger generation of new men from positions of authority. But the founding of branches of UNIP provided the new men with a vehicle for translating their social status into political power and economic opportunity. The basic discontent of returned labor migrants provided the necessary source of political support which the new leaders could use to challenge the power of the chief and his ruling clique. The drive for control of chiefdom affairs was facilitated by rivalries within the royal clan. In more general terms, one may suggest that marked cleavages within a traditional ruling group facilitate the development of new political movements. These may at first take root in the interstitial zone between structures, and, if they gain widespread popular support, they may challenge the traditional ruling group. In Uyombe the struggle for power was not as clearly defined as the above formulation suggests. Though UNIP did pose a threat to the royal clan as a body, royals were also members of the party. The principal struggle was between the "new men" and the "old guard," the chief and his supporters. Edwall Wowo exemplifies or personifies the thrust of new men who are themselves of royal birth, and Eric Enda that of the more educated commoners. Though these two men represent two prongs of a political alliance, on many issues they were on opposite sides. They did, however, stand together in opposing the old guard. The conflict between the old guard and the new men was only one facet of the struggle for power.

Among the new men there was an important division which was indicative of the growing social distinctions within Yombe society itself—the division between the more and the less educated. The distinction was not primarily one of wealth (many of the more educated were unemployed and relied upon cultivation for subsistence), but of level of education, previous occupation and experience, and possibilities of future employment. The more educated leaders were potentially employable in the Zambian civil service, in UNIP posts, or as clerks and managers of commercial enterprises, while the less educated, lacking Western qualifications, were not potentially mobile. These attributes, related to achieved qualifications, were important determinants for political behavior. The more educated tended to support the policies of the central government and of national UNIP. Their present interests and future opportunities were more intimately tied to those of the national Zambian community and their decisions reflected more universalistic considerations. The less educated political leaders had few prospects of leaving Uyombe or gaining local salaried posts. Their interests were thus tied to those of the local community, and their political behavior was parochial and particularistic. They sought to gain control of the new sources of wealth entering Uyombe. Local commercial interests were also important in this elite configuration. Though many local shop owners and traders were highly educated, their interests lay within the community. The chief neither originated local development schemes nor demanded that the central government do so. Because the new men changed this situation, most shop owners and traders backed them.

The struggle for Zambian independence and the founding of branches of a national mass party in Uyombe provided new opportunities for gaining political power. The new men used the party as a means of acquiring positions of authority, power, influence, and prestige. Their activities undermined the power of the chief, traditional ruling groups and cliques, and produced new political alignments. The party-based elite gained considerable power and, having gained it, began to entrench itself. With independence the more qualified of the new men received political appointments as civil servants or regional party officers and left the community, leaving local affairs in the hands of the less qualified and the traditional ruling group who were more parochial in their orientation. I would suggest that the Yombe case illustrates the way in which a mass party, having securely established itself, may then enter into a phase of entrenchment, if not conservatism. Within Uyombe this process of consolidation has led to the strengthening of the alliance between political and commercial interests and produced a conservative trend. However, new forces have been released, and pressure is gradually building up from beneath; this pressure may lead to the rejection of the present party leaders for new ones.

The New Men and the Villagers

At the same time that the less educated political leaders were attempting to consolidate power, headmen and villagers were increasing their demands. Most headmen and villagers supported development schemes but were opposed to the use of their labor and skills to develop Muyombe as the center of basic services. They wanted development schemes in their areas and a share of the paying jobs which arose from government projects such as the building of school blocks and teachers' houses in Muyombe. Moreover, carpenters and bricklayers began to protest because, in addition to the less specialized labor required of everyone, they were expected to contribute their skills and thus felt doubly exploited.

The growing demands of villagers for local development have put pressure on all those chiefdom leaders whose power is based primarily on popular support. The legitimacy of these leaders is constantly being reevaluated in terms of the extent to which their actions have met popular standards and fulfilled expectations. Hence the leadership of the new men is precarious, and in order to meet local expectations they must increase their demands on the government for assistance in developing Uyombe. At the same time that there was growing emphasis on parochial interests, the new leaders were forced into what might at first appear to be a more radical stance. Villagers were demanding more basic services and a better standard of living. If the new leaders could not provide them, they would lose public support. In attempting to retain their power, local leaders were forced to take up positions which the central government might consider radical. As Uyombe was moving toward one continuity, other social forces were operating toward another. At the very time when the new leaders were consolidating their gains, the basis of their power was threatened.

The chief and the royal clan have remained an important element in this fluid situation. If the party-based elite is unable to provide for local demands, the chief and royal clan stand as a potential alternative source of leadership. As the less educated consolidate their power and are no longer able to meet or become insensitive to local demands, villagers may seek new leadership. The party which had operated to bring a new elite into positions of power and to extend popular participation may no longer serve this function. The party may lose touch with its base of support, and villagers may turn to the former ruling elements which, to retain a modicum of power, have become part of the coalition with the party-based elite. If this assessment of developing trends is correct, what one may observe is the national, mass party beginning to wither at the level of grass roots politics.

10
Epilogue

At the time of my fieldwork it was difficult to assess the full impact of the social trends observed—to determine whether they were merely adjustments within an overall constancy of gradual incremental change or whether they might constitute major changes in the preexisting "structural alignment" (Nadel 1957, p. 135).

In 1973 I had the opportunity to return to Uyombe for a short visit and thus to form an initial assessment of the direction of changes suggested in chapter 9. I was not surprised to find that my suggestions had been substantially correct. The key to understanding the political situation of 1973 was to be found in the role which the more educated political leaders had performed in regulating chiefdom politics and in Zambia's policy of rapid Africanization. While living in the towns, the younger, more educated political leaders had been part of the educated section of the growing African urban proletariat. They were the carriers of a "proletarian intellectualism," in Weber's terms (1965, pp. 125-27), and formed part of the intelligentsia of the underprivileged urban working classes. When they returned to the rural areas, they founded local branches of UNIP and sought to rationalize the local government along bureaucratic lines. They tried to adhere to the impartial norms, rules, and regulations of the party, to uphold national party goals, and to subordinate the chief and his ruling clique—the repositories of traditional authority—to more democratic or representative principles of governing. They were the principal adversaries of the chief, and, with the support of the less educated, they were able to control chiefdom politics. The less educated political leaders, while acknowledging party rules and regulations, tended to interpret them in a personal manner. They were parochial in their concerns, pursued personal and local interests, and were primarily concerned with gaining power in the local system, not the national one.

In the preindependence era, new administrative arrangements, based upon councils and committees, were imposed from above by the colonial government. The "new men" were able to use to their advantage this new "collegiate" form of local government to reduce the authority of the chief. This form of rule by committee combined the authority of notables, the practical knowledge of entrepreneurs, and the specialized skills of local representatives of the government departments of the district. It provided for a more representative system of local government and for greater coordination and integration of chiefdom activities. According to Weber, rule based upon collegiate principles is an important prelude to a more rational-legal system of administration (Gerth and Mills 1946, p. 237).

Within local government and the party the inclusion of the more and less educated notables and entrepreneurs produced a representative but counterbalancing mix. The more educated, while responsive to local interests, were oriented toward national party goals; and the less educated, while responsive to national party goals, were oriented toward local interests. The notables, while recognizing change, sought to preserve the traditional authority of chieftainship; and the entrepreneurs, while recognizing traditional authority, were oriented toward changes which would enhance their business opportunities and therefore supported the policies of the young, progressive leaders of rapid development. The Native Administration had encapsulated and helped to preserve many of the particularistic features of the traditional system. But under the leadership of the more educated, local government was on the verge of being transformed into a more bureaucratic and representative system capable of originating self-help schemes and mobilizing the rural peasants to carry them out. A new awareness had been instilled in the common folk, and development was proceeding from beneath.

After independence, the form of local politics, which was used so effectively by the deputy chief and his more educated allies, based upon rule by committees, underwent changes that undermined the effectiveness of the local government as a unit of administration and grass roots development. The two reasons which help to account for these changes are Zambia's policy of rapid Africanization and the loss of effective leadership.

With independence, Zambia became a more open society in that the recruitment and advancement of Africans in all branches of government service and in the mining corporations were no longer restricted by colonial policies or by the color bar. Under colonial rule, few Africans had been career officers in the civil service, and, of a total population of four million in 1965, no more than 150 Africans had received university training. With independence, Zambia's policy of rapid Zambianizaton brought Africans into all levels of government service: the national civil service was staffed by Africans, as was local government. This policy had a number of latent consequences, one of which involved recruiting educated African elites of the urban and rural centers into government service. These elites took advantage of the new opportunities for government service and gradually began to entrench themselves in their new positions of authority and power, thereby hindering the advancement of more qualified persons. Moreover, the siphoning off of the more progressive, educated elements in the rural areas left politics in the hands of the more traditionally oriented and conservative elements, allowing for the emergence of new coalitions of traditional authorities such as chiefs, the less educated, and entrepreneurs. In 1965 this was only a trend but one which became an important reality in the first years of independence.

In the first years of the postindependence era, all of the younger, progressive, more educated members of the party committee and the development committee left Uyombe to take up well-paying jobs in the civil service, the party, and other national organizations; a few were appointed to diplomatic posts in other African countries. The departure of these men left the deputy chief with few allies and the party and the development committee under the control of the less educated, who refused to hold elections, left most posts vacant, and promoted their supporters. They also gained full control over the Uyombe branch of the Kasama Marketing Cooperative and in this way began to translate their political power into economic advantage. The delicate balance between national and local interests ceased to obtain as the less educated entrenched themselves.

The self-help schemes which had already been planned were completed, but new ones were not originated. Development from beneath came to a grinding halt. Since their control depended on popular support, the less educated remained responsive to local interests. Moreover, the chief and his men were waiting in the wings to reassert their leadership. The less educated were ill equipped effectively to represent local interests at the district and national levels. The external relations of the chiefdom were left to the more educated party officers who, as part of the rural intelligentsia, had used their skills and personal contacts to get things done. The less educated possessed neither the skills nor the contacts. The common folk continued to demand development in areas such as education, health, and transport. As pressure built up from beneath, the less educated made increasing demands on the elected representative of Isoka District to the National Assembly of Zambia.

After independence the common folk regarded the central government as theirs and expected it to provide such things as schools and dispensaries. Their expectations were reinforced by the liberal distribution of government loans. In 1969, in the absence of the moderating force of the more educated, the national representative from Isoka District was driven from Uyombe, and its leaders threatened to secede from the district. Leading central government and national party officers came to Uyombe to investigate the popular and almost violent protest. The deputy chief was removed from his post and the post abolished; the development committee was discontinued, and elections were held in the party. The chief was recognized as the sole legal authority of chiefdom government.

In 1970, elections were held in the party in Uyombe. The less educated members of the party committee were soundly defeated, as were many branch officers. They were replaced by younger men, most of whom were of the same educational background but lacked experience in managing party affairs. It was not until the 1973 election that the more educated element began to reassert its political leadership in the party committee, though not in the branches. Six of the eight officers of the party committee had completed seven years or more of schooling. But although the number of branches had increased to seventeen, only two branch secretaries were so qualified. The general low level of education of branch officers has seriously affected the efficiency of the party. The primary efforts of the party committee have been directed toward rebuilding an effective political organization, one which can originate development schemes and mobilize the people to carry them out. From 1965 until 1973 the politics of Uyombe underwent further changes. The less educated, who had taken charge of the party and the committees of local government, could neither control nor meet the demands of the common folk and were therefore removed from office. Under their leadership the party had fallen into disarray, the deputy chief had been deposed, and the chief and his ruling clique had prevailed.

The 1969 protest in Uyombe resulted in major benefits for the common folk and for the elites of Muyombe. The central government built new schools, upgraded old ones, and improved roads. Local labor was employed to construct a new wing for the dispensary, an airstrip to accommodate the small planes of the Flying Doctor Service of Zambia, and a new post office, which was completed in 1973. The Muyombe dispensary was provided with a doctor on a regular basis; running water was laid on in Muyombe. In the summer of 1973 a new road was opened linking the chiefdoms of Ufungwe and Uyombe directly to Isoka District headquarters.

As the capital of Uyombe, Muyombe was the main recipient of government assistance. As a result, its population and shops have almost doubled in number since 1969. The less educated politicians, while suffering a temporary political setback, have benefited from these changes and from their control of the Uyombe Cooperative. The Kasama Cooperative has constructed a new brick building to serve as the headquarters of the Uyombe branch of the cooperative. This building contains a large and efficient grinding machine and sufficient space to store fertilizers, hybrid maize, and dry fish which are sold to cooperative members at a discount. In 1973 the cooperative grinding mill was the only one operating in Uyombe. It was the less educated men who were the officers of the Uyombe Cooperative and who set local policy. They were among those who had received the largest government loans, cultivated large fields, and produced high yields of local and hybrid maize for sale on the local market and to the cooperative. Those who did not receive salaries from the cooperative opened small shops. Simply put, they used their political influence to gain economic advantages within the local system. They represent the new commercial peasants of the rural areas, who have translated their elite status as party leaders into agricultural and commercial wealth. In 1973 these less educated men used their political and economic influence to get themselves elected to posts within the branches. They had shifted their allegiance and become part of a new conservative coalition consisting of the chief and his ruling clique and entrepreneurs.

The remarkable feature of the Uyombe situation is that internal and external forces combined to restore the chief and his ruling clique to positions of power. During the colonial period it was thought by many scholars that the chief was in a dilemma (Gluckman 1968, p. 72, and Fallers 1956) and that chieftainship would be so undermined by colonial rule and by the rise of new elites that it would be swept aside with independence (Wallerstein 1961, pp. 41–43). In African countries such as Malawi and Zambia, which gained their independence through the activities of national mass parties, one might not have expected chiefly rule to persist at the local level. In Zambia, however, UNIP, a mass political party based upon nationalism, has recognized chieftainship as an intimate part of the system of local government. Its policy of rapid Zambianization siphoned off the more educated and progressive elements of the rural centers and thus allowed not only for the resurgence of traditional patterns of authority in the rural areas where most Zambians live, but also for the rise of new but politically conservative coalitions at the local level.

Notes

Chapter 2. The Yombe and Their Country

1 *May/June, 1963 Census of Africans: Village Populations in Northern Rhodesia*. District: Isoka. Minister of Finance, Lusaka, July 1965.
2 For another account of Tumbuka rejection of Ngoni practices, see Fraser 1914, pp. 112–13. Brelsford also mentions the recent creation of an annual ceremony to the alleged founder of the chiefdom of Hewe in Malawi and its royal Chawinga Clan (Brelsford 1956, p. 81).
3 See also the speeches made by Sir Stewart Gore-Brown, the chairman of the Native Land Tenure Committee, in support of the parish system. He gives a clear view of its intended purpose. Northern Rhodesia, Legislative Council Debates, 24 Nov.–20 Dec. 1945, no. 52, p. 358.
4 In Uyombe the post of Deputy Chief was introduced by the Provincial and District Commissioners. But this post was not recognized officially by being recorded in the *Northern Rhodesia Government Gazette*. In 1969 the post was abolished. The reason is explained in the epilogue.

Chapter 3. The Territorial Framework

1 In 1945 the parish system was introduced, removing many previous restrictions on settlement. Villages were organized into parishes, which were the units of taxation, and taxpayers registered by parishes instead of villages. A man was not tied to a village but could move within the parish. Though Uyombe is divided into parishes, they are not administrative units. The basic unit of residence and administration remains the Administrative village. The parish system failed in Uyombe.
2 Southall (1961, p. 1) refers to small towns which have "retained strong links with agriculture and the subsistence economy of the countryside." Middleton (1966, p. 33) identifies a type of small town which is an administrative and trading center in a rural area. However, neither Southall nor Middleton has explored the importance of these small towns. Muyombe provides an illustration of the social and political importance of towns of this type for rural life.
3 In contrast to Muyombe, ethnic diversity is found, for example, in Gondo, Uganda (Vincent 1971), and in Kahama, Tanzania (Abrahams 1961).

167

Chapter 4. The Structure of Political Groups: The Royal Clan

1 The opposite of free people used in this way is not slave, *muzga* (pl. *bazga*). "Free" refers to the superior position of the royal clan as owners of the land. The people of the chiefdom are known as *bantu ba caru*.

2 The *Lists of Yombe Chiefs* names Vinkakanimba as the first and describes him as Mughanga's father.

3 The person referred to as Njera II is in fact Chief Funtukeni of Njera branch; Funtukeni ruled 1904–14.

4 Chief Punyira does not accept that Mwene Vumbo was the first son but considers Kaswanga the eldest.

5 Two local descent groups, the Hungwa Mbamba and the Vidi, claim that their ancestors were the first to settle in Uyombe and that Vinkakanimba arrived at a later time.

6 Richards distinguishes three periods or phases. The first period concerns the founder and establishes the royal clan's right to rule. The second period is characterized by well-known social processes and the enumeration of chiefs or ancestors. The third phase is historical time. She suggests that genealogical manipulation to fit the present is referred back to the second period. But among the Yombe, manipulation may be referred back to any one of the three phases depending on the social groups concerned. Abrahams (1967, p. 111) has made a somewhat similar point.

Chapter 5. The Structure of Political Groups:
            The New Men and the Uyombe UNIP Subregion Branch

1 Bierstedt suggests that power stems from three sources (1) numbers of people, (2) social organization and (3) resources. Although the people of Uyombe were numerous, they lacked a political organization through which they could effectively oppose the chief. The founding of a local party rooted in a national organization changed this situation. The local party was an organization which controlled numbers and resources; it had power.

2 In Ginsberg's (1934) terms, quasi-groups are not groups but categories of persons possessing a cluster of similar attributes or interests. They are a recruiting field for groups or incipient groups, and in Uyombe they often form the basis for coactivity. Harries-Jones (1969) sees little utility in the concept quasi-group. I find it useful, however, for designating, the category of persons who most often come together in support of each other in coalitions.

3 In distinguishing the occupations of the sixty-eight men who were returned labor migrants—most Yombe men spend some time working abroad—I have used Epstein and Mitchell's (1965) occupational categories.

4 During most of my fieldwork the composition of the subregion committee was as I describe it. Although, after independence, most of the more educated were appointed to political posts outside Uyombe—within the party or in the Zambian civil service—their local party posts had not been filled by the time of my departure in September 1965. I therefore use the present tense in describing the members and affairs of this committee.

5 By September 1965, Eric Enda, Simon Nyeka, Ware Ntha, and Gala held important, well-paying civil service posts; only Eric remained in Uyombe as the local credit supervisor. Ado Chila was promoted to the region. None of the less educated members of the committee was promoted.

Chapter 6. Politics in Chiefdom Government:
    The Chief, the Deputy Chief, and the Banangwa Council

1 John (Punyira) Wowo became chief in 1927. His rule predates and spans the Native Administration system. Thus, he has dealt with a number of changes and continues to play an active part in local politics.
2 Michels (1959, p. 46) observes of this type of behavior that "whenever an obstacle is encountered, the leaders are apt to offer to resign, professing that they are weary of office, but really aiming to show the dissentients the indispensability of their own leadership." Edwall then was using a similar technique to gain a demonstration of confidence in him as an indispensable leader.

Chapter 7. Politics in Chiefdom Government:
    The Development and Area Committees

1 The previous chairman, Edward Mbamba, was a village headman who died unexpectedly in 1963. Kenon was of a different segment of the same lineage. Before the election, the local UNIP subregion committee secretary told me who would be elected to these posts.
2 Whenever contributions were needed for local schemes, letters were sent to Yombe living abroad. As might be expected, the highest contributions were made by the largest communities of Yombe working abroad, such as Kitwe. The sum of money indicates in a tangible way the interest of Yombe abroad in "home" affairs.
3 Muyombe upper primary school, which includes standard V and VI was built only in the late 1950s. Until then, Yombe had to go abroad to pursue further education.
4 Kilson (1966) has made a similar observation for Sierra Leone. In the Zambian situation some returned labor migrants may be considered as part of the unemployed lower rungs of the national elite. They may reactivate their status by gaining employment as clerks and teachers in the urban centers.

Bibliography

Abraham, J. C. 1932. *Nyasaland Protectorate: Report on the Census of 1931*. Zomba: Government Printer.

Abrahams, R. G. 1961. "Kahama Township, Western Province, Tanganyika." In A. Southall (ed.), *Social Change in Modern Africa*. London: Oxford University Press.

———. 1967. *The Political Organization of Unyamwezi*. Cambridge: Cambridge University Press.

An Account of the Disturbances in Northern Rhodesia, July to October 1961. 1961. Lusaka: Government Printer.

Bailey, F. G. 1965. "Decisions by Consensus in Councils and Committees," In M. Banton (ed.), *Political Systems and the Distribution of Power*. London: Tavistock.

———. 1969. *Strategems and Spoils*. New York: Schocken Books.

Bierstedt, R. 1950. "An Analysis of Social Power." *American Sociological Review* 15, no. 6 (December).

Bond, G. C. 1972. "Kinship and Conflict in a Yombe Village." *Africa* 52, no. 4 (October).

Brelsford, W. V. 1956. *The Tribes of Northern Rhodesia*. Lusaka: Government Printer.

Evans-Pritchard, E. E. 1940. *The Nuer*. Oxford University Press.

Fallers, L. A. 1965. *Bantu Bureaucracy*. Cambridge: W. Heffer and Son. (Reissue, Chicago: University of Chicago Press, 1965.)

Firth, R. 1964. *Essays on Social Organization and Values*. L. S. E. Monographs on Social Organization and Values. London: The Athlone Press.

Fortes, M. 1957. *The Web of Kinship among the Tallensi*. Oxford University Press.

Fraser, D. 1914. *Winning a Primitive People*. London: Seeley, Service.

Gann, L. H. 1969. *A History of Northern Rhodesia*. New York: Humanities Press.

Gerth, H. H., and Mills, C. W. 1946. *From Max Weber*. New York: Oxford University Press.

Ginsberg, M. 1934. *Sociology*. London: Thornton Butterworth Ltd.

Gluckman, M. 1963. *Order and Rebellion in Tribal Africa*. London: Cohen and West.

———. 1968. "Inter-hierarchical Roles." In Marc Schwartz (ed.), *Local Level Politics*. Chicago: Aldine.

Hailey, L. 1956. *Native Administration in the British African Territories*. Part II. London: H. M. S. O.

Handbook to the Federation of Rhodesia and Nyasaland. 1960. Salisbury: Government Printer.

171

Harries-Jones, P. 1969. "'Home-boy' Ties and Political Organization." In J. C. Mitchell (ed.), *Social Networks in Urban Situations*. Manchester: Manchester University Press.

Hopkins, N. S. 1972. *Popular Government in an African Town*. Chicago: University of Chicago Press.

Hudson, W. J. S. 1965. "Local Government Reorganization in Isoka District." *Journal of Local Administration Overseas* 4, no. 1 (January).

Isoka District Note Book.

Kay, G. 1967a. *A Social Geography of Zambia*. London: University of London Press.

————. 1967b. *Social Aspects of Village Regrouping in Zambia*. Hull: University of Hull.

Kilson, M. L. 1966. *Political Change in a West African State*. Cambridge, Mass.: Harvard University Press.

Kuper, A. 1970. "Gluckman's Village Headman." *American Anthropologist* 72, no. 2 (April).

Laws, R. 1934. *Reminiscences of Livingstonia*. Edinburgh: Oliver and Boyd.

Lévi-Strauss, C. 1966. *The Savage Mind*. London: Weidenfeld and Nicolson; and Chicago: University of Chicago Press.

Livingstone, W. P. 1932. *Laws of Livingstonia*. London: Hodder and Stoughton.

Livingstonia Letter Book. 1906, 1927.

Livingstonia Mission Council Book. 1921.

Lloyd, P. C. 1965. "The Political Structure of African Kingdoms." In M. Banton (ed.), *Political Systems and the Distribution of Power*. London: Tavistock.

Long, N. 1962. "Bandawe Mission Station and Local Politics 1878–86." *Human Problems in British Central Africa* 32.

————. 1968. *Social Change and the Individual*. Manchester: Manchester University Press.

Mair, L. P. 1962. *Primitive Government*. Harmondsworth: Penguin Books.

————. 1963. *New Nations*. Weidenfeld and Nicholson.

————. 1965. "How Small-Scale Societies Change." In J. Gould, *Penguin Survey of the Social Sciences 1965*. Harmondsworth: Penguin Books.

————. 1969. *Anthropology and Social Change*. New York: Humanities Press.

Mbeelo, H. S. 1971. *Reaction to Colonialism*. Manchester: Manchester University Press.

Merton, R. 1961. *Social Theory and Social Structure*. New York: Free Press.

Michels, R. 1959. *Political Parties*. New York: Collier-Macmillan.

Middleton, J. 1966. *The Effects of Economic Development on Traditional Political Systems of the Sahara*. The Hague: Mouton.

Mitchell, J. C., and Epstein, A. L. 1965. "Occupational Prestige and Social Status Among Urban Africans in Northern Rhodesia." In P. L. Van den Berghe (ed.), *Africa*. San Francisco: Chandler Publishing Co.

Mulford, D. C. 1964. *The Northern Rhodesia General Election 1962*. London: Oxford University Press.

————. 1967. *Zambia: The Politics of Independence, 1957-1964*. London: Oxford University Press.

Murray, S. S. 1922. *A Handbook of Nyasaland*. London: Crown Agents for the Colonies.

Nadel, S. F. 1956. "The Concept of Social Elites." *International Social Science Bulletin* 3, no. 3.

————. 1957. *The Theory of Social Structure*. London: Cohen and West.

Northern Rhodesia Government Gazette. Ordinances. Ordinance No. 49 of 1960. Lusaka: Government Printer.

Northern Rhodesia, Legislative Council Debates. 24 November to 20 December 1945. No. 52.

Owusu, M. 1970. *Uses and Abuses of Political Power.* Chicago: University of Chicago Press.

Redfield, R. 1961. *Peasant Society and Culture.* Chicago: University of Chicago Press.

Rex, J. 1968. *Key Problems of Sociological Theory.* London: Routledge and Kegan Paul.

Richards, A. 1960. "Social Mechanisms for the Transfer of Political Rights in Some African Tribes." *Journal of the Royal Anthropological Institute* 90.

———. 1971. "The Nature of the Problem." In A. Richards and A. Kuper (eds.), *Councils in Action.* Cambridge: Cambridge University Press.

Skinner, E. 1968. "The 'Paradox' of Rural Leadership: A Comment." *Journal of African Studies* 6.

Southall, A. W. 1953. *Alur Society.* Cambridge: W. Heffer and Sons, Ltd.

———. 1961. *Social Change in Modern Africa.* London: Oxford University Press.

———. 1966. "The Concepts of Elites and Their Formation in Uganda." In P. C. Lloyd (ed.) *The Elites of Tropical Africa.* London: Oxford University Press.

Swartz, M. 1968. "Introduction." In M. Swartz (ed.), *Local-Level Politics.* Chicago: Aldine.

Swartz, M.; Turner, V. W.; and Tuden, A. 1966. "Introduction." In M. Swartz et al. (eds.), *Political Anthropology.* Chicago: Aldine.

Tew, M. 1950. *Peoples of Lake Nyasa Region.* Ethnographic Survey of Africa. East Central Africa, Part I. London: Oxford University Press.

Turner, V. W. 1964. *Schism and Continuity in an African Society.* Manchester: Manchester University Press.

van Velsen, J. 1959. "The Missionary Factor Among the Lakeside Tonga." *Human Problems in British Central Africa.* Rhodes-Livingstone Journal 26.

———. 1960. "Labour Migration as a Positive Factor in the Continuity of Tonga Tribal Society." *Economic Development and Cultural Change* 3, no. 3.

———. 1964. *The Politics of Kinship.* Manchester: Manchester University Press.

———. 1966. "Some Early Pressure Groups in Malawi." In E. Stokes and R. Brown (eds.), *The Zambian Past.* Manchester: Manchester University Press.

Vincent, J. 1971. *African Elite.* New York: Columbia University Press.

Wallerstein, I. 1961. *Africa.* New York: Vintage Books.

Watson, W. 1958. *Tribal Cohesion in a Money Economy.* Manchester: Manchester University Press.

Weber, M. 1965. *The Sociology of Religion.* London: Methuen and Co.

Wilson, G. 1939. *The Constitution of Ngonde.* (Rhodes-Livingstone Papers, No. 3). Livingstone: Rhodes-Livingstone Institute.

Wilson, M. 1958. *The Peoples of the Nyasa-Tanganyika Corridor.* Communications from the School of African Studies, University of Cape Town, no. 29.

Young, T. C. 1932. *Notes on the History of the Tumbuka-Kamanga Peoples in the Northern Province of Nyasaland.* London: Religious Tract Society.

Zambian African Census. *May/June, 1963, Census of Africans: Village Populations in Norther Rhodesia.* Lusaka: July 1965.

Index